Pastoral Services

Common Worship

Church House Publishing

Pastoral Services

Published by   Church House Publishing
                Church House
                Great Smith Street
                London SW1P 3NZ

Copyright ©   *The Archbishops' Council 2000*

                First published 2000

ISBN   0 7151 2007 7

Printed and bound in the United Kingdom
by Cambridge University Press
on 55gsm Primapages Ivory

Typeset in Gill Sans
by John Morgan and Shirley Thompson/Omnific
Designed by Derek Birdsall RDI

Contents

¶ Authorization

Common Worship: Pastoral Services comprises

¶ alternative services and other material authorized for use until further resolution of the General Synod; and

¶ material commended by the House of Bishops.

For details, see page 403.

Canon B 3 provides that decisions as to which of the authorized services are to be used (other than occasional offices) shall be taken jointly by the incumbent and the parochial church council. In the case of occasional offices (other than Confirmation and Ordination), the decision is to be made by the minister conducting the service, subject to the right of any of the persons concerned to object beforehand to the form of service proposed.

Introduction

We are all on a journey through life. One of the presuppositions on which the Church of England's Pastoral Services are based is that we do not travel alone. Where is God in relation to that journey? He is both the starting point and the ending point, the Alpha and the Omega. Not only that but, as the Psalmist says, in all our rushing around between the beginning and the end, he is there too.

> Where can I go then from your spirit?
> Or where can I flee from your presence?
> If I climb up to heaven, you are there;
> If I make the grave my bed, you are there also.
>
> Psalm 139.6,7

An accompanied journey, with questions

So the journey we take is an accompanied one. God is with us every step of the way. Sometimes the realization of that presence is conveyed to us through the presence of God's people on the journey. As on a medieval pilgrimage, different people on the road have different backgrounds and a variety of family relationships. They engage in different occupations and have varied functions in relation to others on the journey. Not all are travelling at the same speed. Some spend their time specifically helping others along and ministering to them; some imagine their own burdens are too great for them to be able to help others.

The Church is a pilgrim church, a body of people on the move. Even though some people, for example on the funeral and bereavement journey, may feel isolated, what these services do is to put that journey in the context of the Church, the Church which prays, which celebrates, which cares. For the sake of those for whom it cares, the Church and its liturgy need to embody that flexibility to adjust to different pastoral situations which is implied by being a church on the move. They also need to reflect that dependability, consistency and stability which is implied by the long history of the Church's worship, traditions and buildings. We serve God, who is the same yesterday, today and for ever, and who is continually doing new things, drawing his new creation to himself.

The order of our journeying

These services are not in the order some might expect.
Thanksgiving for the Gift of a Child could have come first: birth,
and welcome into a human family might seem the obvious starting
point. But there is a logic in placing Marriage before Thanksgiving
for the Gift of a Child. Funeral Services, in all their richness,
are placed towards the end.

Wholeness and Healing

Wholeness and Healing services come first because, as the
Theological Introduction to that section of the book makes clear,
they are as much part of the baptismal liturgy as they are of pastoral
services. Salvation, wholeness, healing and peace with God are part
of the same family of words, revealing the same essential theological
themes as both incarnation and crucifixion: vulnerability and
powerlessness, identification and suffering, being put right, made
whole and restored as part of a new creation. Both in the
Celebration of Wholeness and Healing and in the more personal
ministries of the Laying on of Hands and the Distribution of Holy
Communion, these Gospel themes are made to relate to the real
human condition, with humility and without triumphalism, in a
way that brings people face to face with Jesus Christ.

The Marriage Service

The Marriage Service, unlike Baptism and Funeral Services, is not
for everyone, though here again the Church is present on the
journey, surrounding the couple with love, providing preparation
and promising – for the first time in a Church of England service –
support and prayer. But, down the centuries, not much has changed
in the Marriage Service, and much of the same structure and feel
is retained in the new service. In the Middle Ages there was more
dramatic movement in the service, with most of it happening at the
church door, and the couple entering church for the Wedding Mass.
At the Reformation the wedding proper moved into the body of
the church, and the beginning of the second part of the service was
marked by the procession to the sanctuary. But the main concerns
of the marriage preface (where the reasons for marriage are set
out), have changed little since medieval times – Chaucer uses similar
material in the Parson's Tale, told on another journey in 1387.
Cranmer's 1549 service included 'quietness, sobriety and peace' as
the ideal of Christian married life, and later social changes included

those in the 1928 service (the basis for the Series 1 Marriage Service) making 'the causes for which matrimony was ordained' acceptable to a more refined generation, and the (optional) omission of the word 'obey' in the bride's promises.

Thanksgiving for the Gift of a Child
The short service of Thanksgiving for the Gift of a Child may be used on a wide variety of occasions, both private and public, as part of the journey towards baptism. It is at such key moments in people's lives that they are often prompted to ask serious questions and even to turn to God. Here there is also provision for those who accompany others on the journey, as words are given for supporting friends, standing alongside the parents welcoming a new member of the family.

The Funeral Service
The Funeral Service is both the end of the human journey in this world and a whole series of journeys in itself. From the eighth century or earlier, the Funeral rite was a continuum, broken by movements from place to place, from home to church, to the place of burial and back to the home. This pattern was severely truncated at the Reformation, but today's pastoral needs suggest a return to it. As grieving is a process marked by different stages, we believe that one helpful contribution the Church can make pastorally is to have a series of services and resources in which some of these different stages can be recognized, spoken of in advance or recapitulated.

So the Funeral Service is part of a longer continuum, though it stands perfectly well on its own if necessary. Following on from ministry to the sick we move into ministry at the time of death, through the possibility of prayers in the house after someone has died, prayers in church or at home before the funeral, through the journey which brings the body to the dead person's spiritual home on earth, the church, for the funeral itself, and then on to some prayers at home after the funeral, a later Memorial Service and the provision for annual memorials. The bereaved will need to be able to say different things to God and to one another at each of these different stages.

The structure within the Funeral Service itself moves from the human to the divine, from earth to heaven. It begins with an acknowledgement of the different groups of people who come to mourn, for some of whom the early part of the service will be a recapitulation of those stages since the death which they have not been able to witness. The service provides an opportunity for the celebration of the life of the person who has died, and moves from this into the reading of Scripture and prayer, before reaching its climax in the commendation and the committal.

Conclusion
Through all of these resources runs the theme of being accompanied on the journey by the Church, by the people who, in surrounding us and supporting us, reveal the personal love and care of Jesus Christ, whose death put an end to death for eternity.

The pastoral task of the Christian Church, all the people of God, ministers and laity, is to provide company on the journey, towards baptism, marriage, welcoming children and at death itself. This is the kind of company, using these and other resources, which, in revealing the love of Christ, will draw people to put their faith in him and to serve him in the fellowship of his Church until they come to their eternal home in the company of all the saints.

Wholeness and Healing

Contents

For General Rules, see page 402.

¶ *Theological Introduction*

Baptism witnesses to God's gift of salvation, in which he gathers people into the new creation in Jesus Christ. Baptism points to the way in which God in Jesus Christ is overthrowing an order of life corrupted by sin and death and bringing to birth a renewed creation, a creation alive with the healing presence of God's Spirit. Baptism is a sign of individual and corporate forgiveness and renewal within the life of the baptized. That life proclaims not only the risen power won by Christ for us in his resurrection and exaltation, but also our identification as human beings with the constraints and suffering borne by Christ in his incarnation and on the cross.

With the incarnation of Jesus, God begins the renewal of our alienated, weakened and fragmented human condition (Romans 8.3,4). In St Matthew's Gospel Jesus' baptism expresses his solidarity with us in our weakness (Matthew 3.14,15) and his healing ministry is seen as the outworking of the suffering servant who 'took our infirmities and bore our diseases' (Matthew 8.17). The death and resurrection of Jesus Christ promise both the judgement of all that is flawed in human life and the recreation of our humanity. A powerful biblical image portrays the sufferings of the Messiah, of the creation, and of God's people, as the birth pains that herald the new age in which peace and righteousness reign (Luke 12.50; John 16.21; Romans 8.18-30; Colossians 1.24; Revelation 12). The Christ, the anointed one, is clothed with the Holy Spirit to bring good news to the afflicted and to proclaim the day of the Lord's favour (Luke 4.18-21).

It is apparent in Scripture that the physical, emotional, social and spiritual well-being of human beings are closely interconnected. Christ's work of reconciliation extends beyond the purely personal and relational to the social order and the whole creation (cf Colossians 1.15-27). The Gospels use the term 'healing' both for physical healing and for the broader salvation that Jesus brings. A common New Testament term for sickness is 'weakness' (*asthenia*) (Luke 5.15; 13.11,12; John 5.5); it carries broad associations of powerlessness and vulnerability, including human vulnerability in the face of the dominion of sin and death (Romans 5.6; 8.3). As Christians face weakness, they receive God's grace, expressed sometimes in an experience of healing and sometimes through the strength that comes in the bearing of weakness (2 Corinthians 12.9).

Furthermore, the New Testament also presents us with a picture of Christians in a running battle with forces of evil that are external to us but bear heavily upon our lives. Although the principalities and powers (Ephesians 6.12) are not always forces of evil, they can have an impact on the social and political order; the evil one not only brings temptation but takes people captive (Gospels, *passim*); the power of idols enslaves consciences (1 Corinthians 8); and pagan sacrifices are offered to demons with whom we must not be participants (1 Corinthians 10). This series of pictures, while not absolving us from personal responsibility for our actions, also strongly implies that without the grace of God we are at risk of being in the grip of an array of forces beyond our powers to resist or break. Yet there is victory in Christ, and we also learn that, in the final analysis, 'an idol is nothing in the world and there is no God but one' (1 Corinthians 8.4); and that victorious discernment categorizes all forces of spiritual evil as provisional and counterfeit. Their 'power' lies in their impact on us, and their 'reality' therefore is shadowy and interim only. But we nonetheless need deliverance from that power, and the language of healing and wholeness is entirely appropriate to that process.

Acts of healing in the Gospels are intimately related to the restoring of individuals to a place of worth within the social order (cf Mark 1.44; 5.15-20; 6.32-34; Luke 13.10-17). 'By his wounds you have been healed' (1 Peter 2.24) makes powerful links between human pain and vulnerability and the saving impact of Jesus' own suffering. The same interconnectedness is present where Scripture speaks of God's image in us to point to the way human life is marred and threatened by the impact of evil and is restored by the new creation in Christ (Romans 3.23; 2 Corinthians 3.18; Ephesians 2.13-16).

Healing, reconciliation and restoration are integral to the good news of Jesus Christ. For this reason prayer for individuals, focused through laying on of hands or anointing with oil, has a proper place within the public prayer of the Church. God's gracious activity of healing is to be seen both as part of the proclaiming of the good news and as an outworking of the presence of the Spirit in the life of the Church.

Such prayer needs to be sensitive to a number of simplifications or misunderstandings. It should not imply a simple link between sickness and sin; Jesus himself warned against the direct association of disability and sin (John 9.3). The receiving of forgiveness and the act of forgiving others may open the way to healing and wholeness. Prayer for healing and strengthening should not involve the rejection of the skills and activity of medicine which are also part of God's faithfulness to creation (cf Ecclesiasticus 38.9-12; Psalm 147.3). Prayer for healing needs to take seriously the way in which individual sickness and vulnerability are often the result of injustice and social oppression. Equally importantly such prayer should not imply that the restoration of physical wholeness is the only way in which Christ meets human need. Healing has always to be seen against the background of the continuing anguish of an alienated world and the hidden work of the Holy Spirit bringing God's new order to birth. It is a way of partaking in God's new life that will not be complete until it includes the whole creation and the destruction of death itself.

¶ Introductory Note

These forms of service are intended to recognize the links between prayer for healing and the wider celebration in the Church of reconciliation and renewal in the gospel of Jesus Christ.

¶ The first is a service most suitable for a diocesan or deanery occasion.

¶ The second, the Laying on of Hands with Prayer and Anointing at a Celebration of Holy Communion, is intended for occasional use, when appropriate, as part of the regular liturgical life of a parish.

¶ The third, Prayer for Individuals in Public Worship, is primarily intended for use in churches where such prayer for individuals is a regular feature of Sunday worship.

¶ The fourth, Ministry to the Sick, is intended for use in the sickroom, whether in hospital or at home.

¶ The fifth comprises prayers for protection and peace for use with or by individuals at need.

Those who come for prayer with Laying on of Hands and/or Anointing should make careful preparation. They may receive the Laying on of Hands on behalf of others who are not present as well as for themselves.

Where prayer is offered for those who will minister to others, this should be seen as prayer for the grace and discernment of the Holy Spirit, as well as prayer for healing. All who minister to others in need should have careful regard for the duty of confidentiality which this privilege brings. As part of their preparation, those who minister need to be ready to recognize where specialist skills may be required.

If a need for a more particular ministry of exorcism or deliverance is perceived, then the bishop's instructions should be followed and his authorized advisor consulted.

A Celebration of Wholeness and Healing

(especially suitable for a diocesan or deanery occasion)

Structure

Optional parts of the service are indicated by square brackets.

¶ **The Gathering**
The Greeting
Dialogue
The Collect

¶ **The Liturgy of the Word**
Readings and Psalm
Gospel Reading
Sermon

¶ **Prayer and Penitence**
[Introduction]
Prayers of Intercession
Prayers of Penitence

¶ **Laying on of Hands and Anointing**
Prayer over the Oil
Laying on of Hands
[Anointing]
The Lord's Prayer – *unless Holy Communion is celebrated*

¶ **[The Liturgy of the Sacrament**
The Peace
Preparation of the Table
Taking of the Bread and Wine
The Eucharistic Prayer
The Lord's Prayer
Breaking of the Bread
Giving of Communion
Prayer after Communion]

¶ **The Sending Out**
Proclamation of the Gospel
The Peace – *unless Holy Communion is celebrated*
[Blessing – *if Holy Communion is celebrated*]
The Dismissal

For Notes, see pages 24–25.

A Celebration of Wholeness and Healing

(especially suitable for a diocesan or deanery occasion)

¶ *The Gathering*

At the entrance of the ministers, a hymn or chant may be sung.

The Greeting

The president greets the people using these or other suitable words

In the name of Christ, we welcome you.
We have been called out of darkness into God's marvellous light.
Grace and peace be with you

All **and also with you.**

*The president may introduce the service, using one of the forms
on pages 42–43 or other suitable words.*

This dialogue or another suitable form may be used

The love of God has been poured into our hearts,
through the Holy Spirit who has been given to us:
we dwell in him and he lives in us.

Give thanks to the Lord and call upon his name:

All **make known his deeds among the peoples.**

Sing to God, sing praises to his name:

All **and speak of all his marvellous works.**

Holy, holy, holy, is the Lord God almighty:

All **who was and is and is to come.**

The Collect

Silence may be kept.

Heavenly Father,
you anointed your Son Jesus Christ
with the Holy Spirit and with power
to bring to us the blessings of your kingdom.
Anoint your Church with the same Holy Spirit,
that we who share in his suffering and victory
may bear witness to the gospel of salvation;
through Jesus Christ, your Son our Lord,
who is alive and reigns with you
in the unity of the Holy Spirit,
one God, now and for ever.

All **Amen.**

¶ The Liturgy of the Word

*If this celebration takes place on a Sunday or Principal Festival
the readings of the day are normally used. For other occasions
a table of readings is provided on pages 44–45.*

*Either one or two readings from Scripture precede the Gospel reading.
At the end of each, the reader may say*

This is the word of the Lord.

All **Thanks be to God.**

*The psalm or canticle follows the first reading, and other hymns and
songs may be used between the readings.*

Gospel Reading

An acclamation may herald the Gospel reading.

When the Gospel is announced, the reader says

Hear the Gospel of our Lord Jesus Christ according to *N.*

All **Glory to you, O Lord.**

At the end

This is the Gospel of the Lord.

All **Praise to you, O Christ.**

Sermon

¶ Prayer and Penitence

As an introduction to this section, a minister may use one of the forms on pages 42–43, if it has not already been used at the beginning of the service.

Prayers of Intercession

At the Prayers of Intercession, the following Litany of Healing may be used. Additional petitions, including names, may be included.

God the Father, your will for all people is health and salvation.

All **We praise and bless you, Lord.**

God the Son, you came that we might have life,
and might have it more abundantly.

All **We praise and bless you, Lord.**

God the Holy Spirit, you make our bodies
   the temple of your presence.

All **We praise and bless you, Lord.**

Holy Trinity, one God, in you we live and move and have our being.

All **We praise and bless you, Lord.**

Lord, grant your healing grace to all who are sick, injured
   or disabled,
that they may be made whole.

All **Hear us, Lord of life.**

Grant to all who are lonely, anxious or depressed
a knowledge of your will and an awareness of your presence.

All **Hear us, Lord of life.**

Grant to all who minister to those who are suffering
wisdom and skill, sympathy and patience.

All **Hear us, Lord of life.**

Mend broken relationships, and restore to those in distress
soundness of mind and serenity of spirit.

All **Hear us, Lord of life.**

Sustain and support those who seek your guidance
and lift up all who are brought low by the trials of this life.

All **Hear us, Lord of life.**

Grant to the dying peace and a holy death,
and uphold by the grace and consolation of your Holy Spirit
   those who are bereaved.

All **Hear us, Lord of life.**

Restore to wholeness whatever is broken by human sin,
in our lives, in our nation, and in the world.

All **Hear us, Lord of life.**

You are the Lord who does mighty wonders.

All **You have declared your power among the peoples.**

With you, Lord, is the well of life

All **and in your light do we see light.**

Hear us, Lord of life:

All **heal us, and make us whole.**

Let us pray.

A period of silence follows.

O Lord our God, accept the fervent prayers of your people;
in the multitude of your mercies look with compassion
   upon us and all who turn to you for help;
for you are gracious, O lover of souls,
and to you we give glory, Father, Son, and Holy Spirit,
now and for ever.

All **Amen.**

Prayers of Penitence

The gospel calls us to turn away from sin
and be faithful to Christ.
As we offer ourselves to him in penitence and faith,
we renew our confidence and trust in his mercy.

Cast your burden upon the Lord

All **and he will sustain you.**

In returning and rest

All **you shall be saved.**

In quietness and trust

All **shall be your strength.**

There follows a period of silent reflection and self-examination.

One or other of the following or another suitable form may be used

You raise the dead to life in the Spirit:
Lord, have mercy.

All **Lord, have mercy.**

You bring pardon and peace to the sinner:
Christ, have mercy.

All **Christ, have mercy.**

You bring light to those in darkness:
Lord, have mercy.

All **Lord, have mercy.**

(or)

All **Most merciful God,**
Father of our Lord Jesus Christ,
we confess that we have sinned
in thought, word and deed.
We have not loved you with our whole heart.
We have not loved our neighbour as ourselves.
In your mercy
forgive what we have been,
help us to amend what we are,
and direct what we shall be;
that we may do justly,
love mercy,
and walk humbly with you, our God.
Amen.

Absolution

The president says the Absolution, using this or any other authorized form

God, the Father of mercies,
has reconciled the world to himself
through the death and resurrection of his Son, Jesus Christ,
not holding our sins against us,
but sending his Holy Spirit
to shed abroad his love among us.
By the ministry of reconciliation
entrusted by Christ to his Church,
receive his pardon and peace
to stand before him in his strength alone
this day and for evermore.

All **Amen.**

A hymn or chant may be sung.

¶ Laying on of Hands and Anointing

Oil for anointing is brought before the president.

Our help is in the name of the Lord
All **who has made heaven and earth.**

Blessed be the name of the Lord:
All **now and for ever. Amen.**

(or)

Praise God who made heaven and earth,
All **who keeps his promise for ever.**

Let us give thanks to the Lord our God,
All **who is worthy of all thanksgiving and praise.**

Blessed are you, sovereign God, gentle and merciful,
creator of heaven and earth.
Your Word brought light out of darkness,
and daily your Spirit renews the face of the earth.

When we turned away from you in sin,
your anointed Son took our nature and entered our suffering
to bring your healing to those in weakness and distress.
He broke the power of evil and set us free from sin and death
that we might become partakers of his glory.

His apostles anointed the sick in your name,
bringing wholeness and joy to a broken world.
By your grace renewed each day
you continue the gifts of healing in your Church
that your people may praise your name for ever.
By the power of your Spirit may your blessing rest
on those who are anointed with this oil in your name;
may they be made whole in body, mind and spirit.

Hear the prayer we offer for all your people.
Remember in your mercy those for whom we pray:
heal the sick, raise the fallen, strengthen the fainthearted
and enfold in your love the fearful and those who have no hope.

In the fullness of time complete your gracious work.
Reconcile all things in Christ and make them new,
that we may be restored in your image, renewed in your love,
and serve you as sons and daughters in your kingdom.

Through your anointed Son, Jesus Christ, our Lord,
to whom with you and the Holy Spirit
we lift our voices of thanks and praise:

All **Blessed be God, our strength and our salvation,
now and for ever. Amen.**

Alternative prayers may be used (pages 46–47).

*The laying on of hands is administered, using these or other
suitable words*

In the name of God and trusting in his might alone,
receive Christ's healing touch to make you whole.

May Christ bring you wholeness
of body, mind and spirit,
deliver you from every evil,
and give you his peace.

All **Amen.**

Anointing may be administered. The minister says

N, I anoint you in the name of God who gives you life.
Receive Christ's forgiveness, his healing and his love.

May the Father of our Lord Jesus Christ
grant you the riches of his grace,
his wholeness and his peace.

All **Amen.**

After the laying on of hands and anointing, the president says

The almighty Lord,
who is a strong tower for all who put their trust in him,
whom all things in heaven, on earth, and under the earth obey,
be now and evermore your defence.
May you believe and trust that the only name under heaven
given for health and salvation
is the name of our Lord Jesus Christ.

All **Amen.**

*Unless the Liturgy of the Sacrament follows immediately,
the president introduces the Lord's Prayer*

In confidence let us pray to the Father
for the coming of the kingdom among us:

All **Our Father in heaven,
hallowed be your name,
your kingdom come,
your will be done,
on earth as in heaven.
Give us today our daily bread.
Forgive us our sins
as we forgive those who sin against us.
Lead us not into temptation
but deliver us from evil.
For the kingdom, the power,
and the glory are yours
now and for ever.
Amen.**

(or)

All **Our Father, who art in heaven,
hallowed be thy name;
thy kingdom come;
thy will be done;
on earth as it is in heaven.
Give us this day our daily bread.
And forgive us our trespasses,
as we forgive those who trespass against us.
And lead us not into temptation;
but deliver us from evil.
For thine is the kingdom,
the power and the glory,
for ever and ever.
Amen.**

*If the Liturgy of the Sacrament follows, the president continues with
the Peace (see Note 2 on page 24).*

A hymn or song of thanksgiving may be sung.

¶ *The Sending Out*

The president may say

God who said: 'Let light shine out of darkness'

All **has caused his light to shine within us**

to give the light of the knowledge of the glory of God

All **revealed in the face of Jesus Christ.**

We have this treasure in earthen vessels

All **to show that the power belongs to God.**

A minister says

Hear the words of the Gospel according to *N.*

All **Glory to you, O Lord.**

A short passage from the Gospels is read (suggested passages are given on page 45).

At the end

This is the Gospel of the Lord.

All **Praise to you, O Christ.**

The Peace and Dismissal

God has made us one in Christ.

He has set his seal upon us

and, as a pledge of what is to come,

has given the Spirit to dwell in our hearts.

The peace of the Lord be always with you

All **and also with you.**

A minister says

Go in the joy and peace of Christ. [Alleluia, alleluia.]

All **Thanks be to God. [Alleluia, alleluia.]**

A sign of peace may be exchanged.

The ministers and people depart.

Notes

1 **Occasion**
This Order is most suitable for use at a diocesan or deanery occasion. When the ministry of healing is a regular part of a parish's pattern of worship, the rites for the Laying on of Hands with Prayer and Anointing at a Celebration of Holy Communion (pages 26–40) and Prayer for Individuals in Public Worship (pages 48–49) will be more appropriate.

2 **Holy Communion**
When this Order is used within the setting of a celebration of Holy Communion, the Peace follows the Laying on of Hands and Anointing, followed by the Preparation of the Gifts and the Eucharistic Prayer. A Proper Preface, the Post Communion and the blessing from the rite for the Laying on of Hands with Prayer and Anointing at a Celebration of Holy Communion may be used (pages 26–39).

3 **Extended Celebration**
When this Order is used for an extended celebration over a number of hours or a whole day, the Liturgy of the Word may be followed by an extended study period and a time for reflection. Prayer and Penitence may be introduced by the reading of a passage from the Gospels and the period of silence at the Prayers of Penitence may be prolonged. After the conclusion of the Laying on of Hands and Anointing, or after the distribution of communion if Holy Communion is celebrated, there may be a longer period of silence or thanksgiving.

4 **Ministries**
The president of the rite is the bishop, or a priest, who presides over the whole rite. The president may invite others to share in the prayers and the Laying on of Hands, and may delegate the ministry of Anointing to other ministers authorized for this ministry under Canon B 37.

5   Oil
     The oil to be used at this celebration should be pure olive oil
     and normally be consecrated during this service by the bishop
     (or priest) who presides, rather than having been previously blessed.
     This will not only ensure an adequate supply of oil, but provide a
     prayer of thanksgiving at the heart of the rite. If preferred, the
     prayer may be used in the responsive form on pages **46–47**.
     If oil which has previously been blessed is used, then the form of
     thanksgiving in the rite for Laying on of Hands with Prayer and
     Anointing at a Celebration of Holy Communion (page 33) may
     be used.

6   **Introduction to Prayer over the Oil**
     Alternative versicles and responses are suggested at the beginning
     of the prayer over oil for anointing on page 20 (and page 46).
     The introductory dialogue printed first has traditionally been
     a distinctively episcopal text.

Laying on of Hands
with Prayer and Anointing at a
Celebration of Holy Communion

(suitable for occasional use as part of the regular liturgical
life of a parish)

Structure

Optional parts of the service are indicated in square brackets.

¶ **The Gathering**
The Greeting
Prayers of Penitence
The Collect

¶ **The Liturgy of the Word**
Readings and Psalm
Gospel Reading
Sermon

¶ **Prayers of Intercession**
[Litany of Healing]

¶ **Laying on of Hands and Anointing** †
Prayer
Laying on of Hands
[Anointing]

¶ **The Liturgy of the Sacrament**
The Peace
Preparation of the Table
Taking of the Bread and Wine
The Eucharistic Prayer
The Lord's Prayer
Breaking of the Bread
Giving of Communion
Prayer after Communion

¶ **The Dismissal**
Blessing
The Dismissal

*† Where this is offered as part of regular Sunday worship, it may be
done during the Giving of Communion.*

For Notes, see page 40.

Laying on of Hands
with Prayer and Anointing at a
Celebration of Holy Communion

An authorized Order for the Celebration of Holy Communion is used.

¶ The Gathering

At the entry of the ministers a hymn may be sung.

The president may say

In the name of the Father,
and of the Son,
and of the Holy Spirit.

All **Amen.**

The Greeting

The president greets the people

The Lord be with you
All **and also with you.**

(or)

Grace, mercy and peace
from God our Father
and the Lord Jesus Christ
be with you
All **and also with you.**

From Easter Day to Pentecost this acclamation follows

Alleluia. Christ is risen.
All **He is risen indeed. Alleluia.**

The president may introduce the service using one of the forms from pages 42–43, or other suitable words.

Prayer of Preparation

This prayer may be said

All **Almighty God,**
to whom all hearts are open,
all desires known,
and from whom no secrets are hidden:
cleanse the thoughts of our hearts
by the inspiration of your Holy Spirit,
that we may perfectly love you,
and worthily magnify your holy name;
through Christ our Lord.
Amen.

Prayers of Penitence

A minister uses a seasonal invitation to confession or other suitable words.

This form of the Kyrie eleison or an authorized confession may be used

Lord Jesus, you heal the sick:
Lord, have mercy.

All **Lord, have mercy.**

Lord Jesus, you forgive sinners:
Christ, have mercy.

All **Christ, have mercy.**

Lord Jesus, you give yourself to heal us
and bring us strength:
Lord, have mercy.

All **Lord, have mercy.**

The president says

Almighty God,
who forgives all who truly repent,
have mercy upon *you*,
pardon and deliver *you* from all *your* sins,
confirm and strengthen *you* in all goodness,
and keep *you* in life eternal;
through Jesus Christ our Lord.

All **Amen.**

The Gloria in excelsis may be used.

The Collect

*The president introduces a period of silent prayer with the words
'Let us pray' or a more specific bidding.*

*On a Sunday or Principal Festival, the Collect of the Day is used;
otherwise this Collect may be used*

Heavenly Father,
you anointed your Son Jesus Christ
with the Holy Spirit and with power
to bring to us all the blessings of your kingdom.
Anoint your Church with the same Holy Spirit,
that we who share in his suffering and victory
may bear witness to the gospel of salvation;
through Jesus Christ, your Son our Lord,
who is alive and reigns with you
in the unity of the Holy Spirit,
one God, now and for ever.

All **Amen.**

¶ *The Liturgy of the Word*

Readings

The readings and psalmody are either those of the day, or from the table of readings on pages 44–45.

Either one or two readings from Scripture precede the Gospel reading.

At the end of each the reader may say

This is the word of the Lord.

All **Thanks be to God.**

The psalm or canticle follows the first reading; other hymns and songs may be used between the readings.

Gospel Reading

An acclamation may herald the Gospel reading.

When the Gospel is announced the reader says

Hear the Gospel of our Lord Jesus Christ according to *N.*

All **Glory to you, O Lord.**

At the end

This is the Gospel of the Lord.

All **Praise to you, O Christ.**

Sermon

A Creed or authorized Affirmation of Faith may be used.

¶ Prayers of Intercession

The following Litany of Healing may be used.
Additional petitions, including names, may be included.

God the Father, your will for all people is health and salvation.

All **We praise and bless you, Lord.**

God the Son, you came that we might have life,
and might have it more abundantly.

All **We praise and bless you, Lord.**

God the Holy Spirit, you make our bodies
the temple of your presence.

All **We praise and bless you, Lord.**

Holy Trinity, one God, in you we live and move and have our being.

All **We praise and bless you, Lord.**

Lord, grant your healing grace to all who are sick, injured
or disabled,
that they may be made whole.

All **Hear us, Lord of life.**

Grant to all who are lonely, anxious or depressed
a knowledge of your will and an awareness of your presence.

All **Hear us, Lord of life.**

Grant to all who minister to those who are suffering
wisdom and skill, sympathy and patience.

All **Hear us, Lord of life.**

Mend broken relationships, and restore to those in distress
soundness of mind and serenity of spirit.

All **Hear us, Lord of life.**

Sustain and support those who seek your guidance
and lift up all who are brought low by the trials of this life.

All **Hear us, Lord of life.**

Grant to the dying peace and a holy death,
and uphold by the grace and consolation of your Holy Spirit
those who are bereaved.

All **Hear us, Lord of life.**

Restore to wholeness whatever is broken by human sin,
in our lives, in our nation, and in the world.

All **Hear us, Lord of life.**

You are the Lord who does mighty wonders.

All **You have declared your power among the peoples.**

With you, Lord, is the well of life

All **and in your light do we see light.**

Hear us, Lord of life:

All **heal us, and make us whole.**

Let us pray.

A period of silence follows.

O Lord our God, accept the fervent prayers of your people;
in the multitude of your mercies look with compassion
upon us and all who turn to you for help;
for you are gracious, O lover of souls,
and to you we give glory, Father, Son, and Holy Spirit,
now and for ever.

All **Amen.**

¶ *Laying on of Hands and Anointing*

If Anointing is to be administered, oil may be brought before the president.

The president says

Praise God who made heaven and earth,

All **who keeps his promise for ever.**

Let us give thanks to the Lord our God,

All **who is worthy of all thanksgiving and praise.**

Blessed are you, sovereign God, gentle and merciful,
creator of heaven and earth.
Your Word brought light out of darkness,
and daily your Spirit renews the face of the earth.

Your anointed Son brought healing to those in weakness
  and distress.
He broke the power of evil and set us free from sin and death
that we might praise your name for ever.

By the power of your Spirit may your blessing rest
on those who are anointed with this oil in your name;
may they be made whole in body, mind and spirit,
restored in your image, renewed in your love,
and serve you as sons and daughters in your kingdom.

Through your anointed Son, Jesus Christ, our Lord,
to whom with you and the Holy Spirit
we lift our voices of thanks and praise:

All **Blessed be God, our strength and our salvation,
now and for ever. Amen.**

The Laying on of Hands is administered using these or other suitable words

In the name of God and trusting in his might alone,
receive Christ's healing touch to make you whole.

May Christ bring you wholeness
of body, mind and spirit,
deliver you from every evil,
and give you his peace.

All **Amen.**

N, I anoint you in the name of God who gives you life.
Receive Christ's forgiveness, his healing and his love.

May the Father of our Lord Jesus Christ
grant you the riches of his grace,
his wholeness and his peace.

All   **Amen.**

After the Laying on of Hands and Anointing, the president says

The almighty Lord,
who is a strong tower for all who put their trust in him,
whom all things in heaven, on earth, and under the earth obey,
be now and evermore your defence.
May you believe and trust that the only name under heaven
given for health and salvation
is the name of our Lord Jesus Christ.

All   **Amen.**

¶ *The Liturgy of the Sacrament*

The Peace

The president may introduce the Peace with a suitable sentence.
The following may be used

God has made us one in Christ.
He has set his seal upon us
and as a pledge of what is to come
has given the Spirit to dwell in our hearts.

The peace of the Lord be always with you

All **and also with you.**

These words may be added

Let us offer one another a sign of peace.

All may exchange a sign of peace.

The service continues with the Preparation of the Table. Presidential texts for the rest of the service are to be found in Common Worship: Services and Prayers for the Church of England *(pages 155–335) and the President's edition (pages 381–524).*

Preparation of the Table

Taking of the Bread and Wine

The Eucharistic Prayer

An authorized Eucharistic Prayer is used.

One of these Proper Prefaces may be used.

Short Proper Prefaces

For general use

1   And now we give you thanks
because you call us out of darkness into your marvellous light,
and by the power of your redeeming love you make us whole,
that we may be the first fruits of your new creation.

(traditional language)
And now we give thee thanks
because thou dost call us out of darkness into thy marvellous light,
and by the power of thy redeeming love dost make us whole,
that we may be the first fruits of thy new creation.

2   And now we give you thanks
that, taking upon himself our human nature,
he shared our joy and our tears,
bore all our sickness,
and carried all our sorrows.
Through death he brought us
to the life of his glorious resurrection,
giving for frailty eternal strength,
and restoring in us the image of your glory.

3   And now we give you thanks
    that you have shown the greatness of your love for us
    by sending him to share our human nature
    and accomplish our forgiveness.
    He embraces us in our weakness,
    he suffers with the sick and the rejected,
    and, bringing your healing to the world,
    he rescues us from every evil.

4   And now we give you thanks
    that through him the sick are healed:
    the blind regain their sight,
    the deaf hear, the lame walk,
    and the outcast are brought home;
    the poor receive good news
    and the dead are raised to life.

5   *For use in particular sickness*
    (especially when the sick have been anointed)
    And now we give you thanks
    because you provide medicine to heal our sickness,
    and the leaves of the tree of life
    for the healing of the nations,
    anointing us with your healing power
    so that we may be the first fruits of your new creation.

For general use

It is right to give you thanks
in sickness and in health,
in suffering and in joy,
through Christ our Saviour and Redeemer,
who as the Good Samaritan
tends the wounds of body and spirit.
He stands by us and pours out for our healing
the oil of consolation and the wine of renewed hope,
turning the darkness of our pain
into the dawning light of his kingdom.
And now we join with saints and angels
for ever praising you and *saying*:

Breaking of the Bread

Giving of Communion

Prayer after Communion

The following Post Communion may be used

God of all compassion,
by the dying and rising of your Christ
you restore us to yourself
and enfold us in your love.
May we who have been refreshed
with the bread of life and the cup of salvation
be renewed by your healing Spirit
and made ready for the coming of your kingdom;
through Jesus Christ our Lord.

All **Amen.**

¶ *The Dismissal*

The president may use the seasonal blessing, or another suitable blessing, or

May God the holy and undivided Trinity
preserve you in body, mind and spirit,
and bring you safe to that heavenly country
where peace and harmony reign;
and the blessing of God almighty,
the Father, the Son, and the Holy Spirit,
be among you and remain with you always.

All **Amen.**

Notes

1   **Ministries**
The president of the celebration of Holy Communion also presides over the ministry of Laying on of Hands and Anointing of the sick. The president may invite others to share in the prayers and the laying on of hands, and may delegate the ministry of anointing to other ministers authorized for this ministry under Canon B 37.

2   **Oil**
Canon B 37 provides that the priest should use 'pure olive oil consecrated by the bishop of the diocese or otherwise by the priest', for which forms are provided in the rite for a celebration of Wholeness and Healing on pages 20–21, and also on pages 46–47.

3   **Holy Communion**
Holy Communion is celebrated in accordance with any authorized rite making use of the special provisions included here.

4   **Celebration at Home or in Hospital**
Where this rite is celebrated at home or in hospital it should be adapted to the form of Holy Communion being followed. The Laying on of Hands and Anointing in this rite or the shorter form on pages 92–93 may be used at the Prayers.

Supplementary Texts

¶ *Introductions*

One of these may be used by the president, either at the Greeting, or to introduce the Prayers of Intercession before the Laying on of Hands and Anointing.

1 We are gathered here in the name of our Lord Jesus Christ, who is present among us by his Spirit. He suffered for us on the cross to bring us healing and reconciliation. Having shared our weakness and learned obedience through suffering, he now lives as our great high priest and is able to save to the uttermost all who draw near to God through him. With our hope set on this great salvation we lay before God our weakness and our need.

2 Jesus sets before us the hope of the kingdom of God. All that is broken will be bound up in God's healing love. All that is marred by weakness and sin will be transformed by God's reconciling love.

   In his humanity, Jesus took on himself our weakness and bore our sins. The Holy Spirit is present in the struggles and groaning of a world subject to decay, bringing to birth the freedom and glory of God's new creation. It is in this hope that we bring to God our prayers and our penitence, and look to God for the new life of the kingdom.

3 Christ taught his disciples to love one another. In his community of love, in praying together, in sharing all things and in caring for the sick, they recalled his words: 'In so far as you did this to one of these, you did it to me.' We gather today to witness to this teaching and to pray in the name of Jesus the healer that the sick may be restored to health and that all among us may know his saving power.

4   Our Lord Jesus Christ went about preaching the gospel and healing. He commanded his disciples to lay hands on the sick that they might be healed. Following his example, and in obedience to his command, we shall lay hands [on N], praying that the Lord will grant healing and peace according to his loving and gracious will.

Saint James writes, 'Is any among you sick? Let him call for the elders of the church, and let them pray over him, anointing him with oil in the name of the Lord; and the prayer of faith will save the sick man, and the Lord will raise him up; and if he has committed sins he will be forgiven.' In fulfilment of this we shall anoint [N] with oil, praying that the Lord will grant healing and restoration and forgiveness according to his loving and gracious will.

¶ Bible Readings

Old Testament	Psalm
Advent	
Isaiah 26.16-19	Psalm 46.1-7
Christmas	
Isaiah 55.1-3,10-11	Psalm 145.14-end
Epiphany	
Isaiah 42.1-7	Psalm 27.1-6 *or* 1-10
Lent	
Isaiah 53.3-6	Psalm 103.1-5,8-14
Lamentations 3.17-24	Psalm 38.9-15
2 Chronicles 28.15	Psalm 23
or Jeremiah 17.5-10,14	
Easter	
1 Kings 17.17-24	Psalm 30.6-12
Pentecost	
Isaiah 61.1-34	Psalm 139.1-17 *or* 1-11
All Saints	
Ezekiel 47.1-12	Psalm 87
Eucharist	
Isaiah 55.1-3,10-11	Psalm 145.14-end
General	
2 Kings 5.9-14	Psalm 66.15-end
2 Kings 20.1-5	Psalm 130
1 Samuel 16.14-23	Psalm 91.1-6,9-13

New Testament	Gospel	Dismissal Gospel	
Advent			
Romans 8.18-23	Matthew 24.3-13	Matthew 5.14-16	
			Birth pangs of new age
Christmas			
Colossians 3.14-17	John 6.47-51	John 6.63-64,66-69	*Bread of Life*
Epiphany			
Acts 9.10-19a	John 9.1-7	John 9.34b-38	
			The opening of eyes
Lent			
Romans 5.6-11	Mark 2.1-12	Mark 5.18-20	*Sin & forgiveness*
2 Corinthians 12.7b-10	Mark 14.32-38	Mark 13.34-36	
			Powerlessness & grace
James 5.14-16	Mark 6.7-13	Mark 6.54-56	*Anointing*
Easter			
Acts 20.7-12	Mark 5.35-end	Mark 6.7-13	*Resurrection*
Pentecost			
Romans 8.12-17	Luke 4.16-21	Luke 4.33-37	*Power of the Spirit*
All Saints			
Revelation 21.22; 22.5	Matthew 28.16-20	Matthew 28.9-10	
			Healing of the nations
Eucharist			
Colossians 3.14-17	John 6.47-51	John 6.63,64,66-69	*Bread of Life*
General			
Romans 10.5-11	Luke 17.11-19	Luke 17.20-21	*Cleansing & response*
James 5.13-16	Mark 9.16-29	Mark 9.38-40	*Prayer*
Acts 10.36-43	Mark 1.21-28 or 5.1-20	Mark 5.25-34	*Deliverance*

¶ *Prayers over the Oil*

Either of these forms may be used.

A Responsive Form of Prayer over the Oil

Our help is in the name of the Lord

All **who has made heaven and earth.**

Blessed be the name of the Lord:

All **now and for ever. Amen.**

(or)

Praise God who made heaven and earth,

All **who keeps his promise for ever.**

Let us give thanks to the Lord our God,

All **who is worthy of all thanksgiving and praise.**

Blessed are you, sovereign God, gentle and merciful,
creator of heaven and earth.
Your Word brought light out of darkness,
and daily your Spirit renews the face of the earth.

All **To you be glory and praise for ever.**

When we turned away from you in sin,
your anointed Son took our nature and entered our suffering
to bring your healing to those in weakness and distress.
He broke the power of evil and set us free from sin and death
that we might become partakers of his glory.

All **To you be glory and praise for ever.**

His apostles anointed the sick in your name,
bringing wholeness and joy to a broken world.
By your grace renewed each day
you continue the gifts of healing in your Church
that your people may praise your name for ever.

All **To you be glory and praise for ever.**

By the power of your Spirit may your blessing rest
on those who are anointed with this oil in your name;
may they be made whole in body, mind and spirit.

All **Hear us, good Lord.**

Hear the prayer we offer for all your people.
Remember in your mercy those for whom we pray:
heal the sick, raise the fallen, strengthen the faint-hearted
and enfold in your love the fearful and those who have no hope.

All **Hear us, good Lord.**

In the fullness of time complete your gracious work.
Reconcile all things in Christ and make them new,
that we may be restored in your image, renewed in your love,
and serve you as sons and daughters in your kingdom.

All **Hear us, good Lord.**

Through your anointed Son, Jesus Christ, our Lord,
to whom with you and the Holy Spirit
we lift our voices of thanks and praise:

All **Blessed be God, our strength and our salvation,
now and for ever. Amen.**

A Short Form of Prayer over the Oil

Lord, holy Father, giver of health and salvation,
as your apostles anointed those who were sick and healed them,
so continue the ministry of healing in your Church.
Sanctify this oil, that those who are anointed with it
may be freed from suffering and distress,
find inward peace, and know the joy of your salvation,
through your Son, our Saviour Jesus Christ.

All **Amen.**

Prayer for Individuals
in Public Worship

1   A ministry of prayer for individuals may be offered in the context of public worship and should be introduced under the procedures required by Canon B 3. Suitable forms of prayer, including any approved under Canon B 4, may be used.

2   This public ministry of prayer may be accompanied by laying on of hands, and may also be accompanied by anointing with oil. It may be helpful to make clear in advance the form of ministry that is intended, which may take a number of forms, such as prayer for individuals who do not explain their particular need; prayer following a brief explanation to those who will pray with them of a person's need or concern; or prayer following an explanation to the whole congregation of a person's need or concern. (The Laying on of Hands may be received on behalf of a third person who is not present.)

3   Those who will be ministering to individuals should be offered appropriate help in preparing for this ministry. Before the service it is normally appropriate for them to pray together for grace and discernment.

4   In the context of a celebration of Holy Communion this personal ministry may be offered at one of the following points:

¶   as part of the Prayers of Intercession (which may, where appropriate, include prayers of penitence)

¶   at the time of the giving of communion

¶   at the end of the service.

5   The Order of the Celebration of Holy Communion may be varied
     as follows:

     ¶   the Prayers of Penitence may be replaced by other
         suitable material

     ¶   on occasion the Creed may be omitted or an authorized
         Affirmation of Faith may be used

     ¶   when ministry to individuals is incorporated into the Prayers
         of Intercession, psalms of lament or hope or other
         appropriate material may be used as a form of introduction
         to such prayer.

6   Whichever pattern is adopted, care needs to be taken to integrate
     ministry to individuals with the corporate prayer of the whole
     people. Where ministry to individuals takes place during or after
     the distribution of communion it is important that the gift and
     promise of communion is not overshadowed by prayer for individual
     needs. In places where ministry to individuals during or after the
     distribution of communion is a regular pattern, it may sometimes
     be helpful to focus such prayer by including prayer for them earlier
     in the service and on occasion to change the pattern to include this
     ministry earlier in the service.

Ministry to the Sick

The Celebration of Holy Communion at Home or in Hospital

with the Sick and Housebound

Note

Forms of service for a celebration of Holy Communion may be modified or shortened in the light of pastoral need and of the context within which they are used. Any material from authorized rites (such as forms of confession and absolution) may be used. When the Holy Communion is celebrated in the presence of the sick an authorized Eucharistic Prayer, the Breaking of the Bread and the Lord's Prayer are always included.

For further Notes, see page 73.

¶ *Two sample services follow, using Order One (pages 53–61) and Order One in Traditional Language (pages 63–72).*

¶ *If Order Two is used, the service follows the pattern in* Common Worship: Services and Prayers for the Church of England, *pages 228–266.*

The Celebration of
Holy Communion
at Home or in Hospital

with the Sick and Housebound

Order One

¶ *The Gathering*

The Greeting

Peace to this house and to all who live in it.

(or)

The peace of the Lord be always with you.

Prayer of Preparation

This prayer may be said

All **Almighty God,**
to whom all hearts are open,
all desires known,
and from whom no secrets are hidden:
cleanse the thoughts of our hearts
by the inspiration of your Holy Spirit,
that we may perfectly love you,
and worthily magnify your holy name;
through Christ our Lord.
Amen.

Prayers of Penitence

This or another invitation to confession may be used

[Come to me, all who labour and are heavy laden,
and I will give you rest.]

God shows his love for us
in that while we were still sinners, Christ died for us.
Let us then show our love for him
by confessing our sins in penitence and faith.

This or another authorized Confession is used

All **Almighty God, our heavenly Father,**
we have sinned against you
and against our neighbour
in thought and word and deed,
through negligence, through weakness,
through our own deliberate fault.
We are truly sorry
and repent of all our sins.
For the sake of your Son Jesus Christ,
who died for us,
forgive us all that is past,
and grant that we may serve you in newness of life
to the glory of your name.
Amen.

The president says

Almighty God,
who forgives all who truly repent,
have mercy upon *you*,
pardon and deliver *you* from all *your* sins,
confirm and strengthen *you* in all goodness,
and keep *you* in life eternal;
through Jesus Christ our Lord.

All **Amen.**

The Collect

*The president introduces a period of silent prayer with the words
'Let us pray' or a more specific bidding.*

The Collect is said, and all respond

All   **Amen.**

¶   *The Liturgy of the Word*

Readings

Either one or two readings from Scripture are used.

The Gospel reading follows.

Prayers of Intercession

Appropriate intercessions may be made.

*The Laying on of Hands with Prayer and Anointing may follow
(pages 92–93).*

¶ *The Liturgy of the Sacrament*

The Peace

If this greeting has not already been used, the president may introduce the Peace with a suitable sentence, and then says

The peace of the Lord be always with you

All **and also with you.**

These words may be added

Let us offer one another a sign of peace.

All may exchange a sign of peace.

Preparation of the Table

Taking of the Bread and Wine

The table is prepared and bread and wine are placed upon it.

At the preparation of the table this or another suitable prayer may be said

Pour upon the poverty of our love
and the weakness of our praise
the transforming fire of your presence.

All **Amen.**

The president takes the bread and wine.

The Eucharistic Prayer

This or another authorized Eucharistic Prayer is used.

Prayer E

The president says

The Lord be with you   *(or)*   The Lord is here.

All   **and also with you.**   **His Spirit is with us.**

Lift up your hearts.

All   **We lift them to the Lord.**

Let us give thanks to the Lord our God.

All   **It is right to give thanks and praise.**

It is right to give you thanks
in sickness and in health,
in suffering and in joy,
through Christ our Saviour and Redeemer,
who as the Good Samaritan
tends the wounds of body and spirit.
He stands by us and pours out for our healing
the oil of consolation and the wine of renewed hope,
turning the darkness of our pain
into the dawning light of his kingdom.

All   **Holy, holy, holy Lord,**
God of power and might,
heaven and earth are full of your glory.
Hosanna in the highest.
[Blessed is he who comes in the name of the Lord.
Hosanna in the highest.]

We praise and bless you, loving Father,
through Jesus Christ, our Lord;
and as we obey his command,
send your Holy Spirit,
that broken bread and wine outpoured
may be for us the body and blood of your dear Son.

On the night before he died he had supper with his friends
and, taking bread, he praised you.
He broke the bread, gave it to them and said:
Take, eat; this is my body which is given for you;
do this in remembrance of me.

When supper was ended he took the cup of wine.
Again he praised you, gave it to them and said:
Drink this, all of you;
this is my blood of the new covenant,
which is shed for you and for many for the forgiveness of sins.
Do this, as often as you drink it, in remembrance of me.

So, Father, we remember all that Jesus did,
in him we plead with confidence his sacrifice
    made once for all upon the cross.

Bringing before you the bread of life and cup of salvation,
we proclaim his death and resurrection
until he comes in glory.

This or another acclamation is used

[Great is the mystery of faith:]

All   **Christ has died:**
Christ is risen:
Christ will come again.

Lord of all life,
help us to work together for that day
when your kingdom comes
and justice and mercy will be seen in all the earth.

Look with favour on your people,
gather us in your loving arms
and bring us with [N and] all the saints
to feast at your table in heaven.

Through Christ, and with Christ, and in Christ,
in the unity of the Holy Spirit,
all honour and glory are yours, O loving Father,
for ever and ever.

All   **Amen.**

The Lord's Prayer

As our Saviour taught us, so we pray

All **Our Father in heaven,**
hallowed be your name,
your kingdom come,
your will be done,
on earth as in heaven.
Give us today our daily bread.
Forgive us our sins
as we forgive those who sin against us.
Lead us not into temptation
but deliver us from evil.
For the kingdom, the power,
and the glory are yours
now and for ever.
Amen.

(or)

Let us pray with confidence as our Saviour has taught us

All **Our Father, who art in heaven,**
hallowed be thy name;
thy kingdom come;
thy will be done;
on earth as it is in heaven.
Give us this day our daily bread.
And forgive us our trespasses,
as we forgive those who trespass against us.
And lead us not into temptation;
but deliver us from evil.
For thine is the kingdom,
the power and the glory,
for ever and ever.
Amen.

Breaking of the Bread

The president breaks the consecrated bread.

The Agnus Dei may be used as the bread is broken.

Giving of Communion

The president says this or another invitation to communion

Jesus is the Lamb of God
who takes away the sin of the world.
Blessed are those who are called to his supper.

All **Lord, I am not worthy to receive you,
but only say the word, and I shall be healed.**

This prayer may be said before the distribution

All **We do not presume
to come to this your table, merciful Lord,
trusting in our own righteousness,
but in your manifold and great mercies.
We are not worthy
so much as to gather up the crumbs under your table.
But you are the same Lord
whose nature is always to have mercy.
Grant us, therefore, gracious Lord,
so to eat the flesh of your dear Son Jesus Christ
and to drink his blood,
that our sinful bodies may be made clean by his body
and our souls washed through his most precious blood,
and that we may evermore dwell in him and he in us.
Amen.**

The president and people receive communion.

Authorized words of distribution are used and the communicant replies

Amen.

Prayer after Communion

Silence is kept.

The Post Communion or the following prayer, or another suitable prayer, is said

All **Almighty God,**
we thank you for feeding us
with the body and blood of your Son Jesus Christ.
Through him we offer you our souls and bodies
to be a living sacrifice.
Strengthen us
in the power of your Spirit
to live and work
to your praise and glory.
Amen.

¶ *Conclusion*

The president may use a suitable blessing, or

The peace of God,
which passes all understanding,
keep your hearts and minds
in the knowledge and love of God,
and of his Son Jesus Christ our Lord;
and the blessing of God almighty,
the Father, the Son, and the Holy Spirit,
be among you and remain with you always.

All **Amen.**

The Celebration of Holy Communion at Home or in Hospital

with the Sick and Housebound

Order One *in Traditional Language*

¶ *The Gathering*

The Greeting

Peace to this house and to all who live in it.

(or)

The peace of the Lord be always with you.

Prayer of Preparation

This prayer may be said

All **Almighty God,**
unto whom all hearts be open,
all desires known,
and from whom no secrets are hid:
cleanse the thoughts of our hearts
by the inspiration of thy Holy Spirit,
that we may perfectly love thee,
and worthily magnify thy holy name;
through Christ our Lord.
Amen.

Prayers of Penitence

This or another invitation to confession may be used

[Come to me, all who labour and are heavy laden,
and I will give you rest.]

God shows his love for us
in that while we were still sinners, Christ died for us.
Let us then show our love for him
by confessing our sins in penitence and faith.

The following or another authorized confession is used

All   **Almighty God, our heavenly Father,**
we have sinned against thee
and against our neighbour,
in thought and word and deed,
through negligence, through weakness,
through our own deliberate fault.
We are heartily sorry
and repent of all our sins.
For the sake of thy Son Jesus Christ,
who died for us,
forgive us all that is past,
and grant that we may serve thee in newness of life
to the glory of thy name.
Amen.

The president says

Almighty God,
who forgives all who truly repent,
have mercy upon *you,*
pardon and deliver *you* from all *your* sins,
confirm and strengthen *you* in all goodness,
and keep *you* in life eternal;
through Jesus Christ our Lord.

All   **Amen.**

The Collect

*The president introduces a period of silent prayer with the words
'Let us pray' or a more specific bidding.*

The Collect is said, and all respond

All   **Amen.**

¶ *The Liturgy of the Word*

Readings

Either one or two readings from Scripture are used.

The Gospel reading follows.

Prayers of Intercession

Appropriate intercessions may be made.

*The Laying on of Hands with Prayer and Anointing may follow
(pages 92–93).*

¶ The Liturgy of the Sacrament

The Peace

If this greeting has not already been used, the president may introduce the Peace with a suitable sentence, and then says

The peace of the Lord be always with you

All **and with thy spirit.**

These words may be added

Let us offer one another a sign of peace.

All may exchange a sign of peace.

Preparation of the Table

Taking of the Bread and Wine

The table is prepared and bread and wine are placed upon it.

At the preparation of the table this or another suitable prayer may be said

Pour upon the poverty of our love
and the weakness of our praise
the transforming fire of thy presence.

All **Amen.**

The president takes the bread and wine.

The Eucharistic Prayer

This or another authorized Eucharistic Prayer is used.

Prayer C

The Lord be with you.   *(or)*   The Lord is here.
All **And with thy spirit.**   **His Spirit is with us.**

Lift up your hearts.
All **We lift them up unto the Lord.**

Let us give thanks unto the Lord our God.
All **It is meet and right so to do.**

It is very meet, right and our bounden duty,
that we should at all times and in all places give thanks unto thee,
O Lord, holy Father,
almighty, everlasting God,
through Jesus Christ thine only Son our Lord.

This or another short Proper Preface may be used

And now we give thee thanks
that thou hast shown the greatness of thy love for us
by sending him to share our human nature
and accomplish our forgiveness.
He embraces us in our weakness,
he suffers with the sick and the rejected,
and, bringing thy healing to the world,
he rescues us from every evil.

Therefore with angels and archangels,
and with all the company of heaven,
we laud and magnify thy glorious name,
evermore praising thee and *saying*:

All **Holy, holy, holy, Lord God of hosts,**
heaven and earth are full of thy glory.
Glory be to thee, O Lord most high.
[Blessed is he that cometh in the name of the Lord.
Hosanna in the highest.]

All glory be to thee,
almighty God, our heavenly Father,
who, of thy tender mercy,
didst give thine only Son Jesus Christ
to suffer death upon the cross for our redemption;
who made there,
by his one oblation of himself once offered,
a full, perfect and sufficient sacrifice, oblation and satisfaction
    for the sins of the whole world;
and did institute,
and in his holy gospel command us to continue,
a perpetual memory of that his precious death,
until his coming again.

Hear us, O merciful Father, we most humbly beseech thee,
and grant that, by the power of thy Holy Spirit,
we receiving these thy creatures of bread and wine,
according to thy Son our Saviour Jesus Christ's holy institution,
in remembrance of his death and passion,
may be partakers of his most blessed body and blood;

who, in the same night that he was betrayed, took bread;
and when he had given thanks to thee,
he broke it and gave it to his disciples, saying:
Take, eat; this is my body which is given for you;
do this in remembrance of me.

Likewise after supper he took the cup;
and when he had given thanks to thee, he gave it to them, saying:
Drink ye all of this;
for this is my blood of the new covenant,
which is shed for you and for many for the forgiveness of sins.
Do this, as oft as ye shall drink it,
in remembrance of me.

One of the following may be used

[Great is the mystery of faith:]
All **Christ has died:**
Christ is risen:
Christ will come again.

(or)

[Jesus Christ is Lord:]

All **O Saviour of the world,**
who by thy cross and precious blood hast redeemed us,
save us, and help us, we humbly beseech thee, O Lord.

Wherefore, O Lord and heavenly Father,
we thy humble servants,
having in remembrance
the precious death and passion of thy dear Son,
his mighty resurrection and glorious ascension,
entirely desire thy fatherly goodness
mercifully to accept this our sacrifice of praise
    and thanksgiving;
most humbly beseeching thee to grant that
by the merits and death of thy Son Jesus Christ,
and through faith in his blood,
we and all thy whole church may obtain remission of our sins,
and all other benefits of his passion.
And although we be unworthy, through our manifold sins,
to offer unto thee any sacrifice,
yet we beseech thee
to accept this our bounden duty and service,
not weighing our merits, but pardoning our offences;
and to grant that all we, who are partakers of this holy communion,
may be fulfilled with thy grace and heavenly benediction;

through Jesus Christ our Lord,
by whom, and with whom, and in whom,
in the unity of the Holy Spirit,
all honour and glory be unto thee,
O Father almighty,
world without end.

All **Amen.**

The Lord's Prayer

Let us pray with confidence as our Saviour has taught us

All   **Our Father, who art in heaven,**
hallowed be thy name;
thy kingdom come;
thy will be done;
on earth as it is in heaven.
Give us this day our daily bread.
And forgive us our trespasses,
as we forgive those who trespass against us.
And lead us not into temptation;
but deliver us from evil.
For thine is the kingdom,
the power and the glory,
for ever and ever.
Amen.

(or)

As our Saviour taught us, so we pray

All   **Our Father in heaven,**
hallowed be your name,
your kingdom come,
your will be done,
on earth as in heaven.
Give us today our daily bread.
Forgive us our sins
as we forgive those who sin against us.
Lead us not into temptation
but deliver us from evil.
For the kingdom, the power,
and the glory are yours
now and for ever.
Amen.

Breaking of the Bread

The president breaks the consecrated bread.

The Agnus Dei may be used as the bread is broken.

Giving of Communion

The president says this or another invitation to communion

Jesus is the Lamb of God
who takes away the sin of the world.
Blessed are those who are called to his supper.

All **Lord, I am not worthy that thou shouldest come
     under my roof,
but speak the word only, and my soul shall be healed.**

This prayer may be said before the distribution

All **We do not presume
to come to this thy table, O merciful Lord,
trusting in our own righteousness,
but in thy manifold and great mercies.
We are not worthy
so much as to gather up the crumbs under thy table.
But thou art the same Lord
whose nature is always to have mercy.
Grant us, therefore, gracious Lord,
so to eat the flesh of thy dear Son Jesus Christ
and to drink his blood,
that our sinful bodies may be made clean by his body
and our souls washed through his most precious blood,
and that we may evermore dwell in him and he in us.
Amen.**

The president and people receive communion.

Authorized words of distribution are used and the communicant replies

Amen.

Prayer after Communion

Silence is kept.

The Post Communion or the following prayer, or another suitable prayer, is said

All **Almighty God,**
we thank thee for feeding us
with the body and blood of thy Son Jesus Christ.
Through him we offer thee our souls and bodies
to be a living sacrifice.
Strengthen us
in the power of thy Spirit
to live and work
to thy praise and glory.
Amen.

¶ *Conclusion*

The president may use a suitable blessing, or

The peace of God,
which passes all understanding,
keep your hearts and minds
in the knowledge and love of God,
and of his Son Jesus Christ our Lord;
and the blessing of God almighty,
the Father, the Son, and the Holy Spirit,
be among you and remain with you always.

All **Amen.**

Notes to the Celebration of Holy Communion at Home or in Hospital

with the Sick and Housebound

1   **Prayers of Penitence**
These may be omitted when the service has been preceded by a penitential rite.

2   **Seasonal Material**
Seasonal or Sunday provision may be used in place of that provided here. At Christmas, Easter and Pentecost some at least of the seasonal provision for the Festival should be used.

3   **Laying on of Hands and Anointing**
The form on pages 92–93 may be used at the Prayers/Prayers of Intercession (Order One) or between the Absolution and Comfortable Words (Order Two).

4   **Anointing**
Canon B 37 provides that the priest should use 'pure oil consecrated by the bishop of the diocese or otherwise by the priest himself' and that the anointing should be made on the forehead with the sign of the cross. In some circumstances it may also be appropriate to anoint on the hands.

5   **Reception of the Consecrated Bread and Wine**
Communion should normally be received in both kinds separately, but where necessary may be received in one kind, whether of bread or, where the communicant cannot receive solid food, wine.

6   **Spiritual Communion**
Believers who cannot physically receive the sacrament are to be assured that they are partakers by faith of the body and blood of Christ and of the benefits he conveys to us by them.

7   **Residential Homes**
These forms may be used in residential homes where pastorally appropriate.

The Distribution of Holy Communion at Home or in Hospital

to the Sick and Housebound

An Outline Order (Order One)

For Notes, see pages 78–79.

The Greeting

This may be

Peace to this house and to all who live in it.

Words of Introduction

These or other suitable words may be used

The Church of God, of which we are members, has taken bread and wine and given thanks over them according to our Lord's command. These holy gifts are now offered to us that, with faith and thanksgiving, we may share in the communion of the body and blood of Christ.

[Prayer of Preparation]

Prayers of Penitence

These may include this invitation to confession

[Come to me, all who labour and are heavy laden, and I will give you rest.]

God shows his love for us
in that when we were still sinners, Christ died for us.
Let us then show our love for him
by confessing our sins in penitence and faith.

The Collect

Reading(s) and Prayers

[Laying on of Hands and Anointing]

The Lord's Prayer

Invitation to Communion

[Prayer of Humble Access]

Giving of Communion

Prayer after Communion

This may include the following varied form

All **Almighty God,**
we thank you for feeding us
with the body and blood of your Son Jesus Christ.
Through him we offer you our souls and bodies
to be a living sacrifice.
Strengthen us
in the power of your Spirit
to live and work
to your praise and glory.
Amen.

The Grace *or* a Blessing

The Distribution of Holy Communion at Home or in Hospital

to the Sick and Housebound

An Outline Order (Order Two)

For Notes, see pages 78–79.

The Greeting

This may be

> Peace be to this house, and to all that dwell in it.

Words of Introduction

These or other suitable words may be used

> The Church of God, of which we are members, has taken bread
> and wine and given thanks over them according to our Lord's
> command. These holy gifts are now offered to us that, with faith
> and thanksgiving, we may share in the communion of the body
> and blood of Christ.

[Prayer of Preparation]

The Collect

Reading(s) and Prayers

Prayers of Penitence

These may include this invitation to confession

> [Come unto me, all that travail and are heavy laden,
> and I will refresh you.]

> God shows his love for us
> in that when we were still sinners, Christ died for us.
> Let us then show our love for him
> by confessing our sins in penitence and faith.

[Laying on of Hands and Anointing]

[Prayer of Humble Access]

Invitation to Communion

Giving of Communion

The Lord's Prayer

Prayer after Communion

This may include the following varied form

All **Almighty God,**
we thank thee for feeding us
with the body and blood of thy Son Jesus Christ.
Through him we offer thee our souls and bodies
to be a living sacrifice.
Strengthen us
in the power of thy Spirit
to live and work
to thy praise and glory.
Amen.

The Grace *or* **a Blessing**

Notes to the Distribution of Holy Communion at Home or in Hospital

to the Sick and Housebound

1 **The Distribution of Communion to the Sick and Housebound**

¶ Ministers may be either ordained or lay persons authorized by the bishop to assist in the distribution of Holy Communion.

¶ When the consecrated bread and wine are to be conveyed directly from a celebration to those not present, they are given to the ministers at the distribution or at the end of the service. The ministers may receive communion either at the celebration or with those to whom they take the elements, or on both occasions.

¶ When Holy Communion is distributed at other times to those absent from a celebration, the minister may receive with them but need not do so.

¶ Words of introduction linking the consecrated elements with the celebration at which they were consecrated must be used.

2 **Prayers of Penitence**
These may be omitted when the service has been preceded by a penitential rite.

3 **Seasonal Material**
Seasonal or Sunday provision may be used in place of that provided here. At Christmas, Easter and Pentecost some at least of the seasonal provision for the Festival should be used.

4 **Laying on of Hands and Anointing**
The form on page 92 may be used at the Prayers/Prayers of Intercession (Order One) or between the Absolution and Comfortable Words (Order Two).

5   **Anointing**
     Canon B 37 provides that the priest should use 'pure oil
     consecrated by the bishop of the diocese or otherwise by the
     priest himself' and that the anointing should be made on the
     forehead with the sign of the cross. In some circumstances it
     may also be appropriate to anoint on the hands.

6   **Reception of the Consecrated Bread and Wine**
     Communion should normally be received in both kinds separately,
     but where necessary may be received in one kind, whether of
     bread or, where the communicant cannot receive solid food, wine.

7   **Spiritual Communion**
     Believers who cannot physically receive the sacrament are to be
     assured that they are partakers by faith of the body and blood of
     Christ and of the benefits he conveys to us by them.

8   **Residential Homes**
     These forms may be used in residential homes where pastorally
     appropriate.

The Distribution of Holy Communion at Home or in Hospital

to the Sick and Housebound

A Sample Service (Order One)

This form of service follows the Outline Order on pages 74–75.

For Notes, see pages 78–79.

The Greeting

Peace to this house and to all who live in it.

(or)

The peace of the Lord be always with you.

Words of Introduction

These or other suitable words may be used

The Church of God, of which we are members, has taken bread and wine and given thanks over them according to our Lord's command. These holy gifts are now offered to us that, with faith and thanksgiving, we may share in the communion of the body and blood of Christ.

Prayer of Preparation

This prayer may be said

All **Almighty God,**
to whom all hearts are open,
all desires known,
and from whom no secrets are hidden:
cleanse the thoughts of our hearts
by the inspiration of your Holy Spirit,
that we may perfectly love you,
and worthily magnify your holy name;
through Christ our Lord.
Amen.

Prayers of Penitence

This or another invitation to confession may be used

[Come to me, all who labour and are heavy laden,
and I will give you rest.]

God shows his love for us
in that while we were still sinners, Christ died for us.
Let us then show our love for him
by confessing our sins in penitence and faith.

This or another authorized confession is used

All **Almighty God, our heavenly Father,**
we have sinned against you
and against our neighbour
in thought and word and deed,
through negligence, through weakness,
through our own deliberate fault.
We are truly sorry
and repent of all our sins.
For the sake of your Son Jesus Christ,
who died for us,
forgive us all that is past,
and grant that we may serve you in newness of life
to the glory of your name.
Amen.

The minister says

Almighty God,
who forgives all who truly repent,
have mercy upon *us*,
pardon and deliver *us* from all *our* sins,
confirm and strengthen *us* in all goodness,
and keep *us* in life eternal;
through Jesus Christ our Lord.

All **Amen.**

The Collect

*The minister introduces a period of silent prayer with the words
'Let us pray' or a more specific bidding.*

The Collect is said, and all respond

All **Amen.**

Reading(s) and Prayers

Either one or two readings from Scripture are read.

The Gospel reading follows.

Appropriate intercessions may be made.

*The Laying on of Hands with Prayer and Anointing may follow
(pages 92–93).*

The Lord's Prayer

As our Saviour taught us, so we pray

All **Our Father in heaven,**
hallowed be your name,
your kingdom come,
your will be done,
on earth as in heaven.
Give us today our daily bread.
Forgive us our sins
as we forgive those who sin against us.
Lead us not into temptation
but deliver us from evil.
For the kingdom, the power,
and the glory are yours
now and for ever.
Amen.

(or)

Let us pray with confidence as our Saviour has taught us

All **Our Father, who art in heaven,**
hallowed be thy name;
thy kingdom come;
thy will be done;
on earth as it is in heaven.
Give us this day our daily bread.
And forgive us our trespasses,
as we forgive those who trespass against us.
And lead us not into temptation;
but deliver us from evil.
For thine is the kingdom,
the power and the glory,
for ever and ever.
Amen.

Giving of Communion

The minister says this or another invitation to communion

Jesus is the Lamb of God
who takes away the sin of the world.
Blessed are those who are called to his supper.

All **Lord, I am not worthy to receive you,**
but only say the word, and I shall be healed.

This prayer may be said before the distribution

All **We do not presume**
to come to this your table, merciful Lord,
trusting in our own righteousness,
but in your manifold and great mercies.
We are not worthy
so much as to gather up the crumbs under your table.
But you are the same Lord
whose nature is always to have mercy.
Grant us, therefore, gracious Lord,
so to eat the flesh of your dear Son Jesus Christ
and to drink his blood,
that our sinful bodies may be made clean by his body
and our souls washed through his most precious blood,
and that we may evermore dwell in him and he in us.
Amen.

The minister and people receive communion.

Authorized words of distribution are used and the communicant replies

Amen.

Prayer after Communion

The following, or another suitable prayer is said

All **Almighty God,
we thank you for feeding us
with the body and blood of your Son Jesus Christ.
Through him we offer you our souls and bodies
to be a living sacrifice.
Strengthen us
in the power of your Spirit
to live and work
to your praise and glory.
Amen.**

Conclusion

The minister says the Grace or a suitable blessing.

The Distribution of Holy Communion at Home or in Hospital

to the Sick and Housebound

A Sample Service (Order Two)

This form of service follows the Outline Order on pages 76–77.

For Notes, see pages 78–79.

The Greeting

Peace be to this house, and to all that dwell in it.

(or)

The peace of the Lord be always with you.

Words of Introduction

These or other suitable words may be used

The Church of God, of which we are members, has taken bread and wine and given thanks over them according to our Lord's command. These holy gifts are now offered to us that, with faith and thanksgiving, we may share in the communion of the body and blood of Christ.

Prayer of Preparation

This prayer may be said

Almighty God,
unto whom all hearts be open,
all desires known,
and from whom no secrets are hid:
cleanse the thoughts of our hearts
by the inspiration of thy Holy Spirit,
that we may perfectly love thee,
and worthily magnify thy holy name;
through Christ our Lord.

All   **Amen.**

Our Lord Jesus Christ said:
Hear, O Israel, the Lord our God is one Lord;
and thou shalt love the Lord thy God with all thy heart,
and with all thy soul, and with all thy mind,
and with all thy strength.
This is the first commandment.

And the second is like, namely this:
Thou shalt love thy neighbour as thyself.
There is none other commandment greater than these.
On these two commandments hang all the law
    and the prophets.

All   **Lord, have mercy upon us,
and write all these thy laws in our hearts, we beseech thee.**

The Collect

The minister says the Collect.

Reading(s) and Prayers

Either one or two readings from Scripture are used.

The Gospel reading follows.

Appropriate intercessions may be made.

Invitation to Confession

This or another invitation to confession may be used

[Come unto me, all that travail and are heavy laden,
and I will refresh you.]

God shows his love for us
in that while we were still sinners, Christ died for us.
Let us then show our love for him
by confessing our sins in penitence and faith.

Confession

All   **Almighty God,**
Father of our Lord Jesus Christ,
maker of all things, judge of all men:
we acknowledge and bewail our manifold sins
    and wickedness,
which we, from time to time,
    most grievously have committed,
by thought, word and deed,
against thy divine majesty,
provoking most justly thy wrath and indignation against us.
We do earnestly repent,
and are heartily sorry for these our misdoings;
the remembrance of them is grievous unto us;
the burden of them is intolerable.
Have mercy upon us,
have mercy upon us, most merciful Father;
for thy Son our Lord Jesus Christ's sake,
forgive us all that is past;
and grant that we may ever hereafter
serve and please thee in newness of life,
to the honour and glory of thy name;
through Jesus Christ our Lord.
Amen.

The minister says

Almighty God, our heavenly Father,
who of his great mercy
hath promised forgiveness of sins
to all them that with hearty repentance and true faith
    turn unto him:
have mercy upon *us*;
pardon and deliver *us* from all *our* sins;
confirm and strengthen *us* in all goodness;
and bring *us* to everlasting life;
through Jesus Christ our Lord.

All   **Amen.**

The Laying on of Hands with Prayer and Anointing may follow
(pages 92–93).

The Comfortable Words

Hear what comfortable words our Saviour Christ saith
unto all that truly turn to him:

Come unto me, all that travail and are heavy laden,
and I will refresh you.   *Matthew 11.28*

So God loved the world, that he gave his only-begotten Son,
to the end that all that believe in him should not perish,
but have everlasting life.   *John 3.16*

Hear also what Saint Paul saith:
This is a true saying, and worthy of all men to be received,
that Christ Jesus came into the world to save sinners. *1 Timothy 1.15*

Hear also what Saint John saith:
If any man sin, we have an advocate with the Father,
Jesus Christ the righteous;
and he is the propitiation for our sins.   *1 John 2.1*

Prayer of Humble Access

This prayer may be said

We do not presume
to come to this thy table, O merciful Lord,
trusting in our own righteousness,
but in thy manifold and great mercies.
We are not worthy
so much as to gather up the crumbs under thy table.
But thou art the same Lord,
whose property is always to have mercy:
grant us therefore, gracious Lord,
so to eat the flesh of thy dear Son Jesus Christ,
and to drink his blood,
that our sinful bodies may be made clean by his body,
and our souls washed through his most precious blood,
and that we may evermore dwell in him,
and he in us.

All   **Amen.**

Giving of Communion

The minister and people receive communion. To each is said

The body of our Lord Jesus Christ, which was given for thee,
preserve thy body and soul unto everlasting life.
Take and eat this in remembrance that Christ died for thee,
and feed on him in thy heart by faith with thanksgiving.

The blood of our Lord Jesus Christ, which was shed for thee,
preserve thy body and soul unto everlasting life.
Drink this in remembrance that Christ's blood was shed for thee,
    and be thankful.

The Lord's Prayer

As our Saviour Christ hath commanded and taught us,
we are bold to say

All   **Our Father, which art in heaven,**
hallowed be thy name;
thy kingdom come;
thy will be done,
in earth as it is in heaven.
Give us this day our daily bread.
And forgive us our trespasses,
as we forgive them that trespass against us.
And lead us not into temptation;
but deliver us from evil.
For thine is the kingdom,
the power and the glory,
for ever and ever.
Amen.

Prayer after Communion

The following or another suitable prayer is said

All   **Almighty God,**
we thank thee for feeding us
with the body and blood of thy Son Jesus Christ.
Through him we offer thee our souls and bodies
to be a living sacrifice.
Strengthen us
in the power of thy Spirit
to live and work
to thy praise and glory.
Amen.

The Blessing

The minister says the Grace or a suitable blessing.

Laying on of Hands
with Prayer and Anointing

*This form may be used at the prayers during the visitation of the sick,
either at Holy Communion with the sick or as part of another form of
prayer at the bedside. If Anointing is administered, the minister must be
authorized for this ministry as required by Canon B 37.*

Blessed are you, sovereign God, gentle and merciful.
Your anointed Son brought healing to those in weakness
    and distress;
he broke the power of evil and set us free from sin and death
that we might become partakers of his glory.
Remember in your mercy all for whom we pray;
in the fullness of time complete your gracious work
that we may be restored in your image, renewed in your love,
and for ever praise your great and holy name,
Father, Son and Holy Spirit.

Holy God, in whom we live and move and have our being,
we make our prayer to you saying,
Lord, hear us.
Lord, graciously hear us.

Grant to [N and] all who seek you
the assurance of your presence, your power and your peace.
Lord, hear us.
Lord, graciously hear us.

Grant your healing grace to [N and] all who are sick,
that they may be made whole in body, mind and spirit.
Lord, hear us.
Lord, graciously hear us.

Grant to all who minister to the suffering
wisdom and skill, sympathy and patience.
Lord, hear us.
Lord, graciously hear us.

Sustain and support the anxious and fearful
and lift up all who are brought low.
Lord, hear us.
Lord, graciously hear us.

Hear us, Lord of life.
Heal us, and make us whole.

A period of silence follows.

O Lord our God, accept the fervent prayers of your people;
in the multitude of your mercies look with compassion
upon us and all who turn to you for help;
for you are gracious, O lover of souls,
and to you we give glory, Father, Son, and Holy Spirit,
now and for ever.
Amen.

The Laying on of Hands is administered.

In the name of God and trusting in his might alone,
receive Christ's healing touch to make you whole.

May Christ bring you wholeness
of body, mind and spirit,
deliver you from every evil,
and give you his peace.
Amen.

These words are used when Anointing is administered

N, I anoint you in the name of God who gives you life.
Receive Christ's forgiveness, his healing and his love.

May the Father of our Lord Jesus Christ
grant you the riches of his grace,
his wholeness and his peace.
Amen.

The minister says

The almighty Lord,
who is a strong tower for all who put their trust in him,
whom all things in heaven, on earth and under the earth obey,
be now and evermore your defence.
May you believe and trust that the only name under heaven
given for health and salvation
is the name of our Lord Jesus Christ.
Amen.

Prayers for Protection and Peace

Notes

1   The following material may be used where it would be pastorally helpful to pray with those suffering from a sense of disturbance or unrest.

2   These pastoral prayers may be used by any minister as appropriate. The ministry of exorcism and deliverance may only be exercised by priests authorized by the bishop, who normally requires that permission be obtained from him for each specific exercise of such a ministry.

3   On occasions when exorcism and deliverance are administered, it is for the bishop to determine the nature of the rite and what form of words should be used.

Prayers for Protection and Peace

May the Lord hear you in the day of trouble,
the name of the God of Jacob defend you;

Send you help from his sanctuary
and strengthen you out of Zion;

Remember all your offerings
and accept your burnt sacrifice;

Grant you your heart's desire
and fulfil all your mind.   *Psalm 20.1-4*
Amen.

Our Lord Jesus Christ,
present with us now in his risen power,
enter into your body and spirit,
take from you all that harms and hinders you,
and fill you with his healing and his peace.
Amen.

Christ be with you: Christ within you;
Christ before you: Christ behind you;
Christ on your right: Christ on your left;
Christ above you: Christ beneath you;
Christ around you: now and ever.

Bind unto yourself the name,
the strong name of the Trinity;
by invocation of the same,
the Three in One and One in Three.
Of whom all nature hath creation,
Eternal Father, Spirit, Word:
praise the Lord of your salvation,
salvation is of Christ the Lord.
Amen.

Almighty God, heavenly Father,
breathe your Holy Spirit into the heart of this your servant *N*
and inspire *him/her* with love for goodness and truth.
May *he/she*, fearing only you, have no other fear;
knowing your compassion, be ever mindful of your love;
and serving you faithfully unto death, live eternally with you;
through Jesus Christ our Lord.
Amen.

For a place
Visit, Lord, we pray, this place
and drive far from it all the snares of the enemy.
Let your holy angels dwell here to keep us in peace,
and may your blessing be upon it evermore;
through Jesus Christ our Lord.
Amen.

Christaraksha – an Indian Prayer

This prayer may be used in any of the following forms

I   *For a person before sleep*
May the cross of the Son of God,
which is mightier than all the hosts of Satan
and more glorious than all the hosts of heaven,
abide with you in your going out and in your coming in.
By day and by night, at morning and at evening,
at all times and in all places may it protect and defend you.
From the wrath of evildoers, from the assaults of evil spirits,
from foes visible and invisible, from the snares of the devil,
from all passions that beguile the soul and body:
may it guard, protect and deliver you.
Amen.

(or)

2 *As a blessing*
May the risen and ascended Christ,
mightier than the hordes of hell,
more glorious than the heavenly hosts,
be with you in all your ways.
Amen.

May the cross of the Son of God
protect you by day and by night,
at morning and at evening,
at all times and in all places.
Amen.

May Christ Jesus guard and deliver you
from the snares of the devil,
from the assaults of evil spirits,
from the wrath of the wicked,
from all base passions
and from the fear of the known and unknown.
Amen.

And the blessing of God almighty,
the Father, the Son, and the Holy Spirit,
be upon you and remain with you always.
Amen.

(or)

3 *For individuals to say before sleep*
May the cross of the Son of God,
which is mightier than all the hosts of Satan,
and more glorious than all the hosts of heaven,
abide with me in my going out and my coming in.
By day and by night, at morning and at evening,
at all times and in all places may it protect and defend me.
From the wrath of evildoers, from the assaults of evil spirits,
from foes visible and invisible, from the snares of the devil,
from all passions that beguile the soul and body:
may it guard, protect and deliver me.
Amen.

Psalm responsories

Based on Psalm 91

Whoever dwells in the shelter of the Most High,
and abides under the shadow of the Almighty,

Shall say to the Lord, 'My refuge and my stronghold,
my God, in whom I put my trust.'

For he shall deliver you from the snare of the fowler
and from the deadly pestilence.

He shall cover you with his wings
    and you shall be safe under his feathers;
his faithfulness shall be my shield and buckler.

You shall not be afraid of any terror by night,
nor of the arrow that flies by day;

Of the pestilence that stalks in darkness,
nor of the sickness that destroys at noonday.

Because you have made the Lord your refuge
and the Most High my stronghold,

There shall no evil happen to you,
neither shall any plague come near my tent.

For he shall give his angels charge over you,
to keep me in all my ways.

Based on Psalm 121

We lift up our eyes to the hills;
from where is our help to come?

Our help comes from the Lord,
the maker of heaven and earth.

He will not suffer your foot to stumble;
he who watches over you will not sleep.

Behold, he who keeps watch over Israel
shall neither slumber nor sleep.

The Lord himself watches over you;
the Lord is your shade at your right hand,

So that the sun shall not strike you by day,
neither the moon by night.

The Lord shall keep you from all evil;
it is he who shall keep your soul.

The Lord shall keep watch over your going out
    and your coming in,
from this time forth for evermore.

Marriage

Contents

For General Rules, see page 402.

The Marriage Service

¶ *Pastoral Introduction*

This may be read by those present before the service begins.

A wedding is one of life's great moments, a time of solemn
commitment as well as good wishes, feasting and joy. St John tells
us how Jesus shared in such an occasion at Cana, and gave there
a sign of new beginnings as he turned water into wine.

Marriage is intended by God to be a creative relationship, as his
blessing enables husband and wife to love and support each other
in good times and in bad, and to share in the care and upbringing
of children. For Christians, marriage is also an invitation to share
life together in the spirit of Jesus Christ. It is based upon a solemn,
public and life-long covenant between a man and a woman, declared
and celebrated in the presence of God and before witnesses.

On this their wedding day the bride and bridegroom face each
other, make their promises and receive God's blessing. You are
witnesses of the marriage, and express your support by your
presence and your prayers. Your support does not end today:
the couple will value continued encouragement in the days and
years ahead of them.

*Love is patient; love is kind; love is not envious or boastful or arrogant
or rude. It does not insist on its own way; it is not irritable or resentful;
it does not rejoice in wrongdoing, but rejoices in the truth. It bears all
things, believes all things, hopes all things, endures all things.*

1 Corinthians 13.4-7

The Marriage Service

Structure

¶ **Introduction**

The Welcome

Preface

The Declarations

The Collect

Readings

Sermon

¶ **The Marriage**

The Vows

The Giving of Rings

The Proclamation

The Blessing of the Marriage

Registration of the Marriage

Prayers

The Dismissal

For Notes, see pages 132–134.

The Marriage Service

¶ *Introduction*

The Welcome

The minister welcomes the people using these
or other appropriate words

The grace of our Lord Jesus Christ,
the love of God,
and the fellowship of the Holy Spirit
be with you

All **and also with you.**

This sentence may be used

God is love, and those who live in love live in God
and God lives in them.   *1 John 4.16*

This prayer may be said

All **God of wonder and of joy:**
grace comes from you,
and you alone are the source of life and love.
Without you, we cannot please you;
without your love, our deeds are worth nothing.
Send your Holy Spirit,
and pour into our hearts
**   that most excellent gift of love,**
that we may worship you now
with thankful hearts
and serve you always with willing minds;
through Jesus Christ our Lord.
Amen.

A hymn may be sung.

Preface

These words or those on page 136 are used

In the presence of God, Father, Son and Holy Spirit,
we have come together
to witness the marriage of N and N,
to pray for God's blessing on them,
to share their joy
and to celebrate their love.

Marriage is a gift of God in creation
through which husband and wife may know the grace of God.
It is given
that as man and woman grow together in love and trust,
they shall be united with one another in heart, body and mind,
as Christ is united with his bride, the Church.

The gift of marriage brings husband and wife together
in the delight and tenderness of sexual union
and joyful commitment to the end of their lives.
It is given as the foundation of family life
in which children are [born and] nurtured
and in which each member of the family,
in good times and in bad,
may find strength, companionship and comfort,
and grow to maturity in love.

Marriage is a way of life made holy by God,
and blessed by the presence of our Lord Jesus Christ
with those celebrating a wedding at Cana in Galilee.
Marriage is a sign of unity and loyalty
which all should uphold and honour.
It enriches society and strengthens community.
No one should enter into it lightly or selfishly
but reverently and responsibly in the sight of almighty God.

N and N are now to enter this way of life.
They will each give their consent to the other
and make solemn vows,
and in token of this they will [each] give and receive a ring.
We pray with them that the Holy Spirit will guide
    and strengthen them,
that they may fulfil God's purposes
for the whole of their earthly life together.

The Declarations

The minister says to the congregation

First, I am required to ask anyone present who knows a reason
why these persons may not lawfully marry, to declare it now.

The minister says to the couple

The vows you are about to take are to be made in the presence
   of God,
who is judge of all and knows all the secrets of our hearts;
therefore if either of you knows a reason why you may not
   lawfully marry,
you must declare it now.

The minister says to the bridegroom

N, will you take N to be your wife?
Will you love her, comfort her, honour and protect her,
and, forsaking all others,
be faithful to her as long as you both shall live?

He answers

I will.

The minister says to the bride

N, will you take N to be your husband?
Will you love him, comfort him, honour and protect him,
and, forsaking all others,
be faithful to him as long as you both shall live?

She answers

I will.

The minister says to the congregation

Will you, the families and friends of N and N,
support and uphold them in their marriage
now and in the years to come?

All   **We will.**

The Collect

*The minister invites the people to pray, silence is kept
and the minister says the Collect*

God our Father,
from the beginning
you have blessed creation with abundant life.
Pour out your blessings upon *N* and *N*,
that they may be joined in mutual love and companionship,
in holiness and commitment to each other.
We ask this through our Lord Jesus Christ your Son,
who is alive and reigns with you,
in the unity of the Holy Spirit,
one God, now and for ever.

All **Amen.**

Readings

*At least one reading from the Bible is used.
A selection of readings is found on pages 137–149.*

Sermon

¶ The Marriage

A hymn may be sung.

The couple stand before the minister.

The Vows

The minister introduces the vows in these or similar words

N and N, I now invite you to join hands and make your vows,
in the presence of God and his people.

The bride and bridegroom face each other.
The bridegroom takes the bride's right hand in his.

These words, or those on page 150, are used

I, N, take you, N,
to be my wife,
to have and to hold
from this day forward;
for better, for worse,
for richer, for poorer,
in sickness and in health,
to love and to cherish,
till death us do part;
according to God's holy law.
In the presence of God I make this vow.

They loose hands.
The bride takes the bridegroom's right hand in hers, and says

I, N, take you, N,
to be my husband,
to have and to hold
from this day forward;
for better, for worse,
for richer, for poorer,
in sickness and in health,
to love and to cherish,
till death us do part;
according to God's holy law.
In the presence of God I make this vow.

They loose hands.

The Giving of Rings

The minister receives the ring(s), and says this prayer
or the prayer on page 151

Heavenly Father, by your blessing
let *these rings* be to N and N
a symbol of unending love and faithfulness,
to remind them of the vow and covenant
which they have made this day
through Jesus Christ our Lord.

All **Amen.**

The bridegroom places the ring on the fourth finger of the
bride's left hand and, holding it there, says

N, I give you this ring
as a sign of our marriage.
With my body I honour you,
all that I am I give to you,
and all that I have I share with you,
within the love of God,
Father, Son and Holy Spirit.

If rings are exchanged, they loose hands and the bride places a ring on
the fourth finger of the bridegroom's left hand and, holding it there, says

N, I give you this ring
as a sign of our marriage.
With my body I honour you,
all that I am I give to you,
and all that I have I share with you,
within the love of God,
Father, Son and Holy Spirit.

If only one ring is used, before they loose hands the bride says

N, I receive this ring
as a sign of our marriage.
With my body I honour you,
all that I am I give to you,
and all that I have I share with you,
within the love of God,
Father, Son and Holy Spirit.

The Proclamation

The minister addresses the people

In the presence of God, and before this congregation,
N and N have given their consent
and made their marriage vows to each other.
They have declared their marriage by the joining of hands
and by the giving and receiving of *rings*.
I therefore proclaim that they are husband and wife.

The minister joins their right hands together and says

Those whom God has joined together let no one put asunder.

The Blessing of the Marriage

The husband and wife kneel. The minister may use the following blessing or one of those on pages 152–155.

Blessed are you, O Lord our God,
for you have created joy and gladness,
pleasure and delight, love, peace and fellowship.
Pour out the abundance of your blessing
upon N and N in their new life together.
Let their love for each other be a seal upon their hearts
and a crown upon their heads.
Bless them in their work and in their companionship;
awake and asleep,
in joy and in sorrow,
in life and in death.
Finally, in your mercy, bring them to that banquet
where your saints feast for ever in your heavenly home.
We ask this through Jesus Christ your Son, our Lord,
who lives and reigns with you and the Holy Spirit,
one God, now and for ever.

All **Amen.**

The minister says to the couple

God the Father,
God the Son,
God the Holy Spirit,
bless, preserve and keep you;
the Lord mercifully grant you the riches of his grace,
that you may please him both in body and soul,
and, living together in faith and love,
may receive the blessings of eternal life.

All **Amen.**

Registration of the Marriage

See Note 10 on page 134.

A hymn or psalm may be used (see pages 148–149).

Prayers

These or other suitable prayers are used (see Note 9 on page 133 and pages 156–168). The prayers usually include these concerns and may follow this sequence:

¶ *Thanksgiving*

¶ *Spiritual growth*

¶ *Faithfulness, joy, love, forgiveness and healing*

¶ *Children, other family members and friends*

Faithful God,
holy and eternal,
source of life and spring of love,
we thank and praise you for bringing *N* and *N* to this day,
and we pray for them.
Lord of life and love:

All **hear our prayer.**

May their marriage be life-giving and life-long,
enriched by your presence and strengthened by your grace;
may they bring comfort and confidence to each other
in faithfulness and trust.
Lord of life and love:

All **hear our prayer.**

May the hospitality of their home
bring refreshment and joy to all around them;
may their love overflow to neighbours in need
and embrace those in distress.
Lord of life and love:

All **hear our prayer.**

May they discern in your word
order and purpose for their lives;
and may the power of your Holy Spirit
lead them in truth and defend them in adversity.
Lord of life and love:

All **hear our prayer.**

May they nurture their family with devotion,
see their children grow in body, mind and spirit
and come at last to the end of their lives
with hearts content and in joyful anticipation of heaven.
Lord of life and love:

All **hear our prayer.**

The prayers conclude with the Lord's Prayer.

As our Saviour taught us, so we pray

All **Our Father in heaven,**
hallowed be your name,
your kingdom come,
your will be done,
on earth as in heaven.
Give us today our daily bread.
Forgive us our sins
as we forgive those who sin against us.
Lead us not into temptation
but deliver us from evil.
For the kingdom, the power,
and the glory are yours
now and for ever.
Amen.

(or)

Let us pray with confidence as our Saviour has taught us

All **Our Father, who art in heaven,**
hallowed be thy name;
thy kingdom come;
thy will be done;
on earth as it is in heaven.
Give us this day our daily bread.
And forgive us our trespasses,
as we forgive those who trespass against us.
And lead us not into temptation;
but deliver us from evil.
For thine is the kingdom,
the power and the glory,
for ever and ever.
Amen.

A hymn may be sung.

The Dismissal

The minister says

God the Holy Trinity make *you* strong in faith and love,
defend *you* on every side, and guide *you* in truth and peace;
and the blessing of God almighty,
the Father, the Son, and the Holy Spirit,
be among *you* and remain with *you* always.

All **Amen.**

The Marriage Service within a Celebration of Holy Communion

Structure

¶ **The Gathering**
The Welcome
Prayers of Penitence
Preface
The Declarations
The Collect

¶ **The Liturgy of the Word**
Readings
Gospel Reading
Sermon

¶ **The Marriage**
The Vows
The Giving of Rings
The Proclamation
† The Blessing of the Marriage
Registration of the Marriage
Prayers

¶ **The Liturgy of the Sacrament**
The Peace
Preparation of the Table
Taking of the Bread and Wine
The Eucharistic Prayer
The Lord's Prayer
    † The Blessing of the Marriage
Breaking of the Bread
Giving of Communion
Prayer after Communion

¶ **The Dismissal**

† indicates alternative position allowed and shown indented in italics

The Marriage Service within a Celebration of Holy Communion

¶ *The Gathering*

The Welcome

*The minister welcomes the people using these
or other appropriate words*

The grace of our Lord Jesus Christ,
the love of God,
and the fellowship of the Holy Spirit
be with you

All **and also with you.**

This sentence may be used

God is love, and those who live in love live in God
and God lives in them.   *1 John 4.16*

This prayer may be said

All **God of wonder and of joy:**
grace comes from you,
and you alone are the source of life and love.
Without you, we cannot please you;
without your love, our deeds are worth nothing.
Send your Holy Spirit,
and pour into our hearts
**   that most excellent gift of love,**
that we may worship you now
with thankful hearts
and serve you always with willing minds;
through Jesus Christ our Lord.
Amen.

A hymn may be sung.

Prayers of Penitence

A minister may use these or other suitable words

As we prepare to hear God's word
and to celebrate the marriage of N and N,
we remember our human frailty
and our need for God's help in all that we do.

(or)

Gathered together as God's family,
let us ask forgiveness from our heavenly Father,
for he is full of gentleness and compassion.

(or)

We come to God as one from whom no secrets are hidden,
to ask for his forgiveness and peace.

Confession and Absolution

Either

All **Lord our God,**
in our sin we have avoided your call.
Our love for you is like a morning cloud,
like the dew that goes away early.
Have mercy on us;
deliver us from judgement;
bind up our wounds
and revive us;
in Jesus Christ our Lord.
Amen.

The president says

The Lord forgive *you your* sin,
unite *you* in the love which took Christ to the cross,
and bring *you* in the Spirit to his wedding feast in heaven.

All **Amen.**

(or)

Lord, in our weakness you are our strength.
Lord, have mercy.

All **Lord, have mercy.**

Lord, when we stumble, you raise us up.
Christ, have mercy.

All **Christ, have mercy.**

Lord, when we fail, you give us new life.
Lord, have mercy.

All **Lord, have mercy.**

The president says

May God in his goodness forgive *us our* sins,
grant *us* strength in *our* weakness,
and bring *us* to eternal life,
through Jesus Christ our Lord.

All **Amen.**

Preface

These words or those on page 136 are used

In the presence of God, Father, Son and Holy Spirit
we have come together
to witness the marriage of *N* and *N*,
to pray for God's blessing on them,
to share their joy
and to celebrate their love.

Marriage is a gift of God in creation
through which husband and wife may know the grace of God.
It is given
that as man and woman grow together in love and trust,
they shall be united with one another in heart, body and mind,
as Christ is united with his bride, the Church.

The gift of marriage brings husband and wife together
in the delight and tenderness of sexual union
and joyful commitment to the end of their lives.
It is given as the foundation of family life
in which children are [born and] nurtured
and in which each member of the family,
in good times and in bad,
may find strength, companionship and comfort,
and grow to maturity in love.

Marriage is a way of life made holy by God,
and blessed by the presence of our Lord Jesus Christ
with those celebrating a wedding at Cana in Galilee.
Marriage is a sign of unity and loyalty
which all should uphold and honour.
It enriches society and strengthens community.
No one should enter into it lightly or selfishly
but reverently and responsibly in the sight of almighty God.

N and *N* are now to enter this way of life.
They will each give their consent to the other
and make solemn vows,
and in token of this they will [each] give and receive a ring.
We pray with them that the Holy Spirit will guide
    and strengthen them,
that they may fulfil God's purposes
for the whole of their earthly life together.

The Declarations

The minister says to the congregation

First, I am required to ask anyone present who knows a reason
why these persons may not lawfully marry, to declare it now.

The minister says to the couple

The vows you are about to take are to be made in the presence
    of God,
who is judge of all and knows all the secrets of our hearts;
therefore if either of you knows a reason why you may not
    lawfully marry,
you must declare it now.

The minister says to the bridegroom

N, will you take N to be your wife?
Will you love her, comfort her, honour and protect her,
and, forsaking all others,
be faithful to her as long as you both shall live?

He answers

I will.

The minister says to the bride

N, will you take N to be your husband?
Will you love him, comfort him, honour and protect him,
and, forsaking all others,
be faithful to him as long as you both shall live?

She answers

I will.

The minister says to the congregation

Will you, the families and friends of N and N,
support and uphold them in their marriage
now and in the years to come?

All   **We will.**

The Collect

The minister invites the people to pray, silence is kept and the minister says the Collect

God our Father,
from the beginning
you have blessed creation with abundant life.
Pour out your blessings upon *N* and *N,*
that they may be joined in mutual love and companionship,
in holiness and commitment to each other.
We ask this through our Lord Jesus Christ your Son,
who is alive and reigns with you,
in the unity of the Holy Spirit,
one God, now and for ever.

All **Amen.**

¶ The Liturgy of the Word

Readings

*Either one or two readings from Scripture precede the Gospel reading
(see pages 137–149).*

At the end of each the reader may say

This is the word of the Lord.

All **Thanks be to God.**

*The psalm or canticle (pages 169–172) follows the first reading;
other hymns and songs may be used between the readings.*

Gospel Reading

*An acclamation may herald the Gospel reading.
One of the following may be used*

Alleluia, alleluia.
God made them male and female
and the two will become one.

All **Alleluia.** *cf Mark 10.8*

(or)

Alleluia, alleluia.
God is love;
let us love one another
as God has loved us.

All **Alleluia.** *cf 1 John 4.8-11*

When the Gospel is announced the reader says

Hear the Gospel of our Lord Jesus Christ according to *N.*

All **Glory to you, O Lord.**

At the end

This is the Gospel of the Lord.

All **Praise to you, O Christ.**

Sermon

¶ *The Marriage*

A hymn may be sung.

The couple stand before the minister.

The Vows

The minister introduces the vows in these or similar words

N and N, I now invite you to join hands and make your vows,
in the presence of God and his people.

The bride and bridegroom face each other.
The bridegroom takes the bride's right hand in his.

These words, or those on page 150 are used

I, N, take you, N,
to be my wife,
to have and to hold
from this day forward;
for better, for worse,
for richer, for poorer,
in sickness and in health,
to love and to cherish,
till death us do part;
according to God's holy law.
In the presence of God I make this vow.

They loose hands.
The bride takes the bridegroom's right hand in hers, and says

I, N, take you, N,
to be my husband,
to have and to hold
from this day forward;
for better, for worse,
for richer, for poorer,
in sickness and in health,
to love and to cherish,
till death us do part;
according to God's holy law.
In the presence of God I make this vow.

They loose hands.

The Giving of Rings

*The minister receives the ring(s), and says this prayer
or the prayer on page 151*

Heavenly Father, by your blessing
let *these rings* be to N and N
a symbol of unending love and faithfulness,
to remind them of the vow and covenant
which they have made this day
through Jesus Christ our Lord.

All   **Amen.**

*The bridegroom places the ring on the fourth finger of the
bride's left hand, and, holding it there, says*

N, I give you this ring
as a sign of our marriage.
With my body I honour you,
all that I am I give to you,
and all that I have I share with you,
within the love of God,
Father, Son and Holy Spirit.

*If rings are exchanged, they loose hands and the bride places a ring on
the fourth finger of the bridegroom's left hand, and, holding it there, says*

N, I give you this ring
as a sign of our marriage.
With my body I honour you,
all that I am I give to you,
and all that I have I share with you,
within the love of God,
Father, Son and Holy Spirit.

If only one ring is used, before they loose hands the bride says

N, I receive this ring
as a sign of our marriage.
With my body I honour you,
all that I am I give to you,
and all that I have I share with you,
within the love of God,
Father, Son and Holy Spirit.

The Proclamation

The minister addresses the people

In the presence of God, and before this congregation,
N and *N* have given their consent
and made their marriage vows to each other.
They have declared their marriage by the joining of hands
and by the giving and receiving of *rings*.
I therefore proclaim that they are husband and wife.

The minister joins their right hands together and says

Those whom God has joined together let no one put asunder.

The Blessing of the Marriage

The Blessing of the Marriage may be used here or after the Lord's Prayer.

The husband and wife kneel. The minister may use the following blessing or one of those on pages 152–155.

Blessed are you, O Lord our God,
for you have created joy and gladness,
pleasure and delight, love, peace and fellowship.
Pour out the abundance of your blessing
upon N and N in their new life together.
Let their love for each other be a seal upon their hearts
and a crown upon their heads.
Bless them in their work and in their companionship;
awake and asleep,
in joy and in sorrow,
in life and in death.
Finally, in your mercy, bring them to that banquet
where your saints feast for ever in your heavenly home.
We ask this through Jesus Christ your Son, our Lord,
who lives and reigns with you and the Holy Spirit,
one God, now and for ever.

All **Amen.**

The minister says to the couple

God the Father,
God the Son,
God the Holy Spirit,
bless, preserve and keep you;
the Lord mercifully grant you the riches of his grace,
that you may please him both in body and soul,
and, living together in faith and love,
may receive the blessings of eternal life.

All **Amen.**

Registration of the Marriage

See Note 10 on page 134.

A hymn or psalm may be used (see pages 148–149).

Prayers

*These or other suitable prayers are used (see Note 9 on page 133
and pages 156–168). The prayers usually include these concerns
and may follow this sequence:*

¶   *Thanksgiving*

¶   *Spiritual growth*

¶   *Faithfulness, joy, love, forgiveness and healing*

¶   *Children, other family members and friends*

Faithful God,
holy and eternal,
source of life and spring of love,
we thank and praise you for bringing *N* and *N* to this day,
and we pray for them.
Lord of life and love:

All   **hear our prayer.**

May their marriage be life-giving and life-long,
enriched by your presence and strengthened by your grace;
may they bring comfort and confidence to each other
in faithfulness and trust.
Lord of life and love:

All   **hear our prayer.**

May the hospitality of their home
bring refreshment and joy to all around them;
may their love overflow to neighbours in need
and embrace those in distress.
Lord of life and love:

All   **hear our prayer.**

May they discern in your word
order and purpose for their lives;
and may the power of your Holy Spirit
lead them in truth and defend them in adversity.
Lord of life and love:

All   **hear our prayer.**

May they nurture their family with devotion,
see their children grow in body, mind and spirit
and come at last to the end of their lives
with hearts content and in joyful anticipation of heaven.
Lord of life and love:

All **hear our prayer.**

Father of all,
in Jesus Christ you open to us
the treasures of your kingdom;
guide us by your Holy Spirit
that we may receive your redeeming grace
and reflect the perfect unity of your love,
for you live and reign,
one God, now and for ever.

All **Amen.**

A hymn may be sung.

¶ *The Liturgy of the Sacrament*

The Peace

The president may introduce the Peace with a suitable sentence.
The following may be used

To crown all things there must be love.
Let the peace of Christ rule in your hearts.
The peace of the Lord be always with you

All **and also with you.**

(or)

We have celebrated the love of *N* and *N*.
We now celebrate God's love for all of us.
Peace, in Christ, to all of you   *cf 1 Peter 5.14*

All **and also with you.**

These words may be added

Let us offer one another a sign of peace.

All may exchange a sign of peace.

The service continues with the Preparation of the Table. Presidential
texts for the rest of the service are to be found in Common Worship:
Services and Prayers for the Church of England *(pages 155–335)*
and the President's edition (pages 381–524).

Preparation of the Table
Taking of the Bread and Wine

The following prayer may be used

In your goodness, Lord,
accept the gift of our love,
and with a father's affection watch over this couple
you have joined in the covenant of marriage;
through Jesus Christ our Lord.

All **Amen.**

The Eucharistic Prayer

An authorized Eucharistic Prayer is used.

One of these Proper Prefaces may be used

Short Proper Preface

And now we give you thanks
because you have made the union between Christ and his Church
a pattern for the marriage between husband and wife.
Therefore with angels ...

Extended Proper Preface

All glory, honour, thanks and praise
be given to you, creator of heaven and earth.
When you made us in your image,
creating us male and female,
you gave us the gift of marriage.
When sin marred that image
you healed our brokenness,
giving your Son to die for us.
Therefore we raise our voices,
with all who have served you in every age,
to proclaim the glory of your name:

The Lord's Prayer

The Blessing of the Marriage

(if not used earlier)

Breaking of the Bread

Giving of Communion

Prayer after Communion

The following Post Communion may be used

Gracious God,
may *N* and *N*, who have been bound together
in these holy mysteries,
become one in body and soul.
May they live in faithfulness and peace
and obtain those eternal joys
prepared for all who love you;
through your Son Jesus Christ our Lord.

All **Amen.**

¶ *The Dismissal*

The minister says

The Lord bless you and keep you:

All **Amen.**
The Lord make his face to shine upon you,
and be gracious to you:

All **Amen.**
The Lord lift up his countenance upon you
and give you peace: *Numbers 6.24-26*

All **Amen.**
The Lord God almighty, Father, Son, and Holy Spirit,
the holy and undivided Trinity,
guard you, save you,
and bring you to that heavenly city,
where he lives and reigns for ever and ever.

All **Amen.**

Notes to the Marriage Service

1 **Preparation**
It is the custom and practice of the Church of England to offer preparation for marriage for couples who are soon to be married, as well as to be available for support and counselling in the years that follow.

2 **The Banns**
The banns are to be published in the church on three Sundays at the time of Divine Service by the officiant in the form set out in *The Book of Common Prayer* or in the following form:

> I publish the banns of marriage between NN of … and NN of … This is the *first / second / third* time of asking. If any of you know any reason in law why they may not marry each other you are to declare it.
> We pray for these couples *(or N and N)* as they prepare for their wedding(s).

A suitable prayer may be said (see page 135).

3 **Hymns and Canticles**
These may be used at suitable points during the service.

4 **Entry**
The bride may enter the church escorted by her father or a representative of the family, or the bride and groom may enter church together.

5 **Readings and Sermon**
At least one reading from the Bible must be used. Suggested readings are printed on pages 137–149. If occasion demands, either the Sermon or the Readings and Sermon may come after the Blessing of the Marriage. Chairs may be provided for the bride and bridegroom.

6   'Giving Away'
     This traditional ceremony is optional. Immediately before
     the couple exchange vows (pages 108 and 123), the minister may ask:

>   Who brings this woman to be married to this man?

     The bride's father (or mother, or another member of her family
     or a friend representing the family) gives the bride's right hand to
     the minister who puts it in the bridegroom's right hand.
     Alternatively, after the bride and bridegroom have made their
     Declarations, the minister may ask the parents of bride and
     bridegroom in these or similar words:

>   N and N have declared their intention towards each other.
>   As their parents,
>   will you now entrust your son and daughter to one another
>   as they come to be married?

     Both sets of parents respond:

>   We will.

7   The Declarations and the Vows
     The *Book of Common Prayer* version of the Declarations, and / or the
     alternative vows on pages 150–151, may be used. The couple repeat
     the vows after the minister, or may read them. If preferred, the
     question to the bride, and her vow, may come before the question
     to the bridegroom and his vow.

8   The Giving of Rings
     If desired, the bride and bridegroom may each place a ring on the
     fourth finger of the other's hand, and may then say together the
     words 'N, I give you this ring …'. The prayer on page 151 may be
     used instead of the prayer on pages 109 and 124.

9   The Prayers
     Several forms of intercession are provided. Other suitable forms
     may be used, especially prayers which the couple have written or
     selected in co-operation with the minister. Whatever form is used,
     silence may be kept as part of the intercession. Free prayer may be
     offered.

10 **Registration of the Marriage**
The law requires that the Registers are filled in immediately after the solemnization of a marriage. This may take place either after the Proclamation or at the end of the service.

11 **Holy Communion**
For communicant members of the Church it is appropriate that they receive communion soon after their marriage. For some this may make it appropriate for the marriage to take place within the context of a Celebration of Holy Communion.

12 **The Marriage Service within a Celebration of Holy Communion**
The Notes to the Order for the Celebration of Holy Communion, as well as the Notes to the Marriage Service, apply equally to this service. Texts are suggested at different points, but other suitable texts may be used. Authorized Prayers of Penitence may be used. In the Liturgy of the Word, there should be a Gospel reading, preceded by either one or two other readings from the Bible. If desired, the Blessing of the Marriage may take place between the Lord's Prayer and the Breaking of the Bread.

13 **Ecumenical Provisions**
Where a minister of another Christian Church is invited to assist at the Solemnization of Matrimony, the permissions and procedures set out in Canon B 43 are to be followed. The Church of England minister who solemnizes the marriage must establish the absence of impediment, direct the exchange of vows, declare the existence of the marriage, say the final blessing, and sign the registers. A minister invited to assist may say all or part of the opening address, lead the declarations of intent, supervise the exchange of rings, and join in the blessing of the marriage. He or she may also read a lesson and lead all or part of the prayers. Where the couple come from different Christian communions the bishop may authorize such variations to the marriage service as are set out in *An Order for the Marriage of Christians from Different Churches*, which is published separately.

Supplementary Texts

¶   *Prayers at the Calling of the Banns*

Prayers such as the following may be used

Lord,
the source of all true love,
we pray for *these couples.*
Grant to them
joy of heart,
seriousness of mind
and reverence of spirit,
that as they enter into the oneness of marriage
they may be strengthened and guided by you,
through Jesus Christ our Lord.

All   **Amen.**

Lord of love,
we pray for *N* and *N.*
Be with them in all their preparations
and on their wedding day.
Give them your love in their hearts
throughout their married life together,
through Jesus Christ our Lord.

All   **Amen.**

¶ *Alternative Preface*

We have come together in the presence of God, to witness the marriage of N and N, to ask his blessing on them, and to share in their joy. Our Lord Jesus Christ was himself a guest at a wedding in Cana of Galilee, and through his Spirit he is with us now.

The Bible teaches us that marriage is a gift of God in creation and a means of his grace, a holy mystery in which man and woman become one flesh. It is God's purpose that, as husband and wife give themselves to each other in love throughout their lives, they shall be united in that love as Christ is united with his Church.

Marriage is given, that husband and wife may comfort and help each other, living faithfully together in need and in plenty, in sorrow and in joy. It is given, that with delight and tenderness they may know each other in love, and, through the joy of their bodily union, may strengthen the union of their hearts and lives. It is given as the foundation of family life in which children may be born and nurtured in accordance with God's will, to his praise and glory.

In marriage husband and wife belong to one another, and they begin a new life together in the community. It is a way of life that all should honour; and it must not be undertaken carelessly, lightly, or selfishly, but reverently, responsibly, and after serious thought.

This is the way of life, created and hallowed by God, that N and N are now to begin. They will each give their consent to the other; they will join hands and exchange solemn vows, and in token of this they will [each] give and receive a ring.

Therefore, on this their wedding day we pray with them, that, strengthened and guided by God, they may fulfil his purpose for the whole of their earthly life together.

¶ Readings and Psalms

Any suitable translation may be used.

Old Testament and Apocrypha

Genesis 1.26-28

Then God said, 'Let us make humankind in our image, according to our likeness; and let them have dominion over the fish of the sea, and over the birds of the air, and over the cattle, and over all the wild animals of the earth, and over every creeping thing that creeps upon the earth.'

So God created humankind in his image,
in the image of God he created them;
male and female he created them.

God blessed them, and God said to them, 'Be fruitful and multiply, and fill the earth and subdue it; and have dominion over the fish of the sea and over the birds of the air and over every living thing that moves upon the earth.'

Song of Solomon 2.10-13; 8.6,7

My beloved speaks and says to me:
'Arise, my love, my fair one,
and come away;
for now the winter is past,
the rain is over and gone.
The flowers appear on the earth;
the time of singing has come,
and the voice of the turtle dove
is heard in our land.
The fig tree puts forth its figs,
and the vines are in blossom;
they give forth fragrance.
Arise, my love, my fair one,
and come away.'

Set me as a seal upon your heart,
as a seal upon your arm;
for love is strong as death,
passion fierce as the grave.
Its flashes are flashes of fire,
a raging flame.
Many waters cannot quench love,
neither can floods drown it.
If one offered for love
all the wealth of one's house,
it would be utterly scorned.

Jeremiah 31.31-34

The days are surely coming, says the Lord, when I will make a new covenant with the house of Israel and the house of Judah. It will not be like the covenant that I made with their ancestors when I took them by the hand to bring them out of the land of Egypt – a covenant that they broke, though I was their husband, says the Lord. But this is the covenant that I will make with the house of Israel after those days, says the Lord: I will put my law within them, and I will write it on their hearts; and I will be their God, and they shall be my people. No longer shall they teach one another, or say to each other, 'Know the Lord', for they shall all know me, from the least of them to the greatest, says the Lord; for I will forgive their iniquity, and remember their sin no more.

Tobit 8.4-8

When the parents had gone out and shut the door of the room, Tobias got out of bed and said to Sarah, 'Sister, get up, and let us pray and implore our Lord that he grant us mercy and safety.' So she got up, and they began to pray and implore that they might be kept safe. Tobias began by saying,
'Blessed are you, O God of our ancestors,
and blessed is your name in all generations for ever.
Let the heavens and the whole creation bless you for ever.
You made Adam, and for him you made his wife Eve
as a helper and support.
From the two of them the human race has sprung.
You said, "It is not good that the man should be alone;
let us make a helper for him like himself."

I now am taking this kinswoman of mine,
not because of lust,
but with sincerity.
Grant that she and I may find mercy
and that we may grow old together.'

And they both said, 'Amen, amen.'

Epistle

Romans 7.1,2,9-18

Do you not know, brothers and sisters – for I am speaking to those who know the law – that the law is binding on a person only during that person's lifetime? Thus a married woman is bound by the law to her husband as long as he lives; but if her husband dies, she is discharged from the law concerning the husband.

I was once alive apart from the law, but when the commandment came, sin revived and I died, and the very commandment that promised life proved to be death to me. For sin, seizing an opportunity in the commandment, deceived me and through it killed me. So the law is holy, and the commandment is holy and just and good.

Did what is good, then, bring death to me? By no means! It was sin, working death in me through what is good, in order that sin might be shown to be sin, and through the commandment might become sinful beyond measure.

For we know that the law is spiritual; but I am of the flesh, sold into slavery under sin. I do not understand my own actions. For I do not do what I want, but I do the very thing I hate. Now if I do what I do not want, I agree that the law is good. But in fact it is no longer I that do it, but sin that dwells within me. For I know that nothing good dwells within me, that is, in my flesh. I can will what is right, but I cannot do it.

Romans 8.31-35,37-39

What then are we to say about these things? If God is for us, who is against us? He who did not withhold his own Son, but gave him up for all of us, will he not with him also give us everything else? Who will bring any charge against God's elect? It is God who justifies. Who is to condemn? It is Christ Jesus, who died, yes, who was raised, who is at the right hand of God, who indeed intercedes for us. Who will separate us from the love of Christ? Will hardship, or distress, or persecution, or famine, or nakedness, or peril, or sword?

No, in all these things we are more than conquerors through him who loved us. For I am convinced that neither death, nor life, nor angels, nor rulers, nor things present, nor things to come, nor powers, nor height, nor depth, nor anything else in all creation, will be able to separate us from the love of God in Christ Jesus our Lord.

Romans 12.1,2,9-13

I appeal to you therefore, brothers and sisters, by the mercies of God, to present your bodies as a living sacrifice, holy and acceptable to God, which is your spiritual worship. Do not be conformed to this world, but be transformed by the renewing of your minds, so that you may discern what is the will of God – what is good and acceptable and perfect.

Let love be genuine; hate what is evil, hold fast to what is good; love one another with mutual affection; outdo one another in showing honour. Do not lag in zeal, be ardent in spirit, serve the Lord. Rejoice in hope, be patient in suffering, persevere in prayer. Contribute to the needs of the saints; extend hospitality to strangers.

Romans 15.1-3,5-7,13

We who are strong ought to put up with the failings of the weak, and not to please ourselves. Each of us must please our neighbour for the good purpose of building up the neighbour. For Christ did not please himself; but, as it is written, 'The insults of those who insult you have fallen on me.'

May the God of steadfastness and encouragement grant you to live in harmony with one another, in accordance with Christ Jesus, so that together you may with one voice glorify the God and Father of our Lord Jesus Christ. Welcome one another, therefore, just as Christ has welcomed you, for the glory of God.

May the God of hope fill you with all joy and peace in believing, so that you may abound in hope by the power of the Holy Spirit.

1 Corinthians 13

If I speak in the tongues of mortals and of angels, but do not have love, I am a noisy gong or a clanging cymbal. And if I have prophetic powers, and understand all mysteries and all knowledge, and if I have all faith, so as to remove mountains, but do not have love, I am nothing. If I give away all my possessions, and if I hand over my body so that I may boast, but do not have love, I gain nothing.

Love is patient; love is kind; love is not envious or boastful or arrogant or rude. It does not insist on its own way; it is not irritable or resentful; it does not rejoice in wrongdoing, but rejoices in the truth. It bears all things, believes all things, hopes all things, endures all things.

Love never ends. But as for prophecies, they will come to an end; as for tongues, they will cease; as for knowledge, it will come to an end. For we know only in part, and we prophesy only in part; but when the complete comes, the partial will come to an end. When I was a child, I spoke like a child, I thought like a child, I reasoned like a child; when I became an adult, I put an end to childish ways. For now we see in a mirror, dimly, but then we will see face to face. Now I know only in part; then I will know fully, even as I have been fully known. And now faith, hope, and love abide, these three; and the greatest of these is love.

Ephesians 3.14-end

I bow my knees before the Father, from whom every family in heaven and on earth takes its name. I pray that, according to the riches of his glory, he may grant that you may be strengthened in your inner being with power through his Spirit, and that Christ may dwell in your hearts through faith, as you are being rooted and grounded in love. I pray that you may have the power to comprehend, with all the saints, what is the breadth and length and height and depth, and to know the love of Christ that surpasses knowledge, so that you may be filled with all the fullness of God.

Now to him who by the power at work within us is able to accomplish abundantly far more than all we can ask or imagine, to him be glory in the church and in Christ Jesus to all generations, for ever and ever. Amen.

Ephesians 4.1-6

I, the prisoner in the Lord, beg you to lead a life worthy of the calling to which you have been called, with all humility and gentleness, with patience, bearing with one another in love, making every effort to maintain the unity of the Spirit in the bond of peace. There is one body and one Spirit, just as you were called to the one hope of your calling, one Lord, one faith, one baptism, one God and Father of all, who is above all and through all and in all.

Ephesians 5.21-end

Be subject to one another out of reverence for Christ.

Wives, be subject to your husbands as you are to the Lord. For the husband is the head of the wife just as Christ is the head of the church, the body of which he is the Saviour. Just as the church is subject to Christ, so also wives ought to be, in everything, to their husbands.

Husbands, love your wives, just as Christ loved the church and gave himself up for her, in order to make her holy by cleansing her with the washing of water by the word, so as to present the church to himself in splendour, without a spot or wrinkle or anything of the kind – yes, so that she may be holy and without blemish. In the same way, husbands should love their wives as they do their own bodies. He who loves his wife loves himself. For no one ever hates his own body, but he nourishes and tenderly cares for it, just as Christ does for the church, because we are members of his body. 'For this reason a man will leave his father and mother and be joined to his wife, and the two will become one flesh.' This is a great mystery, and I am applying it to Christ and the church. Each of you, however, should love his wife as himself, and a wife should respect her husband.

Philippians 4.4-9

Rejoice in the Lord always; again I will say, Rejoice. Let your gentleness be known to everyone. The Lord is near. Do not worry about anything, but in everything by prayer and supplication with thanksgiving let your requests be made known to God. And the peace of God, which surpasses all understanding, will guard your hearts and your minds in Christ Jesus.

Finally, beloved, whatever is true, whatever is honourable, whatever is just, whatever is pure, whatever is pleasing, whatever is commendable, if there is any excellence and if there is anything worthy of praise, think about these things. Keep on doing the things that you have learned and received and heard and seen in me, and the God of peace will be with you.

Colossians 3.12-17

As God's chosen ones, holy and beloved, clothe yourselves with compassion, kindness, humility, meekness, and patience. Bear with one another and, if anyone has a complaint against another, forgive each other; just as the Lord has forgiven you, so you also must forgive. Above all, clothe yourselves with love, which binds everything together in perfect harmony. And let the peace of Christ rule in your hearts, to which indeed you were called in the one body. And be thankful. Let the word of Christ dwell in you richly; teach and admonish one another in all wisdom; and with gratitude in your hearts sing psalms, hymns, and spiritual songs to God. And whatever you do, in word or deed, do everything in the name of the Lord Jesus, giving thanks to God the Father through him.

Little children, let us love, not in word or speech, but in truth and action. And by this we will know that we are from the truth and will reassure our hearts before him whenever our hearts condemn us; for God is greater than our hearts, and he knows everything. Beloved, if our hearts do not condemn us, we have boldness before God; and we receive from him whatever we ask, because we obey his commandments and do what pleases him.

And this is his commandment, that we should believe in the name of his Son Jesus Christ and love one another, just as he has commanded us. All who obey his commandments abide in him, and he abides in them. And by this we know that he abides in us, by the Spirit that he has given us.

1 John 4.7-12

Beloved, let us love one another, because love is from God; everyone who loves is born of God and knows God. Whoever does not love does not know God, for God is love. God's love was revealed among us in this way: God sent his only Son into the world so that we might live through him. In this is love, not that we loved God but that he loved us and sent his Son to be the atoning sacrifice for our sins. Beloved, since God loved us so much, we also ought to love one another. No one has ever seen God; if we love one another, God lives in us, and his love is perfected in us.

Gospel

Matthew 5.1-10

When Jesus saw the crowds, he went up the mountain; and after
he sat down, his disciples came to him. Then he began to speak,
and taught them, saying:

'Blessed are the poor in spirit, for theirs is the kingdom of heaven.
Blessed are those who mourn, for they will be comforted.
Blessed are the meek, for they will inherit the earth.
Blessed are those who hunger and thirst for righteousness,
    for they will be filled.
Blessed are the merciful, for they will receive mercy.
Blessed are the pure in heart, for they will see God.
Blessed are the peacemakers, for they will be called children of God.
Blessed are those who are persecuted for righteousness' sake,
    for theirs is the kingdom of heaven.'

Matthew 7.21,24-end

Jesus said, 'Not everyone who says to me, "Lord, Lord", will enter
the kingdom of heaven, but only one who does the will of my
Father in heaven.

'Everyone then who hears these words of mine and acts on them
will be like a wise man who built his house on rock. The rain fell,
the floods came, and the winds blew and beat on that house, but it
did not fall, because it had been founded on rock. And everyone who
hears these words of mine and does not act on them will be like a
foolish man who built his house on sand. The rain fell, and the floods
came, and the winds blew and beat against that house, and it fell –
and great was its fall!'

Now when Jesus had finished saying these things, the crowds
were astounded at his teaching, for he taught them as one having
authority, and not as their scribes.

Mark 10.6-9, 13-16

Jesus said, 'From the beginning of creation, "God made them male and female." "For this reason a man shall leave his father and mother and be joined to his wife, and the two shall become one flesh." So they are no longer two, but one flesh. Therefore what God has joined together, let no one separate.'

People were bringing little children to him in order that he might touch them; and the disciples spoke sternly to them. But when Jesus saw this, he was indignant and said to them, 'Let the little children come to me; do not stop them; for it is to such as these that the kingdom of God belongs. Truly I tell you, whoever does not receive the kingdom of God as a little child will never enter it.' And he took them up in his arms, laid his hands on them, and blessed them.

John 2.1-11

On the third day there was a wedding in Cana of Galilee, and the mother of Jesus was there. Jesus and his disciples had also been invited to the wedding. When the wine gave out, the mother of Jesus said to him, 'They have no wine.' And Jesus said to her, 'Woman, what concern is that to you and to me? My hour has not yet come.' His mother said to the servants, 'Do whatever he tells you.' Now standing there were six stone water-jars for the Jewish rites of purification, each holding twenty or thirty gallons. Jesus said to them, 'Fill the jars with water.' And they filled them up to the brim. He said to them, 'Now draw some out, and take it to the chief steward.' So they took it. When the steward tasted the water that had become wine, and did not know where it came from (though the servants who had drawn the water knew), the steward called the bridegroom and said to him, 'Everyone serves the good wine first, and then the inferior wine after the guests have become drunk. But you have kept the good wine until now.' Jesus did this, the first of his signs, in Cana of Galilee, and revealed his glory; and his disciples believed in him.

John 15.1-8

Jesus said to his disciples: 'I am the true vine, and my Father is the vinegrower. He removes every branch in me that bears no fruit. Every branch that bears fruit he prunes to make it bear more fruit. You have already been cleansed by the word that I have spoken to you. Abide in me as I abide in you. Just as the branch cannot bear fruit by itself unless it abides in the vine, neither can you unless you abide in me. I am the vine, you are the branches. Those who abide in me and I in them bear much fruit, because apart from me you can do nothing. Whoever does not abide in me is thrown away like a branch and withers; such branches are gathered, thrown into the fire, and burned. If you abide in me, and my words abide in you, ask for whatever you wish, and it will be done for you. My Father is glorified by this, that you bear much fruit and become my disciples.'

John 15.9-17

Jesus said to his disciples: 'As the Father has loved me, so I have loved you; abide in my love. If you keep my commandments, you will abide in my love, just as I have kept my Father's commandments and abide in his love. I have said these things to you so that my joy may be in you, and that your joy may be complete.

This is my commandment, that you love one another as I have loved you. No one has greater love than this, to lay down one's life for one's friends. You are my friends if you do what I command you. I do not call you servants any longer, because the servant does not know what the master is doing; but I have called you friends, because I have made known to you everything that I have heard from my Father. You did not choose me but I chose you. And I appointed you to go and bear fruit, fruit that will last, so that the Father will give you whatever you ask him in my name. I am giving you these commands so that you may love one another.'

Psalm 67

1   God be gracious to us and bless us ♦
      and make his face to shine upon us,

2   That your way may be known upon earth, ♦
      your saving power among all nations.

3   *Let the peoples praise you, O God;* ♦
      let all the peoples praise you.

4   O let the nations rejoice and be glad, ♦
      for you will judge the peoples righteously
         and govern the nations upon earth.

5   *Let the peoples praise you, O God;* ♦
      let all the peoples praise you.

6   Then shall the earth bring forth her increase, ♦
      and God, our own God, will bless us.

7   God will bless us, ♦
      and all the ends of the earth shall fear him.

Psalm 121

1   I lift up my eyes to the hills; ♦
      from where is my help to come?

2   My help comes from the Lord, ♦
      the maker of heaven and earth.

3   He will not suffer your foot to stumble; ♦
      he who watches over you will not sleep.

4   Behold, he who keeps watch over Israel ♦
      shall neither slumber nor sleep.

5   The Lord himself watches over you; ♦
      the Lord is your shade at your right hand,

6   So that the sun shall not strike you by day, ♦
      neither the moon by night.

7   The Lord shall keep you from all evil; ♦
      it is he who shall keep your soul.

8   The Lord shall keep watch over your going out
         and your coming in, ♦
      from this time forth for evermore.

Psalm 127

1 Unless the Lord builds the house, ♦
   those who build it labour in vain.

2 Unless the Lord keeps the city, ♦
   the guard keeps watch in vain.

3 It is in vain that you hasten to rise up early
        and go so late to rest, eating the bread of toil, ♦
   for he gives his beloved sleep.

4 Children are a heritage from the Lord ♦
   and the fruit of the womb is his gift.

5 Like arrows in the hand of a warrior, ♦
   so are the children of one's youth.

6 Happy are those who have their quiver full of them: ♦
   they shall not be put to shame
        when they dispute with their enemies in the gate.

Psalm 128

1 Blessed are all those who fear the Lord, ♦
   and walk in his ways.

2 You shall eat the fruit of the toil of your hands; ♦
   it shall go well with you, and happy shall you be.

3 Your wife within your house
        shall be like a fruitful vine; ♦
   your children round your table,
        like fresh olive branches.

4 Thus shall the one be blest ♦
   who fears the Lord.

5 The Lord from out of Zion bless you, ♦
   that you may see Jerusalem in prosperity
        all the days of your life.

6 May you see your children's children, ♦
   and may there be peace upon Israel.

¶ Alternative Vows

The bridegroom takes the bride's right hand in his, and says

I, *N*, take you, *N*,
to be my wife,
to have and to hold
from this day forward;
for better, for worse,
for richer, for poorer,
in sickness and in health,
to love and to cherish,
till death us do part,
according to God's holy law.
In the presence of God I make this vow.

They loose hands.
The bride takes the bridegroom's right hand in hers, and says

I, *N*, take you, *N*,
to be my husband,
to have and to hold
from this day forward;
for better, for worse,
for richer, for poorer,
in sickness and in health,
to love, cherish, and obey,
till death us do part,
according to God's holy law.
In the presence of God I make this vow.

The bridegroom takes the bride's right hand in his, and says

I, *N*, take thee, *N*, to my wedded wife, to have and to hold from this day forward, for better for worse, for richer for poorer, in sickness and in health, to love and to cherish, till death us do part, according to God's holy ordinance; and thereto I plight thee my troth.

They loose hands.
The bride takes the bridegroom's right hand in hers, and says

I, *N*, take thee, *N*, to my wedded husband, to have and to hold from this day forward, for better for worse, for richer for poorer, in sickness and in health, to love, cherish, and to obey, till death us do part, according to God's holy ordinance; and thereto I give thee my troth.

[If desired, the word 'obey' may be omitted, as follows

I, *N*, take thee, *N*, to my wedded husband, to have and to hold from this day forward, for better for worse, for richer for poorer, in sickness and in health, to love and to cherish, till death us do part, according to God's holy ordinance; and thereto I give thee my troth.]

¶ *Prayer at the Giving of the Ring(s)*

Heavenly Father, source of everlasting love,
revealed to us in Jesus Christ
    and poured into our hearts through your Holy Spirit;
that love which many waters cannot quench,
    neither the floods drown;
that love which is patient and kind, enduring all things without end;
by your blessing, let these rings be to *N* and *N*
symbols to remind them of the covenant made this day
through your grace in the love of your Son
and in the power of your Spirit.

All **Amen.**

¶ The Blessing of the Marriage

One of the following forms may be used

1   God of life and beginnings,
you created man and woman in your likeness
and joined them together in union of body and heart;
God of love and forgiveness,
you loved us in Jesus Christ
who humbled himself to death on a cross;
God of grace and strength,
you bring your people to faith
and fill them with your presence.
Blessed are you, O Lord our God,
for you have created joy and gladness,
pleasure and delight, love, peace and fellowship.
Pour out the abundance of your blessing
upon *N* and *N* in their new life together.
Let their love for each other be a seal upon their hearts,
and a crown upon their heads.
Bless them in their work and in their companionship;
awake and asleep,
in joy and in sorrow,
in life and in death.
Finally, in your mercy, bring them to that banquet
where your saints feast for ever in your heavenly home.
We ask this through Jesus Christ your Son, our Lord,
who lives and reigns with you and the Holy Spirit,
one God, now and for ever.

All   **Amen.**

2   All praise and blessing to you, God of love,
    creator of the universe,
    maker of man and woman in your likeness,
    source of blessing for married life.
    All praise to you, for you have created
        courtship and marriage,
        joy and gladness,
        feasting and laughter,
        pleasure and delight.
    May your blessing come in full upon N and N.
    May they know your presence
    in their joys and in their sorrows.
    May they reach old age in the company of friends
    and come at last to your eternal kingdom,
    through Jesus Christ our Lord.

All   **Amen.**

3   Eternal God,
    you create us out of love
    that we should love you and one another.
    Bless this man and this woman, made in your image,
    who today become a sign of your faithful love to us
    in Christ our Lord.

All   **Amen.**

    By your Holy Spirit,
    fill bride and bridegroom with wisdom and hope
    that they may delight in your gift of marriage
    and enrich one another in love and faithfulness;
    through Jesus Christ our Lord.

All   **Amen.**

    Bring them to that table
    where your saints celebrate for ever in your heavenly home;
    through Jesus Christ our Lord,
    who with you and the Holy Spirit lives and reigns,
    one God, for ever and ever.

All   **Amen.**

4 Blessed are you, Lord our God,
God of love, creator of all.

All **Blessed be God for ever.**

Bridegroom Blessed are you, Lord our God,
you make us in your image and likeness.

All **Blessed be God for ever.**

Bride Blessed are you, Lord our God,
you make man and woman to reflect your glory.

All **Blessed be God for ever.**

Bridegroom Blessed are you, Lord our God,
you make us for joy and promise us life.

All **Blessed be God for ever.**

Bride Blessed are you, Lord our God,
you create a people to know your love.

All **Blessed be God for ever.**

Minister May N and N enjoy the blessing of your kingdom.
Give them faith and joy in their marriage.
Blessed are you, Lord our God,
you give joy to bride and groom.

All **Blessed be God for ever.**

May their love be fruitful
and their home a place of peace.
Blessed are you, Lord our God,
you make marriage a sign of your love.

All **Blessed be God for ever.**

May they know the love of the Father,
the life of the Son,
and the joy of the Spirit.
Blessed are you, Lord our God,
Lover, Beloved and Friend of Love.

All **Blessed be God for ever.**

5 *This form may be added to any of the preceding blessings,*
or may be used on its own

Blessed are you, heavenly Father.
All **You give joy to bridegroom and bride.**

Blessed are you, Lord Jesus Christ.
All **You bring life to the world.**

Blessed are you, Holy Spirit of God.
All **You bind us together in love.**

Blessed are you, Father, Son, and Holy Spirit, now and for ever.
All **Amen.**

Longer Prayers and Litanies

I   Eternal God,
    creator and redeemer,
    from whom comes every good and perfect gift,
    fill *N* and *N* with the riches of your grace
    and breathe into their marriage
    the strength of your holy and life-giving Spirit.
    Lord, hear us:

All   **Lord, graciously hear us.**

    Send upon them the gift of love
    that puts no limit to its faith and forbearance.
    Lord, hear us:

All   **Lord, graciously hear us.**

    Sow in their lives the joy that comes from sharing
    and grows with giving.
    Lord, hear us:

All   **Lord, graciously hear us.**

    Let peace spring from their faithfulness to each other
    and flow deeper with the passing years.
    Lord, hear us:

All   **Lord, graciously hear us.**

    Give them patience with their failures
    and persistence with their hopes.
    Lord, hear us:

All   **Lord, graciously hear us.**

    May their kindness, born of a gracious heart,
    be shown to others in a generous spirit.
    Lord, hear us:

All   **Lord, graciously hear us.**

    Let goodness flower with forgiveness
    and be the fruit of their married life.
    Lord, hear us:

All   **Lord, graciously hear us.**

In gentleness let them be tender with each other's dreams
and healing of each other's wounds.
Lord, hear us:

All **Lord, graciously hear us.**

Gracious God,
accept our prayers for N and N,
that as their love ripens
and their marriage matures
they may reap the harvest of the Spirit,
rejoice in your gifts
and reflect your glory in Christ Jesus our Lord.

All **Amen.**

2 **A prayer for all people**
Almighty God, look graciously on the world which you have made
and for which your Son gave his life.
Bless all whom you make one flesh in marriage.
May their life together be a sign of your love to this broken world,
so that unity may overcome estrangement,
forgiveness heal guilt, and joy overcome despair.
Lord, in your mercy

All **hear our prayer.**

May N and N so live together
that the strength of their love may reflect your love
and enrich our common life.
Lord, in your mercy

All **hear our prayer.**

May they be gentle and patient, ready to trust each other,
and, when they fail, willing to recognize and acknowledge their fault
and to give and receive forgiveness.
Lord, in your mercy

All **hear our prayer.**

[May N and N be blessed with the gift of children.
Fill them with wisdom and love as they care for their family.
Lord, in your mercy

All **hear our prayer.]**

May the lonely, the bereaved, and all who suffer want or anxiety,
be defended by you, O Lord.
Lord, in your mercy

All **hear our prayer.**

May those whose lives are today brought together
be given wisdom, patience and courage
to serve one another in Christ's name.
Lord, in your mercy

All **hear our prayer.**

May friends and family gathered here,
and those separated by distance,
be strengthened and blessed this day.
Lord, in your mercy

All **hear our prayer.**

We praise you, merciful God,
for those who have died in the faith of Christ.
May we be strengthened by their example.

Almighty God, you have promised to hear our prayers.

All **Grant that what we have asked in faith
we may by your grace receive,
through Jesus Christ our Lord. Amen.**

3 Eternal God,
creator and preserver of all life and giver of grace;
look with favour on the world you have made,
and especially on this man and this woman
whom you in holy marriage have made one.
Lord, in your mercy

All **hear our prayer.**

Give them wisdom and devotion in ordering their common life,
that each may be to the other
a strength in need, a counsellor in perplexity,
a comfort in sorrow and a companion in joy.
Lord, in your mercy

All **hear our prayer.**

Grant that their wills may be so knit together in your will,
that they may grow together in love and peace
with one another and with you all the days of their life.
Lord, in your mercy

All **hear our prayer.**

Give them grace when they hurt one another
to recognize and acknowledge their fault
and to seek each other's forgiveness
and your pardon and peace.
Lord, in your mercy

All **hear our prayer.**

Make their life together a sign of Christ's love
in this broken and disordered world,
that unity may overcome estrangement,
forgiveness heal injury
and joy overcome despair.
Lord, in your mercy

All **hear our prayer.**

[Bestow on them, if it is your will,
the heritage and gift of children
and the grace to bring them up
to know you, to love you and to serve you.
Lord, in your mercy

All **hear our prayer.**]

Give them such fulfilment of their affection
that they may reach out in love and concern for others.
Lord, in your mercy

All **hear our prayer.**

Grant that all those who have witnessed these vows
may find their lives strengthened
and their loyalties confirmed.
Lord, in your mercy

All **hear our prayer.**

Grant that the bonds of our common humanity
by which all your children are united to one another
may be so transformed by your grace
that your will may be done on earth as it is in heaven;
where, O Father, with your Son and the Holy Spirit,
you live and reign in perfect unity, now and for ever.

All **Amen.**

4   Almighty God, our heavenly Father,
     we lift up our hearts to you
     through Jesus Christ our Lord.
     Through him you have made a covenant of grace with your people
     by the outpouring of your Holy Spirit.

     We praise you for the gift of marriage
     in which the love of husband and wife
     reveals your purposes of love for the world.

     We thank you today for N and N,
     for leading them to each other
     in friendship and love, commitment and trust,
     and for bringing them here for the blessing of their marriage.

     Living God,
     by the presence of your Holy Spirit,
     may they know the risen Christ to be with them now,
     as they celebrate this covenant together.
     May their lives be a witness to your saving love
     in this troubled world.

     As you pour out your love,
     may they grow together in your sight,
     and each be to the other
     a companion in joy, a comfort in sorrow and a strength in need.

     As you blessed the earthly home at Nazareth
     with the presence of your Son,
     may their home be a place of security and peace.
     [Bless this couple with the gift and care of children,
     that they may grow up to know and love you in your Son.]

     And bring us all at the last
     to that great marriage banquet of your Son
     in our home in heaven,
     where, with all your saints and angels,
     in the glory of your presence,
     we will for ever praise you;
     through Jesus Christ our Lord.
All **Amen.**

Thanksgiving

For the sharing of love

5   Father of all,
in Jesus Christ you open to us
the treasures of your kingdom;
guide us by your Holy Spirit
that we may receive your redeeming grace
and reflect the perfect unity of your love,
for you live and reign
Father, Son, and Holy Spirit,
one God, now and for ever.

All   **Amen.**

6   God of love,
we thank you for the gift of marriage and for the joys it brings.
Bless us as we share in this wedding.
We thank you for the love
which has brought *N* and *N* to each other
and for their desire to share that
love for the rest of their lives;
through Jesus Christ our Lord.

All   **Amen.**

Spiritual Growth

7   **For the home**
Lord and Saviour Jesus Christ,
who shared at Nazareth the life of an earthly home:
reign in the home of these your servants as Lord and King;
give them grace to minister to others
      as you have ministered to them,
and grant that by deed and word
they may be witnesses of your saving love
to those among whom they live;
for the sake of your holy name.

All   **Amen.**

8   **For the Holy Spirit**
    Almighty God,
    you send your Holy Spirit
    to be the life and light of all your people.
    Open the hearts of these your servants to the riches of his grace,
    that they may bring forth the fruit of the Spirit
        in love and joy and peace;
    through Jesus Christ our Lord.
All **Amen.**

9   **For grace to live well**
    Faithful God,
    giver of all good things,
    give N and N wisdom and devotion
    in the ordering of their life together.
    May they dwell together in love and peace
    all the days of their life,
        seeking one another's welfare,
        bearing one another's burdens
        and sharing one another's joys;
    through Jesus Christ our Lord.
All **Amen.**

10 **For discipleship**
    Eternal God,
    without your grace nothing is strong, nothing is sure.
    Strengthen N and N with patience, kindness, gentleness
    and all other gifts of the Holy Spirit,
    so that they may fulfil the vows they have made.
    Keep them faithful to each other and to you.
    Fill them with such love and joy
    that they may build a home of peace and welcome.
    Make their life together a sign of Christ's love
        in this broken world,
    that unity may overcome estrangement,
    forgiveness heal guilt,
    and joy conquer despair;
    through Jesus Christ our Lord.
All **Amen.**

11   **For a glimpse of eternal love**
Eternal God, our maker and redeemer,
as you once enriched the wedding at Cana
when your Son turned water into wine,
so by his presence now bring your joy to this day.
May we drink deeply from your boundless love
and know in our hearts the delights of your Holy Spirit.
As we honour the union of a man and a woman,
let the love we celebrate today be a sign of your eternal love,
Father, Son, and Holy Spirit.

All   **Amen.**

12   **For the gift of love**
God of wonder and of joy:
grace comes from you,
and you alone are the source of life and love.
Without you, we cannot please you;
without your love, our deeds are worth nothing.
Send your Holy Spirit,
and pour into our hearts
that most excellent gift of love,
that we may worship you now
with thankful hearts
and serve you always with willing minds;
through Jesus Christ our Lord.

All   **Amen.**

13   **For marriage as a sign to the world**
Almighty God, in whom we live and move and have our being,
look graciously upon the world which you have made
and for which your Son gave his life,
and especially on all whom you make to be one flesh
    in holy marriage.
May their lives together be a sign of your love to this broken world,
so that unity may overcome estrangement,
forgiveness heal guilt,
and joy overcome despair;
through Jesus Christ our Lord.

All   **Amen.**

14   **For the joy of loving**
God our creator,
we thank you for your gift of sexual love
by which husband and wife
may delight in each other
and share with you the joy of creating new life.
By your grace may N and N remain lovers,
rejoicing in your goodness all their days.

All   **Amen.**

15   **For the healing of memory**
Loving God,
you are merciful and forgiving.
Grant that those who are suffering the hurts of the past
     may experience your generous love.
Heal their memories, comfort them,
and send them all from here
renewed and hopeful;
in Jesus Christ our Lord.

All   **Amen.**

16   **For the joy of companionship**
All praise and blessing to you, God of love,
creator of the universe,
maker of man and woman in your likeness,
source of blessing for married life.
All praise to you, for you have created
     courtship and marriage,
     joy and gladness,
     feasting and laughter,
     pleasure and delight.
May your blessing come in full upon N and N.
May they know your presence
in their joys and in their sorrows.
May they reach old age in the company of friends
and come at last to your eternal kingdom;
through Jesus Christ our Lord.

All   **Amen.**

17　**For grace and delight**
God of love, ever gracious and kind,
we pray for N and N as they make the promises of marriage.
Let them know you
as the God of mercy and new beginnings,
who forgives our failures and renews our hope.
May the grace of Christ
be poured into their wedding
for celebration and for joy.
God of love, ever present and faithful,
may N and N know that their marriage is your delight and will.
May the promises they make govern their life together,
as your presence surrounds them,
and your Spirit strengthens and guides them;
through Jesus Christ our Lord.

All　**Amen.**

For faithfulness

18　God of all grace,
friend and companion,
look in favour on N and N,
and all who are made one in marriage.
In your love deepen their love
and strengthen their wills
to keep the promises they have made,
that they may continue
in life-long faithfulness to each other;
through Jesus Christ our Lord.

All　**Amen.**

19　Gracious God,
as you have brought N and N together in love,
enable them through the power of your Holy Spirit
to make and keep the solemn promises of marriage;
through Jesus Christ our Lord.

All　**Amen.**

20   O gracious and ever-living God,
male and female you have created us in your image:
look mercifully upon this man and this woman
who come to you seeking your blessing;
assist them with your grace,
that with true fidelity and steadfast love
they may honour and keep the promises and vows they make;
through Jesus Christ your Son our Lord
who is alive and reigns with you
in the unity of the Holy Spirit, one God, now and for ever.

All   **Amen.**

21   **For faithfulness and peace**
O God of love,
look mercifully upon N and N in the new life
    which they begin together this day.
Unite them evermore in your love.
Keep them faithful to the vows they have made one to the other;
strengthen them with every good gift;
and let your peace be with them,
now and always;
for the sake of Jesus Christ our Lord.

All   **Amen.**

22   **For daily following of Christ**
Heavenly Father,
we thank you that in our earthly lives
you speak to us of your eternal life:
we pray that through their marriage
N and N may know you more clearly,
love you more dearly
and follow you more nearly,
day by day;
through Jesus Christ our Lord.

All   **Amen.**

Children, other Family Members
and Friends

23   **For children and home**
Heavenly Father,
maker of all things,
you enable us to share in your work of creation.
Bless this couple in the gift and care of children,
that their home may be a place of love, security and truth,
and their children grow up to know and love you in your Son
Jesus Christ our Lord.

All   **Amen.**

24   **For children and family**
Lord of life,
you shape us in your image,
and by your gracious gift
the human family is increased.
Grant to *N* and *N* the blessing of children.
Fill them with wisdom and love
as they care for their family,
so that they and their children
may know and love you;
through your Son Jesus Christ our Lord.

All   **Amen.**

25   **For an existing family**
God of all grace and goodness,
we thank you for this new family,
and for everything parents and children have to share;
by your Spirit of peace draw them together
and help them to be true friends to one another.
Let your love surround them
and your care protect them;
through Jesus Christ our Lord.

All   **Amen.**

26   **For the families of the couple**
Gracious Lord,
bless the parents and families of N and N
that they may grow in love and friendship.
Grant that, as they have witnessed these vows today,
they may find their lives enriched and strengthened
and their loyalties confirmed;
in Jesus Christ our Lord.

All   **Amen.**

27   **For the support of friends**
Holy Spirit of God,
you know our strength
and have compassion on our frailty.
Be with N and N
in all they undertake.
And grant that we their friends,
with all who become their friends,
may sense and understand their needs;
through Jesus Christ our Lord.

All   **Amen.**

¶ *Canticles*

A Song of Solomon

Refrain:

All **Many waters cannot quench love;
neither can the floods drown it.**

1   Set me as a seal upon your heart, ♦
    as a seal upon your arm;

2   For love is strong as death, passion fierce as the grave; ♦
    its flashes are flashes of fire, a raging flame.

3   Many waters cannot quench love, ♦
    neither can the floods drown it.

4   If all the wealth of our house were offered for love, ♦
    it would be utterly scorned.   *cf Song of Solomon 8.6-7*

   Glory to the Father and to the Son
   and to the Holy Spirit;
   as it was in the beginning is now
   and shall be for ever. Amen.

A Song of the Bride

Refrain:

All   **God makes righteousness and praise**
       blossom before all the nations.

1   I will greatly rejoice in the Lord, ♦
     my soul shall exult in my God;

2   Who has clothed me with the garments of salvation, ♦
     and has covered me with the cloak of integrity,

3   As a bridegroom decks himself with a garland, ♦
     and as a bride adorns herself with her jewels.

4   For as the earth puts forth her blossom, ♦
     and as seeds in the garden spring up,

5   So shall God make righteousness and praise ♦
     blossom before all the nations.

6   For Zion's sake I will not keep silent, ♦
     and for Jerusalem's sake I will not rest,

7   Until her deliverance shines out like the dawn, ♦
     and her salvation as a burning torch.

8   The nations shall see your deliverance, ♦
     and all rulers shall see your glory;

9   Then you shall be called by a new name ♦
     which the mouth of God will give.

10   You shall be a crown of glory in the hand of the Lord, ♦
     a royal diadem in the hand of your God.   *Isaiah 61.10,11; 62.1-3*

Glory to the Father and to the Son
and to the Holy Spirit;
as it was in the beginning is now
and shall be for ever. Amen.

Magnificat (The Song of Mary)

1   My soul proclaims the greatness of the Lord,
      my spirit rejoices in God my Saviour; ♦
   he has looked with favour on his lowly servant.

2   From this day all generations will call me blessed; ♦
   the Almighty has done great things for me
      and holy is his name.

3   He has mercy on those who fear him, ♦
   from generation to generation.

4   He has shown strength with his arm ♦
   and has scattered the proud in their conceit,

5   Casting down the mighty from their thrones ♦
   and lifting up the lowly.

6   He has filled the hungry with good things ♦
   and sent the rich away empty.

7   He has come to the aid of his servant Israel, ♦
   to remember his promise of mercy,

8   The promise made to our ancestors, ♦
   to Abraham and his children for ever.   *Luke 1.46-55*

Glory to the Father and to the Son
and to the Holy Spirit;
as it was in the beginning is now
and shall be for ever. Amen.

A Song of the Lamb

Refrain:

All **Let us rejoice and exult**
and give glory and homage to our God.

1 Salvation and glory and power belong to our God, ♦
   whose judgements are true and just.

2 Praise our God, all you his servants, ♦
   all who fear him, both small and great.

3 The Lord our God, the Almighty, reigns: ♦
   let us rejoice and exult and give him the glory.

4 For the marriage of the Lamb has come ♦
   and his bride has made herself ready.

5 Blessed are those who are invited ♦
   to the wedding banquet of the Lamb.   *Revelation 19.1b,2b,5b,6b,7,9b*

To the One who sits on the throne and to the Lamb ♦
be blessing and honour and glory and might,
     for ever and ever. Amen.

An Order for Prayer and Dedication after a Civil Marriage

For Notes, see page 183.

Introduction

A hymn may be sung.

The minister may welcome the people and then says

The Lord be with you

All **and also with you.**

Preface

N and N, you stand in the presence of God as man and wife to dedicate to him your life together, that he may consecrate your marriage and empower you to keep the covenant and promise you have solemnly declared.

[The Bible teaches us that marriage is a gift of God in creation and a means of his grace, a holy mystery in which man and woman become one flesh. It is God's purpose that, as husband and wife give themselves to each other in love throughout their lives, they shall be united in that love as Christ is united with his Church.

Marriage is given, that husband and wife may comfort and help each other, living faithfully together in need and in plenty, in sorrow and in joy. It is given, that with delight and tenderness they may know each other in love, and, through the joy of their bodily union, may strengthen the union of their hearts and lives. It is given as the foundation of family life in which children may be [born and] nurtured in accordance with God's will, to his praise and glory. This is the meaning of the marriage you have made.]

You now wish to affirm your desire to live as followers of Christ, and you have come to him, the fountain of grace, that, strengthened by the prayers of the Church, you may be enabled to fulfil your marriage vows in love and faithfulness.

Let us keep silence and remember God's presence with us now.

God is love, and those who live in love live in God
and God lives in them. *1 John 4.16*

This prayer may be said

All **Almighty God,**
to whom all hearts are open,
all desires known,
and from whom no secrets are hidden:
cleanse the thoughts of our hearts
by the inspiration of your Holy Spirit,
that we may perfectly love you,
and worthily magnify your holy name;
through Christ our Lord.
Amen.

Prayers of Penitence

The following Summary of the Law may be said

Our Lord Jesus Christ said:
The first commandment is this:
'Hear, O Israel, the Lord our God is the only Lord.
You shall love the Lord your God with all your heart,
with all your soul, with all your mind,
and with all your strength.'

The second is this: 'Love your neighbour as yourself.'
There is no other commandment greater than these.
On these two commandments hang all the law and the prophets.

All **Amen. Lord, have mercy.**

A minister may use these or other suitable words

God so loved the world
that he gave his only Son Jesus Christ
to save us from our sins,
to be our advocate in heaven,
and to bring us to eternal life.

Let us confess our sins in penitence and faith,
firmly resolved to keep God's commandments
and to live in love and peace with all.

(or)

We come to God as one from whom no secrets are hidden,
to ask for his forgiveness and peace.

Either

All **Lord our God,**
in our sin we have avoided your call.
Our love for you is like a morning cloud,
like the dew that goes away early.
Have mercy on us;
deliver us from judgement;
bind up our wounds and revive us;
in Jesus Christ our Lord.
Amen.

The minister says

The Lord forgive *you your* sin,
unite *you* in the love which took Christ to the cross,
and bring *you* in the Spirit to his wedding feast in heaven.

All **Amen.**

(or)

Lord, in our weakness you are our strength.
Lord, have mercy.

All **Lord, have mercy.**

Lord, when we stumble, you raise us up.
Christ, have mercy.

All **Christ, have mercy.**

Lord, when we fail, you give us new life.
Lord, have mercy.

All **Lord, have mercy.**

The minister says

May God in his goodness forgive *us our* sins,
grant *us* strength in *our* weakness,
and bring *us* to eternal life,
through Jesus Christ our Lord.

All **Amen.**

The Collect

The minister invites the people to pray, silence is kept and the minister says the Collect

God our Father,
you have taught us through your Son
that love is the fulfilling of the law.
Grant to your servants
that, loving one another,
they may continue in your love until their lives' end:
through Jesus Christ your Son our Lord,
who is alive and reigns with you,
in the unity of the Holy Spirit,
one God, now and for ever.

All **Amen.**

Readings

At least one reading from the Bible is used. A selection of readings is found on pages 137–149.

If there are two readings, a psalm or a hymn may be sung between them.

A sermon may be preached here or after the Dedication.

The Dedication

The husband and wife face the minister, who says

N and N, you have committed yourselves to each other in marriage,
and your marriage is recognized by law.
The Church of Christ understands marriage to be,
in the will of God,
the union of a man and a woman,
for better, for worse,
for richer, for poorer,
in sickness and in health,
to love and to cherish,
till parted by death.
Is this your understanding of the covenant and promise
    that you have made?

Husband
and wife   It is.

The minister says to the husband

N, have you resolved to be faithful to your wife,
forsaking all others,
so long as you both shall live?

Husband   That is my resolve, with the help of God.

The minister says to the wife

N, have you resolved to be faithful to your husband,
forsaking all others,
so long as you both shall live?

Wife   That is my resolve, with the help of God.

The minister may say

Heavenly Father, by your blessing
let *these rings* be to N and N
a symbol of unending love and faithfulness
and of the promises they have made to each other;
through Jesus Christ our Lord.

All   **Amen.**

The minister says to the congregation

N and N have here affirmed
their Christian understanding and resolve
in the marriage which they have begun.
Will you, their families and friends,
support and uphold them in their marriage,
now and in the years to come?

All **We will.**

The congregation remains standing.

The husband and wife kneel and say together

Heavenly Father,
we offer you our souls and bodies,
our thoughts and words and deeds,
our love for one another.
Unite our wills in your will,
that we may grow together
in love and peace
all the days of our life;
through Jesus Christ our Lord. Amen.

The minister says

Almighty God give you grace to persevere,
that he may complete in you
the work he has already begun,
through Jesus Christ our Lord.

All **Amen.**

The Lord bless and watch over you,
the Lord make his face shine upon you
and be gracious to you,
the Lord look kindly on you and give you peace
all the days of your life.

All **Amen.**

A sermon may be preached.

A hymn may be sung.

Prayers

One or more of the following prayers may be used

Almighty God,
you send your Holy Spirit
to be the life and light of all your people.
Open the hearts of these your servants to the riches of his grace,
that they may bring forth the fruit of the Spirit
in love and joy and peace;
through Jesus Christ our Lord.

All **Amen.**

For the gift of children

Heavenly Father,
maker of all things,
you enable us to share in your work of creation.
Bless this couple in the gift and care of children,
that their home may be a place of love, security and truth
and their children grow up to know and love you in your Son
Jesus Christ our Lord.

All **Amen.**

For families

Father of all life,
whose promise is to be the God of all the families of your people,
give your grace to *N* and *N* in their new life together
and bless those for whom they care.
Enfold them in your love
as they share in their new family,
that they may grow up in all things into Christ,
who gave himself that all humanity might be made one in him.

All **Amen.**

For families
Heavenly Father,
we are your children, made in your image.
Hear our prayer
that fathers and mothers, sons and daughters,
may find together the perfect love that casts out fear,
walk together in the way that leads to eternal life
and grow up together into the full humanity
of your Son Jesus Christ our Lord.

All **Amen.**

Concluding prayer
Eternal God, true and loving Father,
in holy marriage you make your servants one.
May their life together witness to your love in this troubled world;
may unity overcome division,
forgiveness heal injury
and joy triumph over sorrow,
through Jesus Christ our Lord.

All **Amen.**

The Lord's Prayer is said.

As our Saviour taught us, so we pray

All **Our Father in heaven,**
hallowed be your name,
your kingdom come,
your will be done,
on earth as in heaven.
Give us today our daily bread.
Forgive us our sins
as we forgive those who sin against us.
Lead us not into temptation
but deliver us from evil.
For the kingdom, the power,
and the glory are yours
now and for ever.
Amen.

(or)

Let us pray with confidence as our Saviour has taught us

All **Our Father, who art in heaven,**
hallowed be thy name;
thy kingdom come;
thy will be done;
on earth as it is in heaven.
Give us this day our daily bread.
And forgive us our trespasses,
as we forgive those who trespass against us.
And lead us not into temptation;
but deliver us from evil.
For thine is the kingdom,
the power and the glory,
for ever and ever.
Amen.

A hymn may be sung.

God the Holy Trinity make *you* strong in faith and love,
defend *you* on every side, and guide *you* in truth and peace;
and the blessing of God almighty,
the Father, the Son, and the Holy Spirit,
be among *you* and remain with *you* always.

All   **Amen.**

Notes

1   **The Nature of the Service**
The service is one in which the couple – already married –
wish to dedicate to God their life together. Because it is not a
marriage service, banns may not be called nor any entry made
in the Register of Marriages.

2   **Entrance of the Couple**
Husband and wife should enter the church together without
ceremony and sit together at the front of the church.

3   **The Prayers**
Other prayers may be used, especially when they form part of
the particular Christian tradition of the husband or wife.

4   **The Rings**
Because the marriage has already taken place, no ring is to be
given or received in the course of the service. If a ring is worn and
the prayer of blessing is to be used, the hand should be extended
towards the minister.

5   **The Minister**
When the service is not led by a priest, the Grace is used
in place of the Blessing.

6   **Holy Communion**
The structure of the Marriage Service within the Order for
the Celebration of Holy Communion should be followed. The
Introduction in this service replaces the Introduction; Prayers of
Penitence must be used; also, in the Liturgy of the Word, there
must be a Gospel reading, preceded by either one or two other
readings from Scripture and followed by a sermon. This is followed
by the Dedication and the Prayers, and the Liturgy of the Sacrament
follows. Any of the proper material in the Marriage Service within
the Order for the Celebration of Holy Communion may be used.

Thanksgiving for Marriage

Note

This outline service is designed for a number of different occasions. It may be used:

¶ on occasions when a number of couples reaffirm their vows together;

¶ to celebrate an anniversary;

¶ after a time of separation or difficulty in marriage;

¶ either at home or in church;

¶ combined with another service, such as the Holy Communion.

For each occasion, suitable prayers and other words should be chosen – with the couple if that is appropriate – from the resources which follow, or elsewhere. One way of amplifying the Outline Order for the first occasion above, which might be a major church occasion where some formality is right, is provided in the service which follows on page 185. On other occasions much may be done informally or extempore.

Thanksgiving for Marriage: An Outline Order

Introduction

1 Welcome

2 Prayer of Preparation

3 Preface

4 Readings

5 Psalms, Songs or Hymns

6 Sermon

Renewal of Vows

7 The couple(s) are invited to renew their marriage vows in a suitable form.

8 A ring or rings may be blessed.

9 Prayers are offered, including prayers of thanksgiving and blessing.

Thanksgiving for Marriage: A Sample Service

This sample service is derived from the Outline Order on page 185.

¶ Introduction

The Welcome

The minister welcomes the people, introduces the service informally and invites those present to pray.

The grace of our Lord Jesus Christ,
the love of God,
and the fellowship of the Holy Spirit
be with you

All **and also with you.**

This sentence may be used

God is love, and those who live in love live in God
and God lives in them.

1 John 4.16

Prayer of Preparation

God our Father,
you have taught us through your Son
that love is the fulfilling of the law;
grant to your servants N and N
that, loving one another,
they may continue in your love until their lives' end;
through Jesus Christ our Lord.

All **Amen.**

A hymn or song may be sung.

Preface

We have come together in the presence of God
to give thanks [*with N and N*] for [*… years of*] married life,
[to ask his forgiveness for all that has been amiss,] *
to rejoice together and to ask for God's blessing.
As our Lord Jesus Christ was himself a guest
at the wedding in Cana of Galilee,
so through his Spirit he is with us now.
Marriage is a gift of God in creation
and a means of his grace;
it is given that a husband and wife
may comfort and help each other,
living faithfully together
in times of need as well as in plenty,
in sadness and in joy, in sickness and in health;
it is given that with delight and tenderness
they may know each other in love.
[It is given as the foundation of family life
in which children may be born and nurtured
in accordance with God's will, to his praise and glory.]
In marriage a couple belong together
and live life in the community;
it is a way of life created and hallowed by God,
that all should honour.
Therefore we pray with them
that, strengthened and guided by God,
they may continue to fulfil his purpose for their life together.

*Silence is kept for reflection on the years that have passed
and on shared experiences, good and bad.*

Readings and Sermon

*One or more passages from the Bible is read.
Psalms or hymns may follow the readings. Other songs and readings
may be used.
A sermon may be preached.*

* There may be occasions when this should be omitted; it may be
important to include it when a couple are celebrating their reconciliation.

¶ Renewal of Vows

The minister says to the couple(s)

I invite you now to recall the vows that you made at your wedding.

Husband and wife face each other and hold hands.

The husband says
I, *N*, took you, *N*, to be my wife;
The wife says
I, *N*, took you, *N*, to be my husband;
The couple say together
to have and to hold from that day forward,
for better, for worse, for richer, for poorer,
in sickness and in health, to love and to cherish,
till death us do part, according to God's holy law,
and this was our solemn vow.
Today, in the presence of our family and friends,
we affirm our continuing commitment to this vow.

The minister says to the congregation

Will you, the family and friends of *N* and *N*,
continue to support and uphold them
in their marriage now and in the years to come?
All   **We will.**

The Rings

If a new ring (or new rings) is to be blessed, this prayer may be used

Heavenly Father, source of everlasting love,
revealed to us in Jesus Christ
    and poured into our hearts through your Holy Spirit;
that love which many waters cannot quench,
    neither the floods drown;
that love which is patient and kind, enduring all things without end;
by your blessing, let *these rings* be to N and N
symbols to remind them of the covenant made on their wedding day,
through your grace in the love of your Son
and in the power of your Spirit.

All   **Amen.**

If a ring (or rings) is to be given these words are used

I give you this ring
as a sign of our marriage.
With my body I honour you,
all that I am I give to you,
and all that I have I share with you,
within the love of God,
Father, Son, and Holy Spirit.

Or, if not, each may touch the wedding ring(s) with the words

I gave you this ring
as a sign of our marriage.
With my body I honour you,
all that I am I give to you,
and all that I have I share with you,
within the love of God,
Father, Son, and Holy Spirit.

The couple kneel together. The minister or others may pray, using these or similar prayers

God the Father,
God the Son,
God the Holy Spirit,
bless, preserve and keep you;
the Lord mercifully grant you the riches of his grace
that you may please him both in body and soul,
and, living together in faith and love,
may receive the blessings of eternal life.

All **Amen.**

Blessed are you, heavenly Father.

All **You give joy to husband and wife.**

Blessed are you, Lord Jesus Christ.

All **You have brought new life to mankind.**

Blessed are you, Holy Spirit of God.

All **You bring us together in love.**

Blessed be Father, Son and Holy Spirit.

All **One God, to be praised for ever. Amen.**

Almighty God, our heavenly Father,
we lift up our hearts to you
through Jesus Christ our Lord.
Through him you have made a covenant of grace with your people
by the outpouring of your Holy Spirit.

We praise you for the gift of marriage
in which the love of husband and wife is brought together
and reflects your plan of love for the world.

We thank you today for N and N,
and for leading them to each other
in friendship and love, commitment and trust,
and for bringing them here for the blessing of their marriage.

Living God,
by the presence of your Holy Spirit,
may they know the risen Christ to be with them now,
as they celebrate this covenant together.
May their lives be a witness to your saving love
in this troubled world.

As you pour out your love,
may they grow together in your sight,
and each be to the other
a companion in joy, a comfort in sorrow and a strength in need.

As you blessed the earthly home at Nazareth
with the presence of your Son,
may their home be a place of security and peace.
[Bless this couple with the gift and care of children,
that they may grow up to know and love you in your Son.]

And bring us all at the last
to that great marriage banquet of your Son
in our home in heaven,
where, with all your saints and angels,
in the glory of your presence,
we will for ever praise you;
through Jesus Christ our Lord.

All   **Amen.**

The Lord's Prayer

As our Saviour taught us, so we pray

All　**Our Father in heaven,**
hallowed be your name,
your kingdom come,
your will be done,
on earth as in heaven.
Give us today our daily bread.
Forgive us our sins
as we forgive those who sin against us.
Lead us not into temptation
but deliver us from evil.
For the kingdom, the power,
and the glory are yours
now and for ever.
Amen.

(or)

Let us pray with confidence as our Saviour has taught us

All　**Our Father, who art in heaven,**
hallowed be thy name;
thy kingdom come;
thy will be done;
on earth as it is in heaven.
Give us this day our daily bread.
And forgive us our trespasses,
as we forgive those who trespass against us.
And lead us not into temptation;
but deliver us from evil.
For thine is the kingdom,
the power and the glory
for ever and ever.
Amen.

The Dismissal

The couple may pray together

Heavenly Father,
we offer you our souls and bodies,
our thoughts and words and deeds,
our love for one another.
Unite our wills in your will,
that we may grow together
in love and peace
all the days of our life;
through Jesus Christ our Lord.

All **Amen.**

The minister blesses the couple and the congregation, saying

God the Holy Trinity make *you* strong in faith and love,
defend *you* on every side, and guide *you* in truth and peace;
and the blessing of God almighty,
the Father, the Son, and the Holy Spirit,
be among *you* and remain with *you* always.

All **Amen.**

Emergency Baptism

For Notes, see page 198.

The following form is sufficient.

The minister pours water on the person to be baptized, saying

N, I baptize you in the name of the Father, and of the Son,
and of the Holy Spirit.

All   **Amen.**

The minister may then say the Lord's Prayer and the Grace or a blessing.
If it is appropriate, some of the following may also be used.

Before the Baptism

Jesus says: I have come that you may have life
and have it in all its fullness.   *John 10.10*

All that the Father gives me will come to me;
and whoever comes to me I will not turn away.   *John 6.37*

The Lord is near to the brokenhearted
and will save those who are crushed in spirit.   *Psalm 34.18*

Heavenly Father,
grant that by your Holy Spirit
this child may be born again
and know your love in the new creation
given us in Jesus Christ our Lord.

All   **Amen.**

At the Signing with the Cross

N, may Christ protect and defend you.
Receive the sign of his cross.

Prayer over the Water

Heavenly Father,
bless this water,
that whoever is washed in it
may be made one with Christ
in the fellowship of your Church,
and be brought through every tribulation
to share the risen life
that is ours in Jesus Christ our Lord.

All   **Amen.**

After the Baptism

As our Saviour taught us, so we pray

All   **Our Father in heaven,**
hallowed be your name,
your kingdom come,
your will be done,
on earth as in heaven.
Give us today our daily bread.
Forgive us our sins
as we forgive those who sin against us.
Lead us not into temptation
but deliver us from evil.
For the kingdom, the power,
and the glory are yours
now and for ever.
Amen.

(or)

Let us pray with confidence as our Saviour has taught us

All   **Our Father, who art in heaven,**
hallowed be thy name;
thy kingdom come;
thy will be done;
on earth as it is in heaven.
Give us this day our daily bread.
And forgive us our trespasses,
as we forgive those who trespass against us.
And lead us not into temptation;
but deliver us from evil.
For thine is the kingdom,
the power and the glory,
for ever and ever.
Amen.

Eternal God, our beginning and our end,
preserve in your people the new life of baptism;
as Christ receives us on earth,
so may he guide us through the trials of this world,
and enfold us in the joy of heaven,
where you live and reign,
one God for ever and ever.

All **Amen.**

The grace of our Lord Jesus Christ,
and the love of God,
and the fellowship of the Holy Spirit
be with us all evermore.

All **Amen.**

(or)

May God almighty,
the Father, the Son, and the Holy Spirit,
bless and keep you this day and for evermore.

All **Amen.**

Notes

1   In an emergency, a lay person may be the minister of baptism, and should subsequently inform those who have the pastoral responsibility for the person so baptized.

2   Parents are responsible for requesting emergency baptism for an infant. They should be assured that questions of ultimate salvation or of the provision of a Christian funeral for an infant who dies do not depend upon whether or not the child has been baptized.

3   Before baptizing, the minister should ask the name of the person to be baptized. When, through the absence of parents or for some other reason, there is uncertainty as to the name of the person, the baptism can be properly administered without a name (so long as the identity of the person baptized can be duly recorded).

Service in Church

4   If the person lives, they shall afterwards come to church, or be brought to church, and the service for Holy Baptism followed, except that the Signing with the Cross, the Prayer over the Water and the Baptism are omitted.

5   It may be appropriate to use the prayer of thanksgiving for a child from *Common Worship: Initiation Services* or the President's edition of *Common Worship* (page 50).

6   At the Presentation the president says

> We welcome N, who has been baptized and now comes to take *his/her* place in the company of God's people.

7   Oil mixed with fragrant spices (traditionally called chrism), expressing the blessings of the messianic era and the richness of the Holy Spirit, may be used to accompany the prayer after the baptism. It is appropriate that the oil should have been consecrated by the bishop.

Thanksgiving for the Gift of a Child

Note

This service is provided for a number of different occasions:

¶ the private celebration of a birth or adoption, at home or in church with only family and close friends present;

¶ the public celebration of the birth or adoption of a number of children, perhaps in church on a Sunday afternoon;

¶ the public celebration of the birth or adoption of a number of children as part of a main Sunday act of worship.

It is designed to meet the needs of:

¶ parents who see this as a preliminary to Baptism;

¶ parents who do not wish their children to be baptized immediately;

¶ others, who do not ask for Baptism, but who recognize that something has happened for which they wish to give thanks to God.

¶ *Pastoral Introduction*

This may be read by those present before the service begins.

The birth or adoption of a child is a cause for celebration.
Many people are overcome by a sense of awe at the creation of
new life and want to express their thanks to God. This service
provides an opportunity for parents and families to give thanks
for the birth or adoption of a child and to pray for family life.
It may be a private celebration at home or in hospital, or it may
be a public celebration in church, sometimes with a number
of children.

This service is not the same as Baptism (sometimes called
Christening), which is the sacrament of initiation into membership
of the Church, the Body of Christ. If you are interested in exploring
the Christian faith, or finding out more about preparation for
Baptism, ask the minister taking this service.

Structure

¶   Introduction

¶   Reading(s) and Sermon

¶   Thanksgiving and Blessing

¶   Giving of the Gospel

¶   Prayers

¶   Ending

For Notes, see page 212.

Thanksgiving for the Gift of a Child

Introduction

*The minister welcomes the people using a liturgical greeting
(see page 207) or other suitable words.*

A hymn or song may be sung.

The service may be introduced in these or similar words

We are here today to give thanks for *these children*, with *their* family
and friends, and to support *their* parents in their responsibilities with
prayer and love. God became one of us in Jesus, and understands all
that surrounds the arrival and upbringing of children. It is God's
purpose that children should know love within the stability of their
home, grow in faith, and come at last to the eternal city where his
love reigns supreme.

The following may be used

The works of the Lord are great:

All **his mercy endures for ever.**

Mary gave birth to a child and called him Jesus:

All **he will save his people from their sins.**

He will be called the Prince of Peace:

All **his kingdom will last for ever.**

The minister says

Loving God,
you hold all things in life
and call us into your kingdom of peace;
help us to walk the path of your truth
and fill our lives with gratitude and faith,
through Jesus Christ our Lord.

All **Amen.**

Reading(s) and Sermon

A suitable passage from the Bible is read (see page 207).

A sermon may be preached.

A hymn may be sung.

Thanksgiving and Blessing

Where parents wish to recognize the role of supporting friends it may be appropriate for them to stand with the parents at the thanksgiving. One of them may present the children to the minister, and informal words may be said.

The minister says

Do you receive *these children* as a gift from God?
We do.

Do you wish to give thanks to God and seek his blessing?
We do.

The minister says

God our creator,
we thank you for the wonder of new life
and for the mystery of human love.
We thank you for all whose support and skill
surround and sustain the beginning of life.
We thank you that we are known to you by name
and loved by you from all eternity.
We thank you for Jesus Christ,
who has opened to us the way of love.
We praise you, Father, Son, and Holy Spirit.

All   **Blessed be God for ever.**

The minister may say for each child
What name have you given this child?

A parent or supporting friend replies
His/her name is N.

The minister may take the child.
The minister says

As Jesus took children in his arms and blessed them,
so now we ask God's blessing on N.

Heavenly Father, we praise you for *his/her* birth;
surround *him/her* with your blessing
that *he/she* may know your love,
be protected from evil,
and know your goodness all *his/her* days.

All **May *they* learn to love all that is true,**
grow in wisdom and strength
and, in due time, come through faith and baptism
to the fullness of your grace;
through Jesus Christ our Lord.
Amen.

The minister prays for the parents

May God the Father of all bless *these parents*
and give *them* grace to love and care for *their children*.
May God give *them* wisdom, patience and faith,
help *them* to provide for the *children's* needs
and, by *their* example,
reveal the love and truth that are in Jesus Christ.

All **Amen.**

Giving of the Gospel

A copy of a Gospel is presented, with these words

Receive this book.
It is the good news of God's love.
Take it as your guide.

The minister may address the supporting friends and say

Will you do all that you can to help and support *N and N* in the
bringing up of *N*?
With the help of God, we will.

The minister may address the wider family and friends and say

Will you do all that you can to help and support *this family*?
With the help of God, we will.

Prayers

This prayer may be said by the parents or by the whole congregation

All **God our creator,**
we thank you for the gift of *these* *children*,
entrusted to our care.
May we be patient and understanding,
ready to guide and to forgive,
so that through our love
***they* may come to know your love;**
through Jesus Christ our Lord.
Amen.

The minister may say additional prayers (see pages 208–211), ending with the Lord's Prayer.

Jesus taught us to call God our Father,
and so in faith and trust we say

All **Our Father in heaven,**
hallowed be your name,
your kingdom come,
your will be done,
on earth as in heaven.
Give us today our daily bread.
Forgive us our sins
as we forgive those who sin against us.
Lead us not into temptation
but deliver us from evil.
For the kingdom, the power,
and the glory are yours
now and for ever.
Amen.

(or)

Jesus taught us to call God our Father,
and so we have the courage to say

All   **Our Father, who art in heaven,**
hallowed be thy name;
thy kingdom come;
thy will be done;
on earth as it is in heaven.
Give us this day our daily bread.
And forgive us our trespasses,
as we forgive those who trespass against us.
And lead us not into temptation;
but deliver us from evil.
For thine is the kingdom,
the power and the glory,
for ever and ever.
Amen.

Ending

The minister says one of these or another suitable blessing

The love of the Lord Jesus
draw *you* to himself,
the power of the Lord Jesus
strengthen *you* in his service,
the joy of the Lord Jesus fill *your* hearts;
and the blessing of God almighty,
the Father, the Son, and the Holy Spirit,
be among *you* and remain with *you* always.

All   **Amen.**

(or)

The Lord bless *you* and watch over *you*,
the Lord make his face shine upon *you*
and be gracious to *you*,
the Lord look kindly on *you* and give *you* peace;
and the blessing of God almighty,
the Father, the Son, and the Holy Spirit,
be among *you* and remain with *you* always.

All   **Amen.**

Supplementary Texts

Liturgical Greetings

In the name of Jesus
who was born to be our Saviour, Christ the Lord,
we welcome you.
Grace, mercy and peace be with you

All **and also with you.**

(or)

The grace of our Lord Jesus Christ,
the love of God
and the fellowship of the Holy Spirit
be with you

All **and also with you.**

(or)

The Lord be with you

All **and also with you.**

Bible Readings

One of these, or another suitable passage from the Bible, is read.

Exodus 20.12
Isaiah 9.2,6-7
Psalm 20
Psalm 128
Psalm 139.7-18
Matthew 1.18-25
Matthew 7.24-27
Matthew 18.1-5
Matthew 18.10-14
Mark 10.13-16
Luke 1.39-45
Luke 2.22-24
Luke 2.33-40
John 1.9-14
Ephesians 3.14-21
Ephesians 6.1-4
1 John 2.12-14

Additional Prayers

Additional prayers may include the following or other suitable prayers.

1   **For the child/children**
    God our Father,
    we pray for *this child*
    that in due time
    he/she may be received by baptism
    into the family of your Church,
    and become *an inheritor* of your kingdom;
    through Jesus Christ our Lord.

All   **Amen.**

For the home and family

2   Heavenly Father,
    whose blessed Son shared at Nazareth
        the life of an earthly home:
    bless the home of *this child*,
    and help all the family to live together in your love.
    Teach them to serve you and each other,
    and make them always ready to show your love
        to those in need;
    for the sake of Jesus Christ our Lord.

All   **Amen.**

3   Father in heaven, bless these parents,
    that they may cherish their *child*;
    make them wise and understanding,
    to help *him/her* as *he/she* grows,
    and surround this family
    with the light of your truth
    and the warmth of your love;
    through Jesus Christ our Lord.

All   **Amen.**

4   God our Father, we pray to you
        for all who have the care of *this child*.
     Guide them with your Holy Spirit,
     that they may bring *him/her* up
     in the ways of truth and love.
     Through their care enable *him/her* to grow in grace
     and become daily more like your Son,
     our Saviour Jesus Christ.
All   **Amen.**

5   **For the father**
     Heavenly Father,
     you entrusted your Son Jesus,
     the child of Mary,
     to the care of Joseph, an earthly father.
     Bless *N* [*this man*]
     as he cares for his family.
     Give him strength and wisdom,
         tenderness and patience;
     support him in the work he has to do,
     protecting those who look to him,
     as we look to you for love and salvation,
     through Jesus Christ our rock and defender.
All   **Amen.**

6   **For grandparents and other relatives**
     Father God, from whom every family
         in earth and heaven is named,
     we thank you for the rich variety
         of the families you have created for us,
     and for the relationships
         which we see and enjoy within them.
     Help us to respect and learn from each other,
     that we may come to maturity
     in Christ Jesus our Lord.
All   **Amen.**

7   **For brothers and sisters**
     Living God,
     we pray for *N's brothers and sisters*
     and for all whose lives will be changed by *his/her* arrival;
     grant them friendship and love
     that their home may be an image of your kingdom;
     through Jesus Christ our Lord.
All **Amen.**

8   **After a difficult birth**
     Loving Father,
     you have turned pain into joy
     by the birth of *N* [*this child*].
     May *N* [*this mother*],
     remembering no longer her anguish,
     trust you in all things.
     As she asks for all she would receive,
     may she discover that in you her joy is complete;
     through Jesus your Son.
All **Amen.**

9   **For health workers**
     Father almighty, we give you thanks
     for all concerned with the care of *N* [*this mother*]
     and the safe birth of *N* [*her child*].
     We pray for the doctors and nurses,
          midwives and health visitors,
     and all who will support the health and welfare of this family
          in the coming years.
     May they be filled with your love,
     moved by your compassion
     and supported by your presence.
     We ask this in Jesus' name.
All **Amen.**

10   **When a child is adopted**
      O God of love,
      you have made us your children by adoption and grace;
      as *N* becomes a member of this family
      bind them together by your grace,
      and give them wisdom, joy and faith,
      that together they may grow into your love
      and serve your purposes of peace;
      through Jesus Christ our Lord.
All **Amen.**

11   **For the birth parents of an adopted child**
      Heavenly Father, rich in goodness and mercy,
      look with your love on *N's* natural father and mother.
      Keep them in your good care
      and grant them peace;
      through Jesus Christ our Lord.
All **Amen.**

12   **When a child has special needs**
      Living God, creator of us all,
      we thank you for entrusting *N*
      into the special care of *N and N.*
      Give them and all who surround them
      wisdom and understanding, courage and patience;
      give them grace to put aside fear and anxiety
      and to fulfil your purposes;
      fill their hearts with your unfailing love,
      that *N* may grow up secure in giving and receiving love
      and in the enjoyment of your presence,
      to enrich our lives and the lives of others
      in ways beyond our imagining,
      in Jesus Christ our Lord.
All **Amen.**

Notes

1   To make it clear that the service is one of thanksgiving and not a Baptism, a register shall be kept recording the names of children for whom this thanksgiving service has been conducted, and the family should be given a certificate.

2   The service should be adapted when only one parent is present or to suit particular needs.

3   When several children (from one or more families) have been brought for thanksgiving and blessing, the prayer on page 203 may be said for each child or for each family or for all the children, as is most appropriate. The names of the parents and of the child may be used in the prayer for the parents on page 204.

4   Provision is made on page 203 of the service for supporting friends or relatives to make a commitment to the child and the family. It may be appropriate for them to stand with the family at the thanksgiving. One of them may present the child to the minister, and informal words may be said.

5   Hymns, songs or carols may be sung at points other than those indicated. If occasion requires, the sermon may be omitted.

Funeral

Contents

For General Rules, see page 402.

Ministry at the Time of Death

Structure

The minister and the dying person are alone for

¶ Preparation

¶ Reconciliation

Others may join the minister and the dying person for

¶ Opening Prayer

¶ The Word of God

¶ Prayers

¶ Laying on of Hands and Anointing

¶ Holy Communion

¶ Commendation

¶ Prayer when someone has just died

For Notes, see pages 217 and 235.

Ministry at the Time of Death

Note

Where possible the minister prepares the dying person in private, using the Preparation and Reconciliation sections. The person should be helped to be aware that the time of death is approaching. Family and friends should join the minister and the dying person at the Opening Prayer if they can be present, and it is appropriate that they should receive Holy Communion with the dying person. The different sections of the service may happen at different times, and the last communion may be received on another occasion, and more than once, as pastoral necessity dictates.

See further Notes on page 235.

¶ *Preparation*

One or more of the following short texts may be said with the dying person. They may be softly repeated two or three times.

Who will separate us from the love of Christ?   *Romans 8.35*

Whether we live or whether we die, we are the Lord's.   *Romans 14.8*

Christ died and lived again, so that he might be Lord
of both the dead and the living.   *Romans 14.9*

We know that we have a building from God, a house
not made with hands, eternal in the heavens.   *2 Corinthians 5.1*

We will be with the Lord for ever.   *1 Thessalonians 4.17*

We will see God as he is.   *1 John 3.2*

To you, O Lord, I lift up my soul.   *Psalm 25.1*

The Lord is my light and my salvation; whom then shall I fear?
Psalm 27.1

I believe that I shall see the goodness of the Lord
in the land of the living.
Wait for the Lord;
be strong and he shall comfort your heart;
wait patiently for the Lord. *Psalm 27.13,14*

Into your hands I commend my spirit;
for you have redeemed me, O Lord God of truth. *Psalm 31.5*

My soul is athirst for God, even for the living God. *Psalm 42.2*

Come, you that are blessed by my Father,
inherit the kingdom prepared for you
from the foundation of the world. *Matthew 25.34*

The Lord Jesus says,
'Today you will be with me in Paradise.' *Luke 23.43*

This is indeed the will of my Father,
that all who see the Son and believe in him
may have eternal life;
and I will raise them up on the last day. *John 6.40*

In my Father's house there are many dwelling places. *John 14.2*

I go and prepare a place for you.
And I will come again and will take you to myself,
so that where I am, there you may be also. *John 14.3*

'I desire that those also, whom you have given me,
may be with me where I am, to see my glory,'
says the Lord Jesus. *John 17.24*

Lord Jesus, receive my spirit. *Acts 7.59*

The steadfast love of the Lord never ceases,
his mercies never come to an end;
they are new every morning;
great is your faithfulness. *Lamentations 3.22,23*

The Lord's Prayer

As our Saviour taught us, so we pray

Our Father in heaven,
hallowed be your name,
your kingdom come,
your will be done,
on earth as in heaven.
Give us today our daily bread.
Forgive us our sins
as we forgive those who sin against us.
Lead us not into temptation
but deliver us from evil.
For the kingdom, the power,
and the glory are yours
now and for ever.
Amen.

(or)

Let us pray with confidence as our Saviour has taught us

Our Father, who art in heaven,
hallowed be thy name;
thy kingdom come;
thy will be done;
on earth as it is in heaven.
Give us this day our daily bread.
And forgive us our trespasses,
as we forgive those who trespass against us.
And lead us not into temptation;
but deliver us from evil.
For thine is the kingdom,
the power and the glory,
for ever and ever.
Amen.

¶ Reconciliation

The minister may encourage some expression of penitence, such as

Lord Jesus Christ,
Son of God,
have mercy on me,
a sinner.

(or)

Almighty God, our heavenly Father,
we have sinned against you,
through our own fault,
in thought and word and deed,
and in what we have left undone.
We are heartily sorry,
and repent of all our sins.
For your Son our Lord Jesus Christ's sake,
forgive us all that is past;
and grant that we may serve you in newness of life
to the glory of your name.
Amen.

(or)

Lord, have mercy upon us.
Christ, have mercy upon us.
Lord, have mercy upon us.

The minister may lay hands on the dying person.
If the minister is a priest, either of these absolutions may be used

God, the Father of mercies,
has reconciled the world to himself
    through the death and resurrection of his Son, Jesus Christ,
not counting our trespasses against us,
but sending his Holy Spirit to shed abroad his love among us.
By the ministry of reconciliation
entrusted by Christ to his Church,
receive his pardon and peace
to stand before him in his strength alone,
this day and evermore.
Amen.

If the minister is a deacon or lay person, these words are used

May almighty God have mercy on you,
forgive you your sins,
and bring you to everlasting life.
Amen.

At this point others may join the minister and the dying person.

¶ Opening Prayer

Blessed be the God and Father of our Lord Jesus Christ.
By his great mercy we have been born anew to a living hope
through the resurrection of Jesus Christ from the dead.

[*All* **Blessed be God for ever.**]

Let us pray for …

(Silence)

This prayer may be used

Eternal God,
grant to your servant
[and to us who surround *him/her* with our prayers]
your peace beyond understanding.
Give us faith, the comfort of your presence,
and the words to say to one another and to you,
as we gather in the name of Jesus Christ our Lord.

All **Amen.**

The following may be used

Out of the depths I cry to you:
Lord, hear my voice.
Lord, have mercy.

[*All* **Lord, have mercy.**]

If you should mark what is done amiss:
who may abide it?
Christ, have mercy.

[*All* **Christ, have mercy.**]

Trust in the Lord, for with him there is mercy:
for with him is ample redemption.
Lord, have mercy.

[*All* **Lord, have mercy.**]

¶ *The Word of God*

These or other suitable readings may be used (see pages 383–391)

Romans 8.35,37-39
Psalms 23; 139
John 6.35-40[53-58]

The minister may encourage an act of faith or commitment, such as

Holy God,
Father, Son, and Holy Spirit,
I trust you,
I believe in you,
I love you.

(or)

Jesus, remember me when you come into your kingdom.

(or)

Lord, I believe: help my unbelief.

(or)

Father, into your hands I commend my spirit.

¶ *Prayers*

This litany or some of the prayers with dying people on pages 346–347 may be used, or the minister may pray using his or her own words

God the Father,

All **have mercy upon us.**

God the Son,

All **have mercy upon us.**

God the Holy Spirit,

All **have mercy upon us.**

Holy, blessed and glorious Trinity,

All **have mercy upon us.**

By your holy incarnation, by your cross and passion,
by your precious death and burial,

All **have mercy upon us.**

By your glorious resurrection and ascension,
and by the coming of the Holy Spirit,

All **have mercy upon us.**

Graciously hear us, Lord Jesus Christ,
that it may please you to deliver your servant *N* from all evil
    and from eternal death,

All **hear us, good Lord.**

That it may please you mercifully to pardon all *N*'s sins,

All **hear us, good Lord.**

That it may please you to give *N* peace, rest and gladness,
raising *him/her* to new life in your kingdom,

All **hear us, good Lord.**

That it may please you to bring us, with *N* and all your saints,
to a joyful resurrection,

All **hear us, good Lord.**

Lamb of God, you take away the sin of the world,

All **hear us, good Lord.**

Lamb of God, you take away the sin of the world,

All **hear us, good Lord.**

Lamb of God, you take away the sin of the world,

All **hear us, good Lord.**

All **In darkness and in light,**
in trouble and in joy,
help us, O God, to trust your love,
to seek your purpose
and to praise your name;
through Jesus Christ our Lord.
Amen.

¶ Laying on of Hands and Anointing

The minister, together with others if that is appropriate,
may lay hands on the dying person. This prayer may be used

In the name of our Lord Jesus Christ
I/we lay *my/our* hands on you, N.
May the Lord in his mercy and love uphold you
by the grace and power of the Holy Spirit.
May he deliver you from all evil,
give you light and peace,
and bring you to everlasting life.

All   **Amen.**

The minister may anoint the dying person, making the sign of the cross
in oil on his or her forehead [and hands] (see Note 1 on page 235)

N, I anoint you with oil in the name of our Lord Jesus Christ.
May the Lord in his love and mercy uphold you
by the grace and power of the Holy Spirit.

All   **Amen.**

When the anointing is completed, the minister may add

As you are outwardly anointed with this holy oil,
so may our heavenly Father grant you the inward anointing
        of the Holy Spirit.
Of his great mercy
may he forgive you your sins
and release you from suffering.
May he deliver you from all evil,
preserve you in all goodness
and bring you to everlasting life;
through Jesus Christ our Lord.

All   **Amen.**

¶ Holy Communion

If it is possible, the dying person may receive communion.
Unless the bread and wine have already been consecrated,
an authorized Eucharistic Prayer is used (see Note 1 on page 235).

The Agnus Dei may be used before the giving of communion

Lamb of God,
you take away the sin of the world,
have mercy on us.

Lamb of God,
you take away the sin of the world,
have mercy on us.

Lamb of God,
you take away the sin of the world,
grant us peace.

(or)

Jesus, Lamb of God,
have mercy on us.

Jesus, bearer of our sins,
have mercy on us.

Jesus, redeemer of the world,
grant us peace.

After the words of distribution the following may be added

May the Lord Jesus protect you
and lead you to eternal life.

¶ *Commendation*

The Lord's Prayer

As our Saviour taught us, so we pray

All   **Our Father in heaven,**
hallowed be your name,
your kingdom come,
your will be done,
on earth as in heaven.
Give us today our daily bread.
Forgive us our sins
as we forgive those who sin against us.
Lead us not into temptation
but deliver us from evil.
For the kingdom, the power,
and the glory are yours
now and for ever.
Amen.

(or)

Let us pray with confidence as our Saviour has taught us

All   **Our Father, who art in heaven,**
hallowed be thy name;
thy kingdom come;
thy will be done;
on earth as it is in heaven.
Give us this day our daily bread.
And forgive us our trespasses,
as we forgive those who trespass against us.
And lead us not into temptation;
but deliver us from evil.
For thine is the kingdom,
the power and the glory,
for ever and ever.
Amen.

The minister speaks first to the dying person, using these or other suitable words

N, go forth from this world:
in the love of God the Father who created you,
in the mercy of Jesus Christ who redeemed you,
in the power of the Holy Spirit who strengthens you.
May the heavenly host sustain you
and the company of heaven enfold you.
In communion with all the faithful,
may you dwell this day in peace.

All **Amen.**

(or)

N, go forth upon your journey from this world,
in the name of God the Father almighty who created you;
in the name of Jesus Christ who suffered death for you;
in the name of the Holy Spirit who strengthens you;
in communion with the blessed saints,
and aided by angels and archangels,
and all the armies of the heavenly host.
May your portion this day be in peace,
and your dwelling the heavenly Jerusalem.

All **Amen.**

(and/or)

Holy Lord, almighty and eternal God,
hear our prayers as we entrust to you N,
as you summon *him/her* out of this world.
Forgive *his/her* sins and failings
and grant *him/her* a haven of light, and peace.
Let *him/her* pass unharmed through the gates of death
to dwell with the blessed in light,
as you promised to Abraham and his children for ever.
Accept N into your safe keeping
and on the great day of judgement
raise *him/her* up with all the saints
to inherit your eternal kingdom.
We ask this through Christ our Lord.

All **Amen.**

Gracious God,
nothing in death or life,
nothing in the world as it is,
nothing in the world as it shall be,
nothing in all creation
can separate us from your love.
Jesus commended his spirit into your hands at his last hour.
Into those same hands we now commend your servant N,
that dying to the world and cleansed from sin,
death may be for *him/her* the gate to life
and to eternal fellowship with you;
through the same Jesus Christ our Lord.

All **Amen.**

(and/or)

Into your hands, O merciful Saviour,
we commend your servant N.
Acknowledge, we pray, a sheep of your own fold,
a lamb of your own flock,
a sinner of your own redeeming.
Enfold *him/her* in the arms of your mercy,
in the blessed rest of everlasting peace
and in the glorious company of the saints in light.

All **Amen.**

One or more of the following may also be used

1   Now, Lord, you let your servant go in peace: ♦
    your word has been fulfilled.

2   My own eyes have seen the salvation ♦
    which you have prepared in the sight of every people;

3   A light to reveal you to the nations ♦
    and the glory of your people Israel.   *Luke 2.29-32*

    Glory to the Father and to the Son
    and to the Holy Spirit;
    as it was in the beginning is now
    and shall be for ever.

All **Amen.**

    (or)

1   Lord, now lettest thou thy servant depart in peace :
    according to thy word.

2   For mine eyes have seen :
    thy salvation;

3   Which thou hast prepared :
    before the face of all people;

4   To be a light to lighten the Gentiles :
    and to be the glory of thy people Israel.   *Luke 2.29-32*

    Glory be to the Father, and to the Son :
    and to the Holy Ghost;
    as it was in the beginning, is now, and ever shall be :
    world without end.

All **Amen.**

    (and/or)

All **Give rest, O Christ, to your servant with the saints:**
where sorrow and pain are no more,
neither sighing, but life everlasting.
You only are immortal, the creator and maker of all:
and we are mortal, formed from the dust of the earth,
and unto earth shall we return.
For so you ordained when you created me, saying:
'Dust you are and to dust you shall return.'
All of us go down to the dust,
yet weeping at the grave we make our song:
Alleluia, alleluia, alleluia.

All **Give rest, O Christ, to your servant with the saints:**
where sorrow and pain are no more,
neither sighing, but life everlasting.

(and/or)

At or just after death

1 Jesus, like a mother you gather your people to you; ♦
you are gentle with us as a mother with her children.

2 Often you weep over our sins and our pride, ♦
tenderly you draw us from hatred and judgement.

3 You comfort us in sorrow and bind up our wounds, ♦
in sickness you nurse us, and with pure milk you feed us.

4 Jesus, by your dying we are born to new life; ♦
by your anguish and labour we come forth in joy.

5 Despair turns to hope through your sweet goodness; ♦
through your gentleness we find comfort in fear.

6 Your warmth gives life to the dead, ♦
your touch makes sinners righteous.

7 Lord Jesus, in your mercy heal us; ♦
in your love and tenderness remake us.

8 In your compassion bring grace and forgiveness, ♦
for the beauty of heaven may your love prepare us.

A Song of St Anselm

Blessing

The minister uses one of these blessings

May the eternal God
bless and keep us,
guard our bodies,
save our souls
and bring us safe to the heavenly country,
our eternal home,
where Father, Son, and Holy Spirit reign,
one God for ever and ever.

All **Amen.**

(or)

God grant you to share in the inheritance of his saints in glory;
and the blessing of God almighty,
the Father, the Son, and the Holy Spirit,
be upon you, and remain with you always.

All **Amen.**

¶ *Prayer when someone has just died*

The minister, a family member or a friend may use some or all of these words

In this moment of sorrow the Lord is in our midst
and consoles us with his word:

No eye has seen, nor ear heard, nor the human heart conceived,
what God has prepared for those who love him.

Blessed are the sorrowful; they shall be comforted.

Into your hands, O Lord,
we humbly entrust our *brother/sister N.*
In this life you embraced *him/her* with your tender love,
and opened to *him/her* the gate of heaven.
The old order has passed away,
as you welcome *him/her* into paradise,
where there will be no sorrow, no weeping nor pain,
but the fullness of peace and joy
with your Son and the Holy Spirit for ever and ever.

All **Amen.**

Heavenly Father,
into whose hands Jesus Christ
commended his spirit at the last hour:
into those same hands we now commend your servant *N,*
that death may be for *him/her*
the gate to life and to eternal fellowship with you;
through Jesus Christ our Lord.

All **Amen.**

Remember, O Lord,
this your servant,
who has gone before us with the sign of faith
and now rests in the sleep of peace.
According to your promises,
grant to *him/her* and to all who rest in Christ,
refreshment, light and peace;
through the same Christ our Lord.

All **Amen.**

Most merciful God,
whose wisdom is beyond our understanding,
surround the family of N with your love,
that they may not be overwhelmed by their loss,
but have confidence in your goodness,
and strength to meet the days to come.
We ask this through Christ our Lord.

All **Amen.**

Notes to Ministry at the Time of Death

1 Where the minister is not a bishop or priest

   ¶ anointing is omitted;

   ¶ Holy Communion may be given but not celebrated;

   ¶ the usual alterations are made at the blessing.

2 The laying on of hands may be done by more than one person.

3 Canon B 37 provides that the priest should use 'pure olive oil consecrated by the bishop of the diocese or otherwise by the priest'. If consecrated oil is not available, the priest may use this form:

   Lord, holy Father, giver of health and salvation,
   as your apostles anointed those who were sick and healed them,
   so continue the ministry of healing in your Church.
   Sanctify this oil, that those who are anointed with it
   may be freed from suffering and distress,
   find inward peace, and know the joy of your salvation,
   through your Son, our Saviour Jesus Christ.
   Amen.

4 Wherever possible, care should be taken to use versions of texts familiar to the dying person.

Before the Funeral

Note

This service may be adapted for use

¶   on hearing the news of a death;

¶   as part of the minister's visit to the family before the Funeral.

Hymns may be sung at appropriate points.

Preparation

At this time of sorrow
the Lord is in our midst
and consoles us with his word:
Blessed are the sorrowful; they shall be comforted.

Blessed be God, the Father of our Lord Jesus Christ,
the Father of mercies and the God of all consolation.
He comforts us in all our afflictions
and thus enables us to comfort those who grieve
with the same consolation we have received from him.

We shall not all die
All   **but we shall be changed.**

The trumpet shall sound and the dead will rise immortal
All   **and we shall be changed.**

The perishable must be clothed with the imperishable
All   **and the mortal must be clothed with immortality.**

We shall not all die
All   **but we shall be changed.**

Readings

These or other appropriate readings may be used

We do not want you to be uninformed, brothers and sisters, about those who have died, so that you may not grieve as others do who have no hope. For since we believe that Jesus died and rose again, even so, through Jesus, God will bring with him those who have died. For this we declare to you by the word of the Lord, that we who are alive, who are left until the coming of the Lord, will by no means precede those who have died.   *1 Thessalonians 4.13-15*

1   I lift up my eyes to the hills; ♦
     from where is my help to come?

2   My help comes from the Lord, ♦
     the maker of heaven and earth.

3   He will not suffer your foot to stumble; ♦
     he who watches over you will not sleep.

4   Behold, he who keeps watch over Israel ♦
     shall neither slumber nor sleep.

5   The Lord himself watches over you; ♦
     the Lord is your shade at your right hand,

6   So that the sun shall not strike you by day, ♦
     neither the moon by night.

7   The Lord shall keep you from all evil; ♦
     it is he who shall keep your soul.

8   The Lord shall keep watch over your going out
         and your coming in, ♦
     from this time forth for evermore.   *Psalm 121*

Martha said to Jesus, 'Lord, if you had been here, my brother would not have died. But even now I know that God will give you whatever you ask of him.' Jesus said to her, 'Your brother will rise again.' Martha said to him, 'I know that he will rise again in the resurrection on the last day.'   *John 11.21-24*

Prayers

Memories of the departed may be shared, ending with the following prayer

O God, who brought us to birth,
and in whose arms we die,
in our grief and shock
contain and comfort us;
embrace us with your love,
give us hope in our confusion
and grace to let go into new life;
through Jesus Christ.

All **Amen.**

These or other prayers may follow

Lord, we come into your presence to remember *N*
and to seek your comfort,
for we know that nothing can separate us from your love
and that you support us in our sorrow.
We are sure that the souls of the righteous are with you
and that nothing can harm them.
Although they have died they are in peace.
Give us your strength to rejoice
that you have taken *N* to be with yourself
where *he/she* shall no more be in need.
May we find life and peace and perfect joy with *him/her*
    in your presence;
through Jesus Christ our Lord.

All **Amen.**

God of all consolation,
in your unending love and mercy
you turn the darkness of death
into the dawn of new life.
Your Son, by dying for us, conquered death
and, by rising again, restored to us eternal life.
May we then go forward eagerly to meet our redeemer
and, after our life on earth,
be reunited with all our brothers and sisters
in that place where every tear is wiped away
and all things are made new;
through Jesus Christ our Saviour.

All **Amen.**

Lord, be with us as we open the door.
Come in with us, go out with us.
Do not sleep when we sleep,
but watch over us, protect us and keep us safe,
our only helper and maker.

All **Amen.**   *cf Psalm 121*

Conclusion

And now to him who is able to keep us from falling,
and lift us from the dark valley of despair
to the bright mountain of hope,
from the midnight of desperation
to the daybreak of joy;
to him be power and authority, for ever and ever.

All **Amen.**

¶ For those Unable to be Present at the Funeral

Note

This service may be adapted to suit particular circumstances.
It may be led by a friend or family member or by a minister.
It is deliberately based on the Funeral Service itself.

The Gathering

We meet in the name of Jesus Christ,
who died and was raised to the glory of God the Father.
We join with those in (*place*)
in remembering before God our *brother/sister N*;
to give thanks for *his/her* life;
to commend *him/her* to God our merciful redeemer and judge;
to commit *his/her* body to be *buried/cremated*,
and to comfort one another in our grief.

God of all consolation,
your Son Jesus Christ was moved to tears
at the grave of Lazarus his friend.
Look with compassion on your children in their loss;
give to troubled hearts the light of hope
and strengthen in us the gift of faith,
in Jesus Christ our Lord.

All **Amen.**

Almighty God,
you judge us with infinite mercy and justice
and love everything you have made.
In your mercy
turn the darkness of death into the dawn of new life,
and the sorrow of parting into the joy of heaven;
through our Saviour, Jesus Christ.

All **Amen.**

*Those present may be encouraged to share briefly their memories
of the one who has died.*

*Prayers of Penitence and the Collect may be used from the
Funeral Service.*

Reading

An appropriate reading from the selection on pages 383–391 is read.

Prayers

The prayers from the Funeral Service, or less formal prayer,
may follow as appropriate to the circumstances.

Commendation and Farewell

The prayers in this section of the Funeral Service (page 267)
may be adapted with the addition of a phrase such as 'With those
in (place)' before the words 'We entrust…' or 'We commend…'.

This may be followed by a time of silence, the Lord's Prayer
and a form of dismissal.

¶   *Receiving the Coffin at Church before the Funeral*

Note

The coffin may be received into the church at the beginning of the Funeral Service, or earlier in the day, or on the day before the Funeral. A candle may stand beside the coffin and may be carried in front of the coffin when it is brought into the church.

Receiving the Coffin

The minister meets the coffin at the door of the church and says

We receive the body of our *brother/sister N*
with confidence in God, the giver of life,
who raised the Lord Jesus from the dead.

The coffin may be sprinkled with water, and these words may be used

With this water we call to mind *N*'s baptism.
As Christ went through the deep waters of death for us,
so may he bring us to the fullness of resurrection life
with *N* and all the redeemed.

(or)

Grant, Lord,
that we who are baptized into the death
    of your Son our Saviour Jesus Christ
may continually put to death our evil desires
    and be buried with him;
and that through the grave and gate of death
we may pass to our joyful resurrection;
through his merits,
who died and was buried and rose again for us,
your Son Jesus Christ our Lord.

All   **Amen.**

*These or other suitable sentences of Scripture may be used
(see pages 293–294). The minister may add 'Alleluia' to any of
these sentences.*

'I am the resurrection and the life,' says the Lord. 'Those who
believe in me, even though they die, will live, and everyone who
lives and believes in me will never die.'   *John 11.25,26*

I am convinced that neither death, nor life, nor angels, nor rulers,
nor things present, nor things to come, nor powers, nor height,
nor depth, nor anything else in all creation, will be able to separate
us from the love of God in Christ Jesus our Lord.   *Romans 8.38,39*

Since we believe that Jesus died and rose again, even so, through
Jesus, God will bring with him those who have died. So we will be
with the Lord for ever. Therefore encourage one another with
these words.   *1 Thessalonians 4.14,17b,18*

We brought nothing into the world, and we take nothing out.
The Lord gave, and the Lord has taken away; blessed be the name of
the Lord.   *1 Timothy 6.7; Job 1.21b*

The steadfast love of the Lord never ceases, his mercies never come
to an end; they are new every morning; great is his faithfulness.
                                              Lamentations 3.22,23

Blessed are those who mourn, for they will be comforted.
                                                      Matthew 5.4

God so loved the world that he gave his only Son, so that everyone
who believes in him may not perish but may have eternal life.
                                                       John 3.16

*When the coffin is in place, the minister prays using these or other
suitable words*

God our Father,
by raising Christ your Son you destroyed the power of death
and opened for us the way to eternal life.
As we remember before you our *brother/sister N*,
we ask your help for all who shall gather in *his/her* memory.
Grant us the assurance of your presence and grace,
by the Spirit you have given us;
through Jesus Christ our Lord.

All   **Amen.**

A pall may be placed over the coffin by family, friends or other members of the congregation and these words may be said

We are already God's children,
but what we shall be has not yet been revealed.
Yet we know that when Christ appears we shall be like him,
for we shall see him as he is.

(or)

On Mount Zion the Lord will remove the pall of sorrow
hanging over all nations.
He will destroy death for ever.
He will wipe away the tears from every face.

A Bible may be placed on the coffin, with these words

Lord Jesus Christ,
your living and imperishable word brings us to new birth.
Your eternal promises to us and to N are proclaimed in the Bible.

A cross may be placed on the coffin, with these words

Lord Jesus Christ,
for love of N and each one of us
you bore our sins on the cross.

Other suitable symbols of the life and faith of the departed person may be placed on or near the coffin, with the minister's permission. Those present may be encouraged to share briefly their memories of the one who has died.

Silence is kept.

Readings and Prayers

Heavenly Father,
you have not made us for darkness and death,
but for life with you for ever.
Without you we have nothing to hope for;
with you we have nothing to fear.
Speak to us now your words of eternal life.
Lift us from anxiety and guilt
to the light and peace of your presence,
and set the glory of your love before us;
through Jesus Christ our Lord.

All   **Amen.**

*John 14.1-6 or other appropriate readings may be read,
with psalms and prayers and silence (see pages 345–382
and 383–391).*

Almighty God,
you love everything you have made
and judge us with infinite mercy and justice.
We rejoice in your promises of pardon, joy and peace
to all those who love you.
In your mercy turn the darkness of death into the dawn of new life
and the sorrow of parting into the joy of heaven;
through our Saviour Jesus Christ,
who died, who rose again, and lives for evermore.

All   **Amen.**

Ending

The minister uses one or more of these prayers. The service may end with a time of silence. As they leave, the mourners may come near and touch the coffin, or gather round it and pray.

N has fallen asleep in the peace of Christ.
As we leave *his/her* body here, we entrust *him/her*,
with faith and hope in everlasting life,
to the love and mercy of our Father
and surround *him/her* with our love and prayer.
[In baptism, *he/she* was made by adoption a child of God.
At the eucharist *he/she* was sustained and fed.
God now welcomes *him/her* to his table in heaven
to share in eternal life with all the saints.]

God of all consolation,
your Son Jesus Christ was moved to tears
at the grave of Lazarus his friend.
Look with compassion on your children in their loss;
give to troubled hearts the light of hope
and strengthen in us the gift of faith,
in Jesus Christ our Lord.

All **Amen.**

The Lord God almighty is our Father:
All **he loves us and tenderly cares for us.**

The Lord Jesus Christ is our Saviour:
All **he has redeemed us and will defend us to the end.**

The Lord, the Holy Spirit is among us:
All **he will lead us in God's holy way.**

To God almighty, Father, Son, and Holy Spirit,
All **be praise and glory today and for ever. Amen.**

¶ *A Funeral Vigil*

Note

The vigil may take place as part of a service at church before the Funeral, or it may be a separate service. It may take place in church, at home or in another suitable place, such as a hospital chapel. The Gathering and the Ending may be omitted if the vigil is part of another service.

The Gathering

O Lord, open our lips
All   **and our mouth shall proclaim your praise.**

Blessed are you, God of compassion and mercy,
shepherd and protector of your grieving people,
their beginning and their ending.
Lead us to a place of peace and refreshment;
guide us to springs of life-giving water;
wipe away the tears from our eyes
and bring us to heaven
where there is no more death,
no more grief or crying or pain
in your presence, Father, Son and Holy Spirit:
All   **blessed be God for ever.**

Christ yesterday and today,
the beginning and the end,
Alpha and Omega;
all time belongs to him,
and all ages;
to him be glory and power,
through every age and for ever.
All   **Amen.**

If candles are to be lit

May the light of Christ, rising in glory,
banish all darkness from our hearts and minds.

One of these themes, or a selection from them, may be chosen.

Assurance and Comfort

Old Testament: Isaiah 61.1-3   *To comfort all who mourn*

Psalm: 139

Psalm Prayer
Lord,
you created and fashioned us,
you know us and search us out,
you abide with us through light and dark:
help us to know your presence in this life
and, in the life to come, still to be with you;
where you are alive and reign,
God, for ever and ever.

All **Amen.**

New Testament: 1 Peter 1.3-9   *We have been born anew to*
a living hope

Canticle: A Song of God's Children (page 397)

Gospel: John 14.1-6   *In my Father's house are many rooms*

Prayer

The Faithfulness of God

Old Testament: Isaiah 53.1-10   *The suffering servant*

Psalm: 116.1-8[9-17]

Psalm Prayer
Lord of life,
we walk through eternity in your presence.
Lord of death,
we call to you in grief and sorrow:
you hear us and rescue us.
Watch over us as we mourn the death of your servant,
precious in your sight,
and keep us faithful to our vows to you.

All **Amen.**

New Testament: Romans 8.31-end *Nothing can separate us from the love of Christ*

Revelation 21.1-7 *Behold I make all things new*

Canticle: A Song of the Justified (page 396)

Gospel: John 6.35-40[53-58] *All that the Father gives me will come to me*

Prayer

The Hope of Heaven

Apocrypha: Wisdom 3.1-5,9 *The souls of the righteous are in the hand of God*

Psalm: 25.1-9

Psalm Prayer
God of our salvation,
in our sorrow we lift our hearts to you
and put our faith in you.
Have compassion on us,
forgive us, and love us to eternity,
as you guide us and teach us
in the way that lies ahead
in Jesus Christ our Lord.

All **Amen.**

New Testament: Romans 8.18-25[26-30] *The future glory*
Revelation 21.22-end; 22.3b-5 *The Lord God will be their light*

Canticle: A Song of Faith (page 398)

Gospel: John 14.1-6 *In my Father's house are many rooms*

Prayer

Old Testament: Job 19.23-27   *I know that my Redeemer lives*

Psalm: 32

Psalm Prayer
Lord, our hiding place in times of trouble,
you bring our guilt to mind.
Your hand seems heavy;
our tongues dry up
and we openly confess our guilt.
Embrace us with your mercy.
Teach us to trust you,
and bring us at the last
to rejoice in your presence for ever and ever.

All **Amen.**

New Testament: 2 Timothy 2.8-13   *If we have died with him,*
we shall also live with him

Canticle: A Song of the Redeemed (page 399)

Gospel: John 11.17-27   *I am the resurrection and the life*

Prayer

Advent

Old Testament: Daniel 12.1-3[5-9]   *Everyone whose name shall*
be found written in the book

Psalm: 27

Psalm Prayer
O God our defender,
give us the light of truth and wisdom
that all our hope may be fixed on you,
and on your Son, Jesus the Christ.

All **Amen.**

New Testament: 1 Thessalonians 4.13-18   *So we shall always be*
with the Lord

Canticle: The Song of Manasseh (page 393)

Gospel: Matthew 25.31-end   *The final judgement*

Prayer

An Unexpected Death

Apocrypha: Wisdom 4.8-11,13-15   *Age is not length of time*

Psalm: 6

Psalm Prayer
Our eyes, Lord, are wasted with grief;
you know we are weary with groaning.
As we remember our death
in the dark emptiness of the night,
have mercy on us and heal us;
forgive us and take away our fear
through the dying and rising of Jesus your Son.

All   **Amen.**

New Testament: 2 Corinthians 4.7-15   *We carry in our mortal bodies the death of Jesus*

Canticle: Nunc dimittis (The Song of Simeon) (page 395)

Gospel: Luke 12.35-40   *The coming of the Son of Man*

Prayer

A Child

Old Testament: 2 Samuel 12.16-23   *David's son dies*

Psalm: 38.9-end

Psalm Prayer
Lord, have mercy
on those who go about in mourning all the day long,
who feel numb and crushed
and are filled with the pain of grief,
whose strength has given up
and whose friends and neighbours are distant.
You know all our sighing and longings:
be near to us and teach us to fix our hope on you alone;
through Jesus Christ our Lord.

All   **Amen.**

Apocrypha: Wisdom 4.8-11,13-15   *Age is not length of time*

Canticle: A Song of St Anselm (page 401)

Gospel: Luke 12.35-40   *The coming of the Son of Man*

Prayer

Ending

The Lord's Prayer is said.

The minister says this or another suitable ending

The Lord God almighty is our Father:

All **he loves us and tenderly cares for us.**

The Lord Jesus Christ is our Saviour:

All **he has redeemed us and will defend us to the end.**

The Lord, the Holy Spirit is among us:

All **he will lead us in God's holy way.**

To God almighty, Father, Son, and Holy Spirit,

All **be praise and glory today and for ever. Amen.**

¶ *On the Morning of the Funeral*

Note

This brief form of service is intended to provide a short time of
recollection some time before going to the Funeral. It may be led
by a friend, family member or the minister.

Preparation

As we set out on our journey today,
we pray for the presence of Christ,
who has gone this way before us.

Lord Jesus, you have shown us the way to the Father:
Lord, have mercy.

All **Lord, have mercy.**

Lord Jesus, your word is a light to our path:
Christ, have mercy.

All **Christ, have mercy.**

Lord Jesus, you are the good shepherd,
leading us into everlasting life:
Lord, have mercy.

All **Lord, have mercy.**

The Word

The steadfast love of the Lord never ceases,
his mercies never come to an end;
they are new every morning;
great is your faithfulness.
'The Lord is my portion,' says my soul,
'therefore I will hope in him.'
The Lord is good to those who wait for him,
to the soul that seeks him.
It is good that one should wait quietly
for the salvation of the Lord.

For the Lord will not reject for ever.
Although he causes grief, he will have compassion
according to the abundance of his steadfast love;
for he does not willingly afflict or grieve anyone.

Lamentations 3.22-26,31-33

Prayer

Heavenly Father,
you have not made us for darkness and death,
but for life with you for ever.
Without you we have nothing to hope for;
with you we have nothing to fear.
Speak to us now your words of eternal life.
Lift us from anxiety and guilt
to the light and peace of your presence,
and set the glory of your love before us;
through Jesus Christ our Lord.

All **Amen.**

The Funeral

The Funeral

Pastoral Introduction

This may be read by those present before the service begins.

God's love and power extend over all creation. Every life, including our own, is precious to God. Christians have always believed that there is hope in death as in life, and that there is new life in Christ over death.

Even those who share such faith find that there is a real sense of loss at the death of a loved one. We will each have had our own experiences of their life and death, with different memories and different feelings of love, grief and respect. To acknowledge this at the beginning of the service should help us to use this occasion to express our faith and our feelings as we say farewell, to acknowledge our loss and our sorrow, and to reflect on our own mortality. Those who mourn need support and consolation. Our presence here today is part of that continuing support.

The Outline Order for Funerals

For Notes, see pages 291–292.

The Gathering

1 The coffin may be received at the door by the minister.
2 Sentences of Scripture may be used.
3 The minister welcomes the people and introduces the service.
4 A tribute or tributes may be made.
5 Authorized Prayers of Penitence may be used.
6 The Collect may be said here or in the Prayers.

Readings and Sermon

7 One or more readings from the Bible is used.
   Psalms or hymns may follow the readings.
8 A sermon is preached.

Prayers

9 The prayers usually follow this sequence:

   ¶ Thanksgiving for the life of the departed

   ¶ Prayer for those who mourn

   ¶ Prayers of Penitence (if not already used)

   ¶ Prayer for readiness to live in the light of eternity

Commendation and Farewell

10 The dead person is commended to God with authorized words.

The Committal

11 The body is committed to its resting place with authorized words.

The Dismissal

12 The service may end with a blessing.

   If the Funeral Service takes place within a celebration of Holy Communion, the material on pages 282–290 is followed for that part of the service.

The Funeral Service

¶   **The Gathering**
[Sentences]
Introduction
[Prayer]
[Prayers of Penitence]
The Collect

¶   **Readings and Sermon**

¶   **Prayers**

¶   **Commendation and Farewell**

¶   **The Committal**

¶   **The Dismissal**

For Notes, see pages 291–292.

The Funeral Service

¶ *The Gathering*

The coffin may be received by the minister (see Note 7 on page 292). One or more sentences of Scripture may be used.

'I am the resurrection and the life,' says the Lord. 'Those who believe in me, even though they die, will live, and everyone who lives and believes in me will never die.'　　　　*John 11.25,26*

I am convinced that neither death, nor life, nor angels, nor rulers, nor things present, nor things to come, nor powers, nor height, nor depth, nor anything else in all creation, will be able to separate us from the love of God in Christ Jesus our Lord.　　*Romans 8.38,39*

Since we believe that Jesus died and rose again, even so, through Jesus, God will bring with him those who have died. So we will be with the Lord for ever. Therefore encourage one another with these words.　　　　　*1 Thessalonians 4.14,17b,18*

We brought nothing into the world, and we take nothing out. The Lord gave, and the Lord has taken away; blessed be the name of the Lord.　　　　*1 Timothy 6.7; Job 1.21b*

The steadfast love of the Lord never ceases, his mercies never come to an end; they are new every morning; great is his faithfulness.　　　　*Lamentations 3.22,23*

Blessed are those who mourn, for they will be comforted.　　　　*Matthew 5.4*

God so loved the world that he gave his only Son, so that everyone who believes in him may not perish but may have eternal life.　　　　*John 3.16*

Introduction

The minister says

We meet in the name of Jesus Christ,
who died and was raised to the glory of God the Father.
Grace and mercy be with you.

The minister introduces the service in these or other suitable words

We have come here today
to remember before God our *brother/sister N*;
to give thanks for *his/her* life;
to commend *him/her* to God our merciful redeemer and judge;
to commit *his/her* body to be *buried/cremated,*
and to comfort one another in our grief.

The minister may say one of these prayers

God of all consolation,
your Son Jesus Christ was moved to tears
at the grave of Lazarus his friend.
Look with compassion on your children in their loss;
give to troubled hearts the light of hope
and strengthen in us the gift of faith,
in Jesus Christ our Lord.

All **Amen.**

(or)

Almighty God,
you judge us with infinite mercy and justice
and love everything you have made.
In your mercy
turn the darkness of death into the dawn of new life,
and the sorrow of parting into the joy of heaven;
through our Saviour, Jesus Christ.

All **Amen.**

A hymn may be sung.
A brief tribute may be made (see Note 4 on page 291).

Prayers of Penitence

These or similar words may be used to introduce the confession

As children of a loving heavenly Father,
let us ask his forgiveness,
for he is gentle and full of compassion.

Silence may be kept.

These words may be used

God of mercy,
we acknowledge that we are all sinners.
We turn from the wrong that we have thought and said and done,
and are mindful of all that we have failed to do.
For the sake of Jesus, who died for us,
forgive us for all that is past,
and help us to live each day
in the light of Christ our Lord.

All   **Amen.**

(or)

Lord, have mercy.

All   **Lord, have mercy.**

Christ, have mercy.

All   **Christ, have mercy.**

Lord, have mercy.

All   **Lord, have mercy.**

The minister may say

May God our Father forgive us our sins
and bring us to the eternal joy of his kingdom,
where dust and ashes have no dominion.

All   **Amen.**

The Collect

The minister invites the people to pray, silence is kept and the minister says this or another suitable Collect (see page 350)

Merciful Father,
hear our prayers and comfort us;
renew our trust in your Son,
whom you raised from the dead;
strengthen our faith
that all who have died in the love of Christ
will share in his resurrection;
who lives and reigns with you,
in the unity of the Holy Spirit,
one God, now and for ever.

All **Amen.**

¶ Readings and Sermon

A reading from the Old or New Testament may be read
(see pages 383–391).

This or another psalm or hymn is used (see Note 2 on page 291)

1   The Lord is my shepherd; ♦
therefore can I lack nothing.

2   He makes me lie down in green pastures ♦
and leads me beside still waters.

3   He shall refresh my soul ♦
and guide me in the paths of righteousness for his name's sake.

4   Though I walk through the valley of the shadow of death,
     I will fear no evil; ♦
for you are with me;
     your rod and your staff, they comfort me.

5   You spread a table before me
     in the presence of those who trouble me; ♦
you have anointed my head with oil
     and my cup shall be full.

6   Surely goodness and loving mercy shall follow me
     all the days of my life, ♦
and I will dwell in the house of the Lord for ever.   *Psalm 23*

A reading from the New Testament (which may be a Gospel reading)
is used.

A sermon is preached.

¶ Prrayers

A minister leads the prayers of the people.
The prayers usually follow this sequence:

A minister leads the prayers of the people.
The prayers usually follow this sequence:

¶   *Thanksgiving for the life of the departed*

¶   *Prayer for those who mourn*

¶   *Prayers of Penitence (if not already used)*

¶   *Prayer for readiness to live in the light of eternity*

This form may be used. If occasion demands, the responses may be
omitted and the concluding prayer said by the minister alone. For other
prayers, see pages 351–372.

God of mercy, Lord of life,
you have made us in your image
to reflect your truth and light:
we give you thanks for N,
for the grace and mercy *he/she* received from you,
for all that was good in *his/her* life,
for the memories we treasure today.
[*Especially we thank you* …]
Silence
[Lord, in your mercy
All   **hear our prayer.**]

You promised eternal life to those who believe.
Remember for good this your servant N
as we also remember *him/her.*
Bring all who rest in Christ
into the fullness of your kingdom
where sins have been forgiven
and death is no more.
Silence
[Lord, in your mercy
All   **hear our prayer.**]

Your mighty power brings joy out of grief
and life out of death.
Look in mercy on [... *and*] all who mourn.
Give them patient faith in times of darkness.
Strengthen them with the knowledge of your love.
Silence
[Lord, in your mercy

All **hear our prayer.**]

You are tender towards your children
and your mercy is over all your works.
Heal the memories of hurt and failure.
Give us the wisdom and grace to use aright
the time that is left to us here on earth,
to turn to Christ and follow in his steps
in the way that leads to everlasting life.
Silence
[Lord, in your mercy

All **hear our prayer.**]

All **God of mercy,**
entrusting into your hands all that you have made
and rejoicing in our communion with all your
faithful people,
we make our prayers through Jesus Christ our Saviour.
Amen.

The Lord's Prayer may be said.

As our Saviour taught us, so we pray

All **Our Father in heaven,**
hallowed be your name,
your kingdom come,
your will be done,
on earth as in heaven.
Give us today our daily bread.
Forgive us our sins
as we forgive those who sin against us.
Lead us not into temptation
but deliver us from evil.
For the kingdom, the power,
and the glory are yours
now and for ever.
Amen.

(or)

Let us pray with confidence as our Saviour has taught us

All **Our Father, who art in heaven,**
hallowed be thy name;
thy kingdom come;
thy will be done;
on earth as it is in heaven.
Give us this day our daily bread.
And forgive us our trespasses,
as we forgive those who trespass against us.
And lead us not into temptation;
but deliver us from evil.
For thine is the kingdom,
the power and the glory,
for ever and ever.
Amen.

A hymn may be sung.

¶ Commendation and Farewell

The minister stands by the coffin and may invite others to gather around it.

The minister says

Let us commend N to the mercy of God,
our maker and redeemer.

Silence is kept.

*The minister uses this or another prayer of entrusting
and commending (see pages 373–377)*

God our creator and redeemer,
by your power Christ conquered death
and entered into glory.
Confident of his victory
and claiming his promises,
we entrust N to your mercy
in the name of Jesus our Lord,
who died and is alive
and reigns with you,
now and for ever.

All   **Amen.**

*If the Committal does not follow as part of the same service in the
same place, some sections of the Dismissal (pages 270–273) may be
used here.*

¶ The Committal

Sentences of Scripture may be used (pages 293–294).

The minister says

either

The Lord is full of compassion and mercy,
slow to anger and of great goodness.
As a father is tender towards his children,
so is the Lord tender to those that fear him.
For he knows of what we are made;
he remembers that we are but dust.
Our days are like the grass;
we flourish like a flower of the field;
when the wind goes over it, it is gone
and its place will know it no more.
But the merciful goodness of the Lord endures
    for ever and ever toward those that fear him
and his righteousness upon their children's children.

(or)

We have but a short time to live.
Like a flower we blossom and then wither;
like a shadow we flee and never stay.
In the midst of life we are in death;
to whom can we turn for help,
but to you, Lord, who are justly angered by our sins?
Yet, Lord God most holy, Lord most mighty,
O holy and most merciful Saviour,
deliver us from the bitter pain of eternal death.
Lord, you know the secrets of our hearts;
hear our prayer, O God most mighty;
spare us, most worthy judge eternal;
at our last hour let us not fall from you,
O holy and merciful Saviour.

The minister uses one of the following forms of Committal.

At the burial of a body

We have entrusted our *brother/sister* N to God's mercy,
and we now commit *his/her* body to the ground:
earth to earth, ashes to ashes, dust to dust:
in sure and certain hope of the resurrection to eternal life
through our Lord Jesus Christ,
who will transform our frail bodies
that they may be conformed to his glorious body,
who died, was buried, and rose again for us.
To him be glory for ever.

All   **Amen.**

(or)

in a crematorium, if the Committal is to follow at the Burial of the Ashes

We have entrusted our *brother/sister* N to God's mercy,
and now, in preparation for burial,
we give *his/her* body to be cremated.
We look for the fullness of the resurrection
when Christ shall gather all his saints
to reign with him in glory for ever.

All   **Amen.**

(or)

in a crematorium, if the Committal is to take place then

We have entrusted our *brother/sister* N to God's mercy,
and we now commit *his/her* body to be cremated:
earth to earth, ashes to ashes, dust to dust:
in sure and certain hope of the resurrection to eternal life
through our Lord Jesus Christ,
who will transform our frail bodies
that they may be conformed to his glorious body,
who died, was buried, and rose again for us.
To him be glory for ever.

All   **Amen.**

¶ The Dismissal

The Lord's Prayer

As our Saviour taught us, so we pray

All   **Our Father in heaven,
hallowed be your name,
your kingdom come,
your will be done,
on earth as in heaven.
Give us today our daily bread.
Forgive us our sins
as we forgive those who sin against us.
Lead us not into temptation
but deliver us from evil.
For the kingdom, the power,
and the glory are yours
now and for ever.
Amen.**

(or)

Let us pray with confidence as our Saviour has taught us

All   **Our Father, who art in heaven,
hallowed be thy name;
thy kingdom come;
thy will be done;
on earth as it is in heaven.
Give us this day our daily bread.
And forgive us our trespasses,
as we forgive those who trespass against us.
And lead us not into temptation;
but deliver us from evil.
For thine is the kingdom,
the power and the glory,
for ever and ever.
Amen.**

Nunc dimittis (The Song of Simeon)

1   Now, Lord, you let your servant go in peace: ♦
    your word has been fulfilled.

2   My own eyes have seen the salvation ♦
    which you have prepared in the sight of every people;

3   A light to reveal you to the nations ♦
    and the glory of your people Israel.   *Luke 2.29-32*

    Glory to the Father and to the Son
    and to the Holy Spirit;
    as it was in the beginning is now
    and shall be for ever. Amen.

Prayers

One or more of these prayers, or other suitable prayers, may be used

All   **Heavenly Father,
        in your Son Jesus Christ
        you have given us a true faith and a sure hope.
        Strengthen this faith and hope in us all our days,
        that we may live as those who believe in
              the communion of saints,
              the forgiveness of sins
              and the resurrection to eternal life;
        through Jesus Christ our Lord.
        Amen.**

All   **God be in my head,
        and in my understanding;
        God be in my eyes,
        and in my looking;
        God be in my mouth,
        and in my speaking;
        God be in my heart,
        and in my thinking;
        God be at my end,
        and at my departing.
        Amen.**

Support us, O Lord,
all the day long of this troublous life,
until the shadows lengthen and the evening comes,
the busy world is hushed,
the fever of life is over
and our work is done.
Then, Lord, in your mercy grant us a safe lodging,
a holy rest, and peace at the last;
through Christ our Lord.

All   **Amen.**

Ending

One of these, or another suitable ending, may be used

May God in his infinite love and mercy
bring the whole Church,
living and departed in the Lord Jesus,
to a joyful resurrection
and the fulfilment of his eternal kingdom.

All   **Amen.**

May God give *you*
his comfort and his peace,
his light and his joy,
in this world and the next;
and the blessing of God almighty,
the Father, the Son, and the Holy Spirit,
be among *you* and remain with *you* always.

All   **Amen.**

God will show us the path of life;
in his presence is the fullness of joy:
and at his right hand
there is pleasure for evermore.   *cf Psalm 16.11*

Unto him that is able to keep us from falling,
and to present us faultless before the presence of his glory
    with exceeding joy,
to the only wise God our Saviour,
be glory and majesty,
dominion and power,
both now and ever.

All   **Amen.**   *Jude 24,25*

The Funeral Service within a Celebration of Holy Communion

Structure

¶ **The Gathering**
[Sentences]
[Introduction]
[Prayer]
Prayers of Penitence
The Collect

¶ **The Liturgy of the Word**
Reading(s)
Gospel Reading
Sermon

¶ **Prayers**

¶ **The Liturgy of the Sacrament**
The Peace
Preparation of the Table
Taking of the Bread and Wine
The Eucharistic Prayer
The Lord's Prayer
Breaking of the Bread
Giving of Communion
Prayer after Communion

¶ **Commendation and Farewell**

¶ **The Committal**

¶ **The Dismissal**

For Notes, see pages 291–292.

The Funeral Service within a Celebration of Holy Communion

¶ *The Gathering*

The coffin may be received by the minister (see Note 7 on page 292). One or more sentences of Scripture may be used.

'I am the resurrection and the life,' says the Lord. 'Those who believe in me, even though they die, will live, and everyone who lives and believes in me will never die.'   *John 11.25,26*

I am convinced that neither death, nor life, nor angels, nor rulers, nor things present, nor things to come, nor powers, nor height, nor depth, nor anything else in all creation, will be able to separate us from the love of God in Christ Jesus our Lord.   *Romans 8.38,39*

Since we believe that Jesus died and rose again, even so, through Jesus, God will bring with him those who have died. So we will be with the Lord for ever. Therefore encourage one another with these words.   *1 Thessalonians 4.14,17b,18*

We brought nothing into the world, and we take nothing out. The Lord gave, and the Lord has taken away; blessed be the name of the Lord.   *1 Timothy 6.7; Job 1.21b*

The steadfast love of the Lord never ceases, his mercies never come to an end; they are new every morning; great is his faithfulness.
                                                                                   Lamentations 3.22,23

Blessed are those who mourn, for they will be comforted.
                                                                                               Matthew 5.4

God so loved the world that he gave his only Son, so that everyone who believes in him may not perish but may have eternal life.
                                                                                               John 3.16

Introduction

The minister says

We meet in the name of Jesus Christ,
who died and was raised to the glory of God the Father.
Grace and mercy be with you.

The minister introduces the service in these or other suitable words

We have come here today
to remember before God our *brother/sister N*;
to give thanks for *his/her* life;
to commend *him/her* to God our merciful redeemer and judge;
to commit *his/her* body to be *buried/cremated,*
and to comfort one another in our grief.

The minister may say one of these prayers

God of all consolation,
your Son Jesus Christ was moved to tears
at the grave of Lazarus his friend.
Look with compassion on your children in their loss;
give to troubled hearts the light of hope,
and strengthen in us the gift of faith,
in Jesus Christ our Lord.

All **Amen.**

(or)

Almighty God,
you judge us with infinite mercy and justice
and love everything you have made.
In your mercy
turn the darkness of death into the dawn of new life,
and the sorrow of parting into the joy of heaven;
through our Saviour, Jesus Christ.

All **Amen.**

A hymn may be sung.

A brief tribute may be made (see Note 4 on page 291).

Prayers of Penitence

These or similar words may be used to introduce the confession

As children of a loving heavenly Father,
let us ask his forgiveness,
for he is gentle and full of compassion.

Silence may be kept.

This or another authorized confession is used

God of mercy,
we acknowledge that we are all sinners.
We turn from the wrong that we have thought and said and done,
and are mindful of all that we have failed to do.
For the sake of Jesus, who died for us,
forgive us for all that is past,
and help us to live each day
in the light of Christ our Lord.

All **Amen.**

(or)

Lord, have mercy.

All **Lord, have mercy.**

Christ, have mercy.

All **Christ, have mercy.**

Lord, have mercy.

All **Lord, have mercy.**

This or another authorized absolution is used

May God our Father forgive us our sins
and bring us to the eternal joy of his kingdom,
where dust and ashes have no dominion.

All **Amen.**

The Collect

The minister invites the people to pray, silence is kept and the minister says this or another suitable Collect (see page 350)

Merciful Father,
hear our prayers and comfort us;
renew our trust in your Son,
whom you raised from the dead;
strengthen our faith
that all who have died in the love of Christ
will share in his resurrection;
who lives and reigns with you,
in the unity of the Holy Spirit,
one God, now and for ever.

All   **Amen.**

¶ The Liturgy of the Word

Reading(s)

Either one or two readings from Scripture precede the Gospel reading (see pages 383–391).

At the end of each the reader may say

This is the word of the Lord.

All **Thanks be to God.**

The psalm or canticle (pages 390–401) follows the first reading; other hymns and songs may be used between the readings.

Gospel Reading

An acclamation may herald the Gospel reading.
One of the following may be used

[Alleluia, alleluia.]
God so loved the world
that he gave his only Son.
[Alleluia.]   *cf John 3.16*

(or)

[Alleluia, alleluia.]
Blessed are those who die in the Lord
for they rest from their labour.
[Alleluia.]   *cf Revelation 14.13*

When the Gospel is announced the reader says

Hear the Gospel of our Lord Jesus Christ according to N.

All **Glory to you, O Lord.**

At the end

This is the Gospel of the Lord.

All **Praise to you, O Christ.**

Sermon

¶ *Prayers*

A minister leads the prayers of the people.
The prayers usually follow this sequence:

¶ *Thanksgiving for the life of the departed*

¶ *Prayer for those who mourn*

¶ *Prayers of Penitence (if not already used)*

¶ *Prayer for readiness to live in the light of eternity*

This form may be used. If occasion demands, the responses may be
omitted and the concluding prayer said by the minister alone.

God of mercy, Lord of life,
you have made us in your image
to reflect your truth and light:
we give you thanks for N,
for the grace and mercy *he/she* received from you,
for all that was good in *his/her* life,
for the memories we treasure today.
[*Especially we thank you* ...]
Silence
[Lord in your mercy

All **hear our prayer.**]

You promised eternal life to those who believe.
Remember for good this your servant N
as we also remember *him/her.*
Bring all who rest in Christ
into the fullness of your kingdom
where sins have been forgiven
and death is no more.
Silence
[Lord in your mercy

All **hear our prayer.**]

Your mighty power brings joy out of grief
and life out of death.
Look in mercy on [... *and*] all who mourn.
Give them patient faith in times of darkness.
Strengthen them with the knowledge of your love.
Silence
[Lord in your mercy,

All   **hear our prayer.]**

You are tender towards your children
and your mercy is over all your works.
Heal the memories of hurt and failure.
Give us the wisdom and grace to use aright
the time that is left to us here on earth,
to turn to Christ and follow in his steps
in the way that leads to everlasting life.
Silence
[Lord in your mercy,

All   **hear our prayer.]**

All   **God of mercy,**
entrusting into your hands all that you have made
and rejoicing in our communion with all your
        faithful people,
we make our prayers through Jesus Christ our Saviour.
Amen.

A hymn may be sung.

¶ *The Liturgy of the Sacrament*

The Peace

The president may introduce the Peace with a suitable sentence.
The following may be used

Jesus says:
Peace I leave with you; my peace I give to you.
Not as the world gives do I give you.
Do not let your hearts be troubled,
neither let them be afraid. [Alleluia.]

The peace of the risen Lord be always with you

All **and also with you.**

These words may be added

Let us offer one another a sign of peace.

All may exchange a sign of peace.

The service continues with the Preparation of the Table. Presidential texts for the rest of the service are to be found in Common Worship: Services and Prayers for the Church of England *(pages 155–335) and the President's edition (pages 381–524).*

Preparation of the Table
Taking of the Bread and Wine

The following prayer may be used

May all who are called to a place at your table
follow in the way that leads to the unending feast of life.

All **Amen.**

The Eucharistic Prayer

An authorized Eucharistic Prayer is used.

One of these Proper Prefaces may be used

Short Proper Prefaces

And now we give you thanks
because through him you have given us
the hope of a glorious resurrection;
so that, although death comes to us all,
yet we rejoice in the promise of eternal life;
for to your faithful people life is changed, not taken away;
and when our mortal flesh is laid aside
an everlasting dwelling place is made ready for us in heaven.

(or)

And now we give you thanks
through Jesus Christ our Lord.
In him who rose from the dead
our hope of resurrection dawned.
The sting of death has been removed
by the glorious promise of his risen life.

Blessed are you, gracious God,
creator of heaven and earth,
giver of life, and conqueror of death.
By his death on the cross,
your Son Jesus Christ
    offered the one true sacrifice for sin,
breaking the power of evil
and putting death to flight.
[With all your saints

All   **we give you thanks and praise.]**

Through his resurrection from the dead
you have given us new birth into a living hope,
into an inheritance which is imperishable,
undefiled, and unfading.
[With all your saints

All   **we give you thanks and praise.]**

The joy of resurrection fills the universe,
and so we join with angels and archangels,
with [*N and*] all your faithful people,
evermore praising you and *saying*:

The following acclamation is particularly suitable during the
Eucharistic Prayer

Praise to you, Lord Jesus:

All   **dying you destroyed our death,**
rising you restored our life:
Lord Jesus, come in glory.

The Lord's Prayer

Breaking of the Bread

These words may be used

Every time we eat this bread
and drink this cup,

All **we proclaim the Lord's death
until he comes.**

Giving of Communion

The following invitation may be used

Jesus is the Lamb of God
who takes away the sin of the world.
Happy are those who are called to his supper.

All **Lord, I am not worthy to receive you,
but only say the word and I shall be healed.**

The following words may be used at the giving of communion

The bread of heaven in Christ Jesus.
The cup of life in Christ Jesus.

Prayer after Communion

One or both of the following prayers may be used

Gracious God,
we thank you that in your great love
you have fed us with the spiritual food and drink
   of the body and blood of your Son Jesus Christ
and have given us a foretaste of your heavenly banquet:
grant that this sacrament may be to us
a comfort in affliction
and a pledge of our inheritance
in that kingdom where there is no death,
neither sorrow nor crying,
but fullness of joy with all your saints;
through Jesus Christ our Saviour.

All **Amen.**

All **Heavenly Father,**
in your Son Jesus Christ
you have given us a true faith and a sure hope.
Strengthen this faith and hope in us all our days,
that we may live as those who believe in
   the communion of saints,
   the forgiveness of sins
   and the resurrection to eternal life;
through Jesus Christ our Lord.
Amen.

¶ Commendation and Farewell

The minister stands by the coffin and may invite others to gather around it.

The minister says

Let us commend N to the mercy of God,
our maker and redeemer.

Silence is kept.

The minister uses this or another prayer of entrusting and commending (see pages 373–377)

God our creator and redeemer,
by your power Christ conquered death
and entered into glory.
Confident of his victory
and claiming his promises,
we entrust N to your mercy
in the name of Jesus our Lord,
who died and is alive
and reigns with you,
now and for ever.

All   **Amen.**

If the Committal does not follow as part of the same service in the same place, some sections of the Dismissal (pages 270–274) may be used here.

¶ The Committal

Sentences of Scripture may be used (pages 293–294).

The minister says

either

The Lord is full of compassion and mercy,
slow to anger and of great goodness.
As a father is tender towards his children,
so is the Lord tender to those that fear him.
For he knows of what we are made;
he remembers that we are but dust.
Our days are like the grass;
we flourish like a flower of the field;
when the wind goes over it, it is gone
and its place will know it no more.
But the merciful goodness of the Lord endures
    for ever and ever toward those that fear him
and his righteousness upon their children's children.

(or)

We have but a short time to live.
Like a flower we blossom and then wither;
like a shadow we flee and never stay.
In the midst of life we are in death;
to whom can we turn for help,
but to you, Lord, who are justly angered by our sins?
Yet, Lord God most holy, Lord most mighty,
O holy and most merciful Saviour,
deliver us from the bitter pain of eternal death.
Lord, you know the secrets of our hearts;
hear our prayer, O God most mighty;
spare us, most worthy judge eternal;
at our last hour let us not fall from you,
O holy and merciful Saviour.

The minister uses one of the following forms of Committal.

At the burial of a body

We have entrusted our *brother/sister N* to God's mercy,
and we now commit *his/her* body to the ground:
earth to earth, ashes to ashes, dust to dust:
in sure and certain hope of the resurrection to eternal life
through our Lord Jesus Christ,
who will transform our frail bodies
that they may be conformed to his glorious body,
who died, was buried, and rose again for us.
To him be glory for ever.

All **Amen.**

(or)

in a crematorium, if the Committal is to follow at the Burial of the Ashes

We have entrusted our *brother/sister N* to God's mercy,
and now, in preparation for burial,
we give *his/her* body to be cremated.
We look for the fullness of the resurrection
when Christ shall gather all his saints
to reign with him in glory for ever.

All **Amen.**

(or)

in a crematorium, if the Committal is to take place then

We have entrusted our *brother/sister N* to God's mercy,
and we now commit *his/her* body to be cremated:
earth to earth, ashes to ashes, dust to dust:
in sure and certain hope of the resurrection to eternal life
through our Lord Jesus Christ,
who will transform our frail bodies
that they may be conformed to his glorious body,
who died, was buried, and rose again for us.
To him be glory for ever.

All **Amen.**

¶ *The Dismissal*

The Nunc dimittis (page 395) may be said.

This or another suitable blessing is used

God the Father,
by whose love Christ was raised from the dead,
open to you who believe the gates of everlasting life.

All **Amen.**

God the Son,
who in bursting the grave has won a glorious victory,
give you joy as you share the Easter faith.

All **Amen.**

God the Holy Spirit,
whom the risen Lord breathed into his disciples,
empower you and fill you with Christ's peace.

All **Amen.**

And the blessing of God almighty,
the Father, the Son, and the Holy Spirit,
be among you and remain with you always.

All **Amen.**

Notes to the Funeral Service

1   **Sentences**
    Sentences of Scripture may be used at the entry, after the Introduction, or at other suitable points.

2   **Psalms and Readings**
    Psalms and Readings should normally be drawn from those set out on pages 383–391. A psalm should normally be used. It may be in a metrical or hymn version, or be replaced by a scriptural song (for Canticles, see pages 392–400). There must always be one reading from the Bible.

3   **Hymns**
    Points are suggested for these, but they may be sung at any suitable point.

4   **Tribute**
    Remembering and honouring the life of the person who has died, and the evidence of God's grace and work in them, should be done in the earlier part of the service, after the opening prayer, though if occasion demands it may be woven into the sermon or come immediately before the Commendation. It may be done in conjunction with the placing of symbols, and may be spoken by a family member or friend or by the minister using information provided by the family. It is preferable not to interrupt the flow of the Reading(s) and sermon with a tribute of this kind.

5   **Sermon**
    The purpose of the sermon is to proclaim the gospel in the context of the death of this particular person.

6   **Creed**
    An authorized Creed or an authorized Affirmation of Faith may be said after the sermon.

For Notes 7–9, see over.

7   **Receiving the coffin**
The coffin may be received into the church at the beginning of the service, or earlier in the day, or on the day before the funeral.

¶   A candle may stand beside the coffin and may be carried in front of the coffin when it is brought into the church.

¶   The coffin may be sprinkled with water on entry. This may occur at the Commendation, or at the Committal.

¶   A pall may be placed over the coffin in church by family, friends or other members of the congregation.

¶   Before or at the start of the service or after the opening prayer and hymn, and with the minister's agreement, suitable symbols of the life and faith of the departed person may be placed on or near the coffin.

¶   At the sprinkling, the placing of the pall or symbols, the words on pages 295–296 may be used.

8   **The Committal**
The Committal is used at the point at which it is needed, for example:

¶   at the burial of the body in a cemetery or churchyard,

¶   at the interment of ashes when this follows on the same day or the day following cremation, in which case the second 'preparation for burial' prayer (page 269) is used at the crematorium, or

¶   at a crematorium when the interment of ashes is not to follow immediately.

Forms of Commendation and Committal are provided, but when occasion demands, other authorized forms may be used.

When the body or the ashes are to be deposited in a vault, mausoleum or brick grave, these words may be used at the committal:

We have entrusted our *brother/sister N* to God's mercy, and now we commit *his/her* body to its resting place.

9   **The Funeral Service within Holy Communion**
The Notes to the Order for the Celebration of Holy Communion, as well as the Notes to the Funeral Service, apply equally to this service. Texts are suggested at different points, but other suitable texts may be used. In the Liturgy of the Word, there should be a Gospel reading, preceded by either one or two other readings from the Bible.

Supplementary Texts

¶ *Sentences*

God will show us the path of life; in his presence is the fullness of joy: at his right hand there is pleasure for evermore.   *cf Psalm 16.10*

God is our refuge and strength, a very present help in trouble.
Psalm 46.1

Out of the depths have I cried to you, O Lord; Lord, hear my voice; let your ears consider well the voice of my supplications.
cf Psalm 130.1

I know that my Redeemer lives, and that at the last he will stand upon the earth; and after my skin has been destroyed, then in my flesh I shall see God, whom I shall see for myself, and my eyes shall behold, and not another.   *Job 19.25-27*

As they came from their mother's womb, so they shall go again, naked as they came; they shall take nothing for their toil, which they may carry away with their hands. This also is a grievous ill: just as they came, so shall they go; and what gain do they have from toiling for the wind?   *Ecclesiastes 5.15,16*

The steadfast love of the Lord never ceases, his mercies never come to an end; they are new every morning; great is his faithfulness.
Lamentations 3.22,23

Blessed are those who mourn, for they will be comforted.
Matthew 5.4

The king will say to those at his right hand, 'Come, you that are blessed by my Father, inherit the kingdom prepared for you from the foundation of the world.'   *Matthew 25.34*

Jesus said, 'Truly I tell you, today you will be with me in Paradise.'
Luke 23.43

God so loved the world that he gave his only Son, so that everyone who believes in him may not perish but may have eternal life.
John 3.16

This is indeed the will of my Father, that all who see the Son and believe in him may have eternal life; and I will raise them up on the last day.   *John 6.40*

'I am the resurrection and the life,' says the Lord. 'Those who believe in me, even though they die, will live, and everyone who lives and believes in me will never die.'   *John 11.25,26*

In my Father's house there are many dwelling places. If it were not so, would I have told you that I go to prepare a place for you? And if I go and prepare a place for you, I will come again and will take you to myself, so that where I am, there you may be also.   *John 14.2,3*

I am convinced that neither death, nor life, nor angels, nor rulers, nor things present, nor things to come, nor powers, nor height, nor depth, nor anything else in all creation, will be able to separate us from the love of God in Christ Jesus our Lord.   *Romans 8.38,39*

What no eye has seen, nor ear heard, nor the human heart conceived, what God has prepared for those who love him – these things God has revealed to us through the Spirit.

1 Corinthians 2.9-10a

He must reign until he has put all his enemies under his feet. The last enemy to be destroyed is death.   *1 Corinthians 15.25,26*

Blessed be the God and Father of our Lord Jesus Christ, the Father of mercies and God of all comfort, who comforts us in all our affliction, so that we may be able to comfort those who are in any affliction, with the comfort with which we ourselves are comforted by God.   *2 Corinthians 1.3,4*

We know that if the earthly tent we live in is destroyed, we have a building from God, a house not made with hands, eternal in the heavens.   *2 Corinthians 5.1*

We believe that Jesus died and rose again; and so it will be for those who died as Christians; God will bring them to life with Jesus. Thus we shall always be with the Lord. Comfort one another with these words.   *cf 1 Thessalonians 4.14,17b,18*

We brought nothing into the world, and we take nothing out. The Lord gave, and the Lord has taken away; blessed be the name of the Lord.   *1 Timothy 6.7; Job 1.21b*

At the Celebration of Holy Communion

Jesus said, 'Whoever eats my flesh and drinks my blood has eternal life, and I will raise him up on the last day.' [Alleluia.]   *John 6.54*

¶ Some Texts which may be Used by the Minister

Receiving the coffin

We receive the body of our *brother/sister N*
with confidence in God, the giver of life,
who raised the Lord Jesus from the dead.

Sprinkling the coffin with water

With this water we call to mind *N's* baptism.
As Christ went through the deep waters of death for us,
so may he bring us to the fullness of resurrection life
with *N* and all the redeemed.

(or)

Grant, Lord,
that we who are baptized into the death
    of your Son our Saviour Jesus Christ
may continually put to death our evil desires
    and be buried with him;
and that through the grave and gate of death
we may pass to our joyful resurrection;
through his merits,
who died and was buried and rose again for us,
your Son Jesus Christ our Lord.

All **Amen.**

Covering the coffin with a pall

We are already God's children,
but what we shall be has not yet been revealed.
Yet we know that when Christ appears we shall be like him,
for we shall see him as he is.

(or)

On Mount Zion the Lord will remove the pall of sorrow
hanging over all nations.
He will destroy death for ever.
He will wipe away the tears from every face.

Placing a Bible on the coffin
Lord Jesus Christ,
your living and imperishable word brings us to new birth.
Your eternal promises to us and to *N* are proclaimed in the Bible.

Placing a cross on the coffin
Lord Jesus Christ,
for love of *N* and each one of us
you bore our sins on the cross.

¶   *The Blessing of a Grave*

O God,
whose Son Jesus Christ was laid in a tomb:
bless, we pray, this grave
as the place where the body of *N* your servant
   may rest in peace,
through your Son, who is the resurrection and the life;
who died and is alive and reigns with you
now and for ever.

All   **Amen.**

The Outline Order
for the Funeral of a Child

For Notes, see page 300.

The Gathering

1   The coffin may be received at the door by the minister,
    or it may be in place before the congregation assembles.
2   Sentences of Scripture may be used.
3   The minister welcomes the people and introduces the service.
4   A tribute or tributes may be made.
5   Authorized Prayers of Penitence may be used.
6   The Collect may be said here or in the Prayers.

Readings and Sermon

7   One or more readings from the Bible is used.
    Psalms or hymns may follow the readings.
8   A sermon is preached.

Prayers

9   The prayers usually follow this sequence:

    ¶   Thanksgiving for the child's life, however brief

    ¶   Prayer for those who mourn

    ¶   Prayers of Penitence (if not already used)

    ¶   Prayer for readiness to live in the light of eternity

Commendation and Farewell

10   The child is commended to God with authorized words.

The Committal

11   The child's body is committed to its resting place with
     authorized words.

The Dismissal

12   The service may end with a blessing.

For Resources for the Funeral of a Child, see pages 301–315.

The Outline Order for the Funeral of a Child within a Celebration of Holy Communion

The Gathering

1   The coffin may be received at the door by the minister,
    or it may be in place before the congregation assembles.

2   Sentences of Scripture may be used.

3   The minister welcomes the people and introduces the service.

4   A tribute or tributes may be made.

5   Authorized Prayers of Penitence are used here or in the Prayers.

6   The Collect is said here or in the Prayers.

The Liturgy of the Word

7   One or more readings from the Bible is used.
    Psalms or hymns may follow the readings.

8   A Gospel reading is used

9   A sermon is preached.

Prayers

10 The prayers usually follow this sequence:

    ¶   Thanksgiving for the child's life, however brief

    ¶   Prayer for those who mourn

    ¶   Prayers of Penitence (if not already used)

    ¶   Prayer for readiness to live in the light of eternity

The Liturgy of the Sacrament

11   The Peace

12   Preparation of the Table
        Taking of the Bread and Wine

13   The Eucharistic Prayer (any authorized Eucharistic Prayer
        may be used)

14   The Lord's Prayer (used here rather than in the Prayers)

15   Breaking of the Bread

16   Giving of Communion

17   Prayer after Communion

Commendation and Farewell

18   The child is commended to God with authorized words.

The Committal

19   The child's body is committed to its resting place
        with authorized words.

The Dismissal

20   The service may end with a blessing.

Resources for the Funeral of a Child follow (pages 301–315).

For Notes, see page 300.

Notes

The notes to the Funeral Service (pages 291–292) apply equally to this service.

I   An Outline Order is provided, followed by some suggested resources which may be suitable for different occasions and different ages.

2   The presence of young children at a child's funeral should be welcomed and their needs should be borne in mind.

3   Care should be taken to ensure that there is a clear president throughout, who introduces and concludes the service, and that the number of other speakers, musical items and non-biblical readings does not unbalance the service from its focus on the word of God, prayer and thanksgiving.

4   Wherever possible, the name of the child should be used in the text of the service.

For a Theological Note on the Funeral of a Child Dying near the Time of Birth, see pages 316–317.

Resources for the Funeral of a Child

¶ The Gathering

Words for the Greeting

We meet in the name of Jesus Christ,
who died and was raised to the glory of God the Father.
Grace and mercy be with you.

[*All*   **And also with you.**]

Words for introducing the service

We have come together to worship God,
to thank him for his love,
and to remember the [short] life on earth of *N*;
to share our grief
and to commend *him/her* to the eternal care of God.
[We meet in the faith that death is not the end,
and may be faced without fear,
bitterness or guilt.]

(or)

We have come here today
to remember before God our *brother/sister N*;
to give thanks for *his/her* life;
to commend *him/her* to God our merciful redeemer and judge;
to commit *his/her* body to be *buried/cremated*,
and to comfort one another in our grief.

Introductory sentences

I am convinced that neither death, nor life, nor angels, nor rulers,
nor things present, nor things to come, nor powers, nor height,
nor depth, nor anything else in all creation, will be able to separate
us from the love of God in Christ Jesus our Lord.   *Romans 8.38,39*

The Lamb who is at the throne will be their shepherd, and will
lead them to springs of living water, and God will wipe away all
tears from their eyes.   *Revelation 7.17*

Beloved, we are God's children now; what we will be has not yet
been revealed. What we do know is this: when he is revealed,
we will be like him, for we will see him as he is.   *1 John 3.2*

Let the little children come to me; do not stop them; for it is to
such as these that the kingdom of God belongs.   *Mark 10.14*

I will comfort you, says the Lord, as a mother comforts her child,
and you shall be comforted.   *Isaiah 66.13*

Opening prayers

God of all mercies,
you make nothing in vain
and love all that you have made.
Comfort us in our grief,
and console us by the knowledge of your unfailing love,
through Jesus Christ our Lord.

All   **Amen.**

O God, who brought us to birth,
and in whose arms we die,
in our grief and shock,
contain and comfort us;
embrace us with your love,
give us hope in our confusion
and grace to let go into new life;
through Jesus Christ.

All   **Amen.**

God of love,
you have bound us together in life with *N / those we love*
and opened the door of heaven
through the suffering and resurrection of Jesus;
look upon us in your mercy,
give us courage to face our grief
and bring us all to the fullness of the risen life;
through Jesus Christ our Lord.

All　**Amen.**

¶　*Readings*

One or more passages from the Bible is read.

The following may be suitable for particular occasions

Psalm 23
Psalm 84.1-4

Song of Solomon 2.10-13
Isaiah 49.15-16
Jeremiah 1.4-8
Jeremiah 31.15-17

Matthew 18.1-5,10
Mark 10.13-16
John 6.37-40
John 10.27,28

Romans 8.18,28,35,37-39
1 Corinthians 13.1-13
Ephesians 3.14-19

¶ *Prayers*

The prayers usually follow this sequence:

¶   *Thanksgiving for the child's life, however brief*

¶   *Prayer for those who mourn*

¶   *Prayers of Penitence (if not already used)*

¶   *Prayer for readiness to live in the light of eternity*

Some suggestions follow, from which a choice will need to be made according to age and circumstances.

I   The Lord Jesus is the lover of his people and our only sure hope.
Let us ask him to deepen our faith and sustain us in this dark hour.

You became a little child for our sake, sharing our human life.
To you we pray:

All   **bless us and keep us, O Lord.**

You grew in wisdom, age and grace
and learned obedience through suffering.
To you we pray:

All   **bless us and keep us, O Lord.**

You welcomed children, promising them your kingdom.
To you we pray:

All   **bless us and keep us, O Lord.**

You comforted those who mourned the loss of children and friends.
To you we pray:

All   **bless us and keep us, O Lord.**

You took upon yourself the suffering and death of us all.
To you we pray:

All   **bless us and keep us, O Lord.**

You promised to raise up those who believe in you,
just as you were raised up in glory by the Father.
To you we pray:

All   **bless us and keep us, O Lord.**

2   Father,
    you know our hearts and share our sorrows.
    We are hurt by our parting from *N*, whom we loved:
    when we are angry at the loss we have sustained,
    when we long for words of comfort,
    yet find them hard to hear,
    turn our grief to more patient faith,
    our affliction to firmer hope
    in Jesus Christ our Lord.
All   **Amen.**

3   Father, the death of *N* brings an emptiness into our lives.
    We are separated from *him/her*
    and feel broken and bewildered.
    Give us confidence that *he/she* is safe
    and *his/her* life complete with you,
    and bring us together at the last
    to the wholeness and fullness of your presence in heaven,
    where your saints and angels enjoy you for ever and ever.
All   **Amen.**

4   Lord, we pray for those who mourn,
    for parents and children,
    friends and neighbours.
    Be gentle with them in their grief.
    Show them the depths of your love,
    a glimpse of the kingdom of heaven.
    Spare them the torment of guilt and despair.
    Be with them as they weep beside the empty tomb
        of our risen Saviour.
All   **Amen.**

5   Most merciful God,
     whose wisdom is beyond our understanding,
     surround the family of *N* with your love,
     that they may not be overwhelmed by their loss,
     but have confidence in your love,
     and strength to meet the days to come.
     We ask this through Christ our Lord.
All   **Amen.**

6   O God, you do not willingly grieve or afflict your children.
     Look with pity on the suffering of this family in their loss.
     Sustain them in their anguish;
     and into the darkness of their grief
     bring the light of your love;
     through Jesus Christ we pray.
All   **Amen.**

7   Blessed be the God and Father of our Lord Jesus Christ:
All   **the Father of mercies and the God of all comfort.**

     The Lord is near to those who call upon him:
All   **to all who call upon him faithfully.**

     As a father is tender towards his children:
All   **so is the Lord tender to those that fear him.**

     As a mother comforts her child:
All   **so shall the Lord bring you comfort.**

     Then Jesus took the children in his arms:
All   **he placed his hands on each of them and blessed them.**

     Prayers which may be said by the parents

8   God of love and life,
     you gave *N* to us as our *son/daughter.*
     Give us now the assurance
     that though *he/she* has passed from our sight,
     he/she has not passed from your care.
     Draw near to us in our sadness,
     bring blessing out of grief,
     and help us in our tears and pain
     to know you standing alongside us
     and to experience your love and healing;
     through Jesus Christ our Lord.
All   **Amen.**

9   God of all mystery,
        whose ways are beyond understanding,
        lead us, who grieve at this untimely death,
        to a new and deeper faith in your love,
        which brought your only Son Jesus
        through death into resurrection life.
        We make our prayer in Jesus' name.

All   **Amen.**

10   God of hope,
        we come to you in shock and grief and confusion of heart.
        Help us to find peace
        in the knowledge of your loving mercy to all your children,
        and give us light to guide us out of our darkness
        into the assurance of your love.

All   **Amen.**

11   God of unfailing compassion,
        in your creative love and tenderness you gave us *N*,
        so full of hope for the future.
        You are the source of all our lives,
        the strength of all our days.
        You did not make us for darkness and death
        but to see you face to face
        and to enjoy abundant life.
        Help us to comfort one another
        with the consolation we ourselves receive from you;
        through Jesus Christ our Lord.

All   **Amen.**

12   God of all grace and comfort,
        we thank you for *N*,
        and for the place *he/she* held in all our hearts.
        We thank you
        for the love in which *he/she* was conceived
        and for the care with which *he/she* was surrounded.
        As we remember times of tears and laughter,
        we thank you for the love we shared because of *him/her,*
        reflecting that love which you poured upon us
        in your Son Jesus Christ our Lord.

All   **Amen.**

13   God our Father,
       you know our thoughts and share our sorrows.
       Lead us out of desolation
       to the caring comfort of your love.
       When we forget what happiness is,
       renew in us fresh springs of hope.
       When we feel bereft of peace,
       restore our hearts and calm our fears.
       And when we come at last to our departing,
       bring us home with you for ever,
       the family of God complete;
       through Jesus Christ our Lord.
All   **Amen.**

14   Almighty God, creator and keeper of life,
       we acknowledge that our child *N* is your child,
       loved since before the foundation of the world.
       Grant us such trust
       in the finished work of your Son our Saviour
       that we shall look with hope
       towards a full knowledge of *N*,
       whose earthly life we have so little shared
       but who is now complete with Christ in you.
All   **Amen.**

15   Lord of all, we thank you
       for your work in creation,
       for nourishing life in the womb,
       for your love even in death.
       Thank you for the life of this child *N*,
       whom you gave to us and have taken to yourself.
       Thank you for the arms of your love,
       embracing both us and *N* in your family.
       Thank you for your presence in our sorrow
       and your strength as our family grows older.
       Take our sadness, and fill us with your Spirit
       to serve you on earth
       and join your saints in glory;
       through Jesus Christ our Lord.
All   **Amen.**

For the parents

16   Heavenly Father,
you alone can heal our broken hearts;
you alone can wipe away the tears
    that well up inside us;
you alone can give us the peace we need;
you alone can strengthen us to carry on.
We ask you to be near those whose time of joy
    has been turned into sadness.
Assure them that with you nothing is wasted
    or incomplete,
and uphold them with your tender love.
Supported by your strength,
may our love for one another be deepened
by the knowledge of your love for us all.

All   **Amen.**

17   Loving Father,
in your mercy you have brought your daughter *N*
    through childbirth in safety.
We pray that *N* [*and N*] will know your support
in this time of trouble and sorrow at the loss of their child,
and enjoy your protection always;
through Jesus Christ our Lord.

All   **Amen.**

18   Loving Father,
your servant Mary,
the mother of our Lord and God, Jesus Christ,
stood by the cross while her Son was dying.
May that same Jesus, victorious over death,
risen and ascended,
give comfort to these grieving parents,
and strengthen their faith in you;
through Jesus Christ our Lord.

All   **Amen.**

The children in the family

19　Lord Jesus,
　　we ask you to be close to the children of this family,
　　whose lives have been changed by sorrow.
　　Give them courage to face their loss,
　　and comfort them with your unchanging love.

All　**Amen.**

20　When we are weary and in need of strength,
　　when we are lost and sick at heart,
　　we remember *him/her*.

　　When we have a joy we long to share,
　　when we have decisions that are hard to make,
　　we remember *him/her*.

　　At the blowing of the wind and in the chill of winter,
　　at the opening of the buds and in the rebirth of spring,
　　we remember *him/her*.

　　At the blueness of the skies and in the warmth of summer,
　　at the rustling of the leaves and in the beauty of the autumn,
　　we remember *him/her*.

　　At the rising of the sun and at its setting,
　　we remember *him/her*.

A stillborn child

21　God our creator,
　　from whom all life comes,
　　comfort this family,
　　grieving for the loss of their hoped-for child.
　　Help them to find assurance
　　that with you nothing is wasted or incomplete,
　　and uphold them with your love,
　　through Jesus Christ our Saviour.

All　**Amen.**

22   Gracious God,
      we thank you for the love in which *N* was conceived
      and for the love of the home into which *he/she* was to be born.
      We pray that the love which *his/her* parents
          have for each other
      may grow and deepen as a result of this experience.
      Give us grace, in patience and understanding,
      to listen to each other,
      and to help one another in the days to come.
All **Amen.**

23   **Farewell**
      Heavenly Father, *N* and *N* have named their baby *N*
      – a name to be treasured for ever in their hearts.
      But it was you who formed *him/her* in the womb;
      you knew *him/her* by name before time began.
      Now we commit *N* into your ever-caring and gentle love;
      he/she brought the promise of joy
      to many lives for so short a time;
      enfold *him/her* now in eternal life,
      in the name of our risen Saviour who was born and died
      and lives and reigns with you and the Holy Spirit for ever.
All **Amen.**

¶ Commendation and Farewell

1   God our creator and redeemer,
     by your power Christ conquered death
     and returned to you in glory.
     Confident of your victory
     and claiming his promises,
     we entrust *N* into your keeping
     in the name of Jesus our Lord,
     who, though he died, is now alive
     and reigns with you and the Holy Spirit,
     one God now and for ever.

All   **Amen.**

2   **An older child**
     Into your hands, Lord,
     our faithful creator and most loving redeemer,
     we commend your child *N*,
     for *he/she* is yours in death as in life.
     In your great mercy
     gather *him/her* into your arms
     and fulfil in *him/her* the purpose of your love;
     that, rejoicing in the light and refreshment of your presence,
     he/she may enjoy that life which you have prepared
        for all those who love you,
     through Jesus Christ our Lord.

All   **Amen.**

3   **A young child**
     Heavenly Father,
     whose Son our Saviour
     took little children into his arms and blessed them:
     receive, we pray, your child *N*
     in your never-failing care and love,
     comfort all who have loved *him/her* on earth,
     and bring us all to your everlasting kingdom;
     through Jesus Christ our Lord.

All   **Amen.**

4   **A baby**
To you, gentle Father,
we humbly entrust this child so precious in your sight.
Take *him/her* into your arms
and welcome *him/her* into your presence
where there is no sorrow nor pain,
but the fullness of peace and joy with you
for ever and ever.

All   **Amen.**

5   **Stillbirth**
God of compassion, you make nothing in vain
and love all you have created;
we commend to you *N* and *N*'s child *N*,
for whom they poured out such great love,
for whom they cherished so many hopes and dreams.
We had longed to welcome *him/her* amongst us;
grant us the assurance that *he/she* is now encircled
    in your arms of love,
and shares the resurrection life of your Son, Jesus Christ.

All   **Amen.**

6   **Miscarriage**
God of compassion,
you make nothing in vain,
and we love all that you have created;
we commend to you *N* and *N*'s child *(name child if appropriate)*
for whom they poured out such great love,
for whom they cherished many hopes and dreams.
Grant them the assurance that their child,
though not seen by us, is seen and known by you,
and will share the risen life of your Son, Jesus Christ.

All   **Amen.**

¶ The Committal

The minister uses one of the following forms of Committal.

At the burial of a body

We have entrusted N to God's mercy,
and we now commit *his/her* body to the ground:
earth to earth, ashes to ashes, dust to dust:
in sure and certain hope of the resurrection to eternal life
through our Lord Jesus Christ,
who will transform our frail bodies
that they may be conformed to his glorious body,
who died, was buried, and rose again for us.
To him be glory for ever.

All **Amen.**

(or)

in a crematorium, if the Committal is to follow at the Burial of the Ashes

We have entrusted N to God's mercy,
and now, in preparation for *his/her* burial,
we give *his/her* body to be cremated.
We look for the fullness of the resurrection
when Christ shall gather all his saints
to reign with him in glory for ever.

All **Amen.**

(or)

in a crematorium, if the Committal is to take place then

We have entrusted N to God's mercy,
and we now commit *his/her* body to be cremated:
earth to earth, ashes to ashes, dust to dust:
in sure and certain hope of the resurrection to eternal life
through our Lord Jesus Christ,
who will transform our frail bodies
that they may be conformed to his glorious body,
who died, was buried, and rose again for us.
To him be glory for ever.

All **Amen.**

¶ *The Dismissal*

God be in my head,
and in my understanding;
God be in mine eyes,
and in my looking;
God be in my mouth,
and in my speaking;
God be in my heart,
and in my thinking;
God be at mine end,
and at my departing.

All **Amen.**

Blessings

May Christ the good shepherd
enfold *you* with love,
fill *you* with peace,
and lead *you* in hope,
to the end of *your* days;
and the blessing of God almighty,
the Father, the Son, and the Holy Spirit,
be among *you* and remain with *you* always.

All **Amen.**

May God give *you*
his comfort and his peace,
his light and his joy,
in this world and the next;
and the blessing of God almighty,
the Father, the Son, and the Holy Spirit,
be among *you* and remain with *you* always.

All **Amen.**

May the love of God and the peace of the Lord Jesus Christ
bless and console you,
and all who have known and loved *N*,
this day and for evermore.

All **Amen.**

Theological Note on the Funeral of a Child Dying near the Time of Birth

This Note draws on advice to the Liturgical Commission from the Revd Oliver O'Donovan, Regius Professor of Moral and Pastoral Theology in the University of Oxford.

There has been a growing recognition of the need for particular pastoral care for the parents and families of children dying near the time of birth, evidenced by the work of such bodies as the Stillbirth and Neonatal Death Society and the publication by the Joint Committee for Hospital Chaplaincy of guidelines in pastoral care: *Miscarriage, Stillbirth and Neonatal Death*. Part of this pastoral care is the provision of a full Funeral service which recognizes that the sense of loss and need for space and proper words for mourning is as great as with the death of any other person. In addition to this, the use of some of the Resources for the Funeral of a Child in a memorial service after the disposal of the body might especially help those families who have agreed too rapidly to the disposal of the body and afterwards wish for some way of marking the end of their child's life.

Such deeply felt pastoral needs cannot be met without an awareness of potentially divisive theological questions. The words in the Committal, 'In sure and certain hope of the resurrection to eternal life', raise two questions.

First, is it right to regard an unborn child as a human person, with the capacity for life after death? It would clearly be wrong to hold a Funeral service but to omit these words on the grounds of doubt about whether the corpse was fully human. The decision has already been taken, once it is resolved to hold a Funeral service for a stillbirth, that the parents' grief at this event is to be treated quite seriously as grief at the loss of a *child*. If we cannot speak of a stillborn child as a human being, then we cannot speak of a stillborn child at all. There is certainly no other status (such as that of an animal or a pet) that we can confidently assign to a nascent human being. The terms 'stillborn' and 'stillbirth' are generally used to refer to the death of children in the womb after the stage of viability has been reached, i.e. for practical legal purposes after twenty-four weeks' gestation, when both current law and current medical practice afford the child full protection as a human being.

Second, is it right to speak of a 'sure and certain hope' in the case of someone who has not lived outside the womb, and has not been baptized? You cannot baptize someone who is dead: in any case, to do this would open up enormous areas of debate at the other end of the age-scale. Nor is there provision for baptism *in utero*: not only is it difficult to consider as baptism an event in which water does not touch the person being baptized, it also raises problems about how the decision is taken as to which babies to baptize in this way. It is better to look behind the baptism at the thing signified, namely, in the case of infant baptism, the desire of the parents and the place of the child within the love of God – as one might with an unbaptized child of a few days old. To attribute faith to the dead infant is no more implausible than the assumption made in infant baptism itself. It is possible that this point could be made by requiring the parents to profess that they would have brought the child to baptism had they been able.

We are right to be cautious about a *particular* assertion of the individual child's resurrection. The doubt here, which we feel in the case of an adult given burial by charitable assumption, is compounded by slight speculative doubt that attaches to the human individuality of the child and also by the fact that the child is unbaptized. None of these factors is decisive; however, each detracts in a slight measure from the confidence with which we can assert that this individual will be raised on the last day. The actual text of the Committal, however, does stop short of this assertion. It says that we commit the child's body to the ground in sure and certain hope of *the* resurrection to eternal life. This allows us to claim the significance of the resurrection for our bereavement without dictating precisely to God in what form the resurrection is to restore to us that which we have lost. Surely, this is the correct way to lay hold on the hope of the resurrection, not only in the case of stillborn children but every time that we are bewildered by the mystery of the individual personality and the hiddenness of its destiny.

Those who conduct such services will need to be loving and sensitive, in using the texts as tools at their disposal in giving pastoral help, talking with parents about which prayers they particularly identify with, discovering if there is a name by which parents know their child, facing with them the definiteness of death which such a service marks. No apology is needed for facing the theological questions, because pastoral help cannot realistically be given on the basis of a general lovingness which has doubts or a bad conscience about the words used, but only on the basis of a clear faith in our dead and risen Saviour, Jesus Christ.

After the Funeral

¶ *At Home after the Funeral*

Note

This service may be adapted for use either immediately after
the funeral or later. It may be led by a friend or family member
or by a minister.

At the Door

The minister may say

In the name of God, Father, Son, and Holy Spirit.

All **Amen.**

The peace of God our heavenly Father,
of Jesus Christ the source of peace,
and of the Holy Spirit the comforter
come upon this house and all who live here.

Open, O God, the door of this house;
let your light shine here to drive away all darkness;
through Jesus Christ our Lord.

All **Amen.**

The Word of God

One or more of the following readings may be used

Do not let your hearts be troubled. Believe in God, believe also in
me. In my Father's house there are many dwelling places. If it were
not so, would I have told you that I go to prepare a place for you?
And if I go and prepare a place for you, I will come again and take
you to myself, so that where I am, there you may be also.

John 14.1-3

Come to me, all you that are weary and are carrying heavy burdens, and I will give you rest. Take my yoke upon you, and learn from me; for I am gentle and humble in heart, and you will find rest for your souls. For my yoke is easy, and my burden is light.   *Matthew 11.28-30*

We are citizens of heaven, and from heaven we expect our deliverer to come, the Lord Jesus Christ. He will transform our humble bodies, and give them a form like that of his own glorious body, by that power which enables him to make all things subject to himself. This, my dear friends, whom I love and long for, my joy and my crown, this is what it means to stand firm in the Lord.

Philippians 3.20–4.1

In you, O Lord, do I seek refuge;
let me never be put to shame.

In your righteousness, deliver me and set me free;
incline your ear to me and save me.

Be for me a stronghold to which I may ever resort;
send out to save me, for you are my rock and my fortress.

Deliver me, my God, from the hand of the wicked,
from the grasp of the evildoer and the oppressor.

For you are my hope, O Lord God,
my confidence, even from my youth.

Upon you have I leaned from my birth,
    when you drew me from my mother's womb;
my praise shall be always of you.

O God, you have taught me since I was young,
and to this day I tell of your wonderful works.

Forsake me not, O God,
    when I am old and grey-headed,
till I make known your deeds to the next generation
    and your power to all that are to come.   *Psalm 71.1-6,17,18*

Those who sow in tears
shall reap with songs of joy.

Those who go out weeping, bearing the seed,
will come back with shouts of joy,
    bearing their sheaves with them.   *Psalm 126.5,6*

Where can I go then from your spirit?
Or where can I flee from your presence?

If I climb up to heaven, you are there;
if I make the grave my bed, you are there also.

If I take the wings of the morning
and dwell in the uttermost parts of the sea,

Even there your hand shall lead me,
your right hand hold me fast.

If I say, 'Surely the darkness will cover me
and the light around me turn to night,'

Even darkness is no darkness with you;
    the night is as clear as the day;
darkness and light to you are both alike.   *Psalm 139.7-11*

Prayers

A suitable prayer or prayers from pages 345–382 may be used, or informal prayer for the family may be more appropriate. This prayer may be especially appropriate if there is food after the Funeral

Almighty God, the Father of our Lord Jesus Christ,
whose disciples recognized him as he broke bread
 at their table after the resurrection:
we thank you for your strength upholding us
 in what we have done today,
and now we ask for your presence to be recognized in this home;
bring your peace and joy to each place which stirs the memory;
give your strength and presence in those daily tasks
 which used to be shared,
and in all the changes of life give us grace
 to do your will day by day,
and to look for the glorious coming of Christ,
when you will gather us together to your table in heaven
to be with you for ever and ever.

All   **Amen.**

Conclusion

The minister may say some or all of Psalm 121

I lift up my eyes to the hills;
from where is my help to come?

My help comes from the Lord,
the maker of heaven and earth.

He will not suffer your foot to stumble;
he who watches over you will not sleep.

Behold, he who keeps watch over Israel
shall neither slumber nor sleep.

The Lord himself watches over you;
the Lord is your shade at your right hand,

So that the sun shall not strike you by day,
neither the moon by night.

The Lord shall keep you from all evil;
it is he who shall keep your soul.

The Lord shall keep watch over your going out
    and your coming in,
from this time forth for evermore.

All **Amen.**

The Burial of Ashes

Note

If the service begins in church or chapel, it may be appropriate to invite the mourners to the place of burial at the end of the readings, and to use the psalms at the place of burial.

Preparation

The minister greets the people in these or other suitable words

Grace, mercy and peace
from God our Father and the Lord Jesus Christ
be with you all.

Though we are dust and ashes,
God has prepared for those who love him
    a heavenly dwelling place.
At *his/her* funeral we commended N into the hands
    of almighty God.
As we prepare to commit the remains of N to the earth,
we entrust ourselves and all who love God to his loving care.

Appropriate sentences of Scripture may be used.

The eternal God is our refuge,
and underneath are the everlasting arms.   *cf Deuteronomy 33. 27 AV*

Blessed be the God and Father of our Lord Jesus Christ!
By his great mercy he has given us a new birth into a living hope
    through the resurrection of Jesus Christ from the dead,
and into an inheritance that is imperishable, undefiled, and unfading,
kept in heaven for you.   *1 Peter 1.3,4*

Lord, you have been our refuge
from one generation to another.

Before the mountains were brought forth,
    or the earth and the world were formed,
from everlasting to everlasting you are God.

You turn us back to dust and say:
'Turn back, O children of earth.'

For a thousand years in your sight are but as yesterday,
which passes like a watch in the night.   *Psalm 90.1-4*

Readings

One or more readings follows. The psalms may be used at the place of burial (see Note on page 323).

'O that my words were written down!
O that they were inscribed in a book!
O that with an iron pen and with lead
    they were engraved on a rock for ever!
For I know that my Redeemer lives,
    and that at the last he will stand upon the earth;
and after my skin has been thus destroyed,
then in my flesh I shall see God,
whom I shall see on my side,
    and my eyes shall behold, and not another.
My heart faints within me!'

Job 19.23-27

4   The Lord himself is my portion and my cup; ♦
      in your hands alone is my fortune.

5   My share has fallen in a fair land; ♦
      indeed, I have a goodly heritage.

6   I will bless the Lord who has given me counsel, ♦
      and in the night watches he instructs my heart.

7   I have set the Lord always before me; ♦
      he is at my right hand; I shall not fall.

8   Wherefore my heart is glad and my spirit rejoices; ♦
      my flesh also shall rest secure.

9   For you will not abandon my soul to Death, ♦
      nor suffer your faithful one to see the Pit.

10   You will show me the path of life;
      in your presence is the fullness of joy ♦
    and in your right hand are pleasures for evermore.   *Psalm 16.4-10*

1   O Lord, you have searched me out and known me; ♦
    you know my sitting down and my rising up;
        you discern my thoughts from afar.

2   You mark out my journeys and my resting place ♦
    and are acquainted with all my ways.

3   For there is not a word on my tongue, ♦
    but you, O Lord, know it altogether.

4   You encompass me behind and before ♦
    and lay your hand upon me.

5   Such knowledge is too wonderful for me, ♦
    so high that I cannot attain it.

6   Where can I go then from your spirit? ♦
    Or where can I flee from your presence?

7   If I climb up to heaven, you are there; ♦
    if I make the grave my bed, you are there also.

8   If I take the wings of the morning ♦
    and dwell in the uttermost parts of the sea,

9   Even there your hand shall lead me, ♦
    your right hand hold me fast.

10   If I say, 'Surely the darkness will cover me ♦
    and the light around me turn to night,'

11   Even darkness is no darkness with you;
        the night is as clear as the day; ♦
    darkness and light to you are both alike.

13   I thank you, for I am fearfully and wonderfully made; ♦
    marvellous are your works, my soul knows well.   *Psalm 139.1-11,13*

Someone will ask, 'How are the dead raised? With what kind of body do they come?' Fool! What you sow does not come to life unless it dies. And as for what you sow, you do not sow the body that is to be, but a bare seed, perhaps of wheat or of some other grain. But God gives it a body as he has chosen, and to each kind of seed its own body.

So it is with the resurrection of the dead. What is sown is perishable, what is raised is imperishable. It is sown in dishonour, it is raised in glory. It is sown in weakness, it is raised in power. It is sown a physical body, it is raised a spiritual body.

1 Corinthians 15.35-38, 42-44a

After these things, Joseph of Arimathea, who was a disciple of Jesus, though a secret one because of his fear of the Jews, asked Pilate to let him take away the body of Jesus. Pilate gave him permission; so he came and removed his body. Nicodemus, who had at first come to Jesus by night, also came, bringing a mixture of myrrh and aloes, weighing about a hundred pounds. They took the body of Jesus and wrapped it with the spices in linen cloths, according to the burial custom of the Jews. Now there was a garden in the place where he was crucified, and in the garden there was a new tomb in which no one had ever been laid. And so, because it was the Jewish day of Preparation, and the tomb was nearby, they laid Jesus there.

John 19.38-end

I saw no temple in the city, for its temple is the Lord God the Almighty and the Lamb. And the city has no need of sun or moon to shine on it, for the glory of God is its light, and its lamp is the Lamb. The nations will walk by its light, and the kings of the earth will bring their glory into it. Its gates will never be shut by day – and there will be no night there. People will bring into it the glory and the honour of the nations. But nothing unclean will enter it, nor anyone who practises abomination or falsehood, but only those who are written in the Lamb's book of life.

But the throne of God and of the Lamb will be in it, and his servants will worship him; they will see his face, and his name will be on their foreheads. And there will be no more night; they need no light of lamp or sun, for the Lord God will be their light, and they will reign for ever and ever.

Revelation 21.22-end, 22.3b-5

The minister says

either

We have entrusted our *brother/sister* N to God's mercy,
and we now commit *his/her* mortal remains to the ground:
earth to earth, ashes to ashes, dust to dust:
in sure and certain hope of the resurrection to eternal life
through our Lord Jesus Christ,
who will transform our frail bodies
that they may be conformed to his glorious body,
who died, was buried, and rose again for us.
To him be glory for ever.

All **Amen.**

(or)

God our Father,
in loving care your hand has created us,
and as the potter fashions the clay
you have formed us in your image.
Through the Holy Spirit
you have breathed into us the gift of life.
In the sharing of love you have enriched our knowledge
　　of you and of one another.
We claim your love today,
as we return these ashes to the ground
in sure and certain hope of the resurrection to eternal life.

The congregation may join with the minister in saying

All **Thanks be to God who gives us the victory**
through Jesus Christ our Lord. Amen.

Prayers

The Lord's Prayer

As our Saviour taught us, so we pray

All **Our Father in heaven,**
hallowed be your name,
your kingdom come,
your will be done,
on earth as in heaven.
Give us today our daily bread.
Forgive us our sins
as we forgive those who sin against us.
Lead us not into temptation
but deliver us from evil.
For the kingdom, the power,
and the glory are yours
now and for ever.
Amen.

(or)

Let us pray with confidence as our Saviour has taught us

All **Our Father, who art in heaven,**
hallowed be thy name;
thy kingdom come;
thy will be done;
on earth as it is in heaven.
Give us this day our daily bread.
And forgive us our trespasses,
as we forgive those who trespass against us.
And lead us not into temptation;
but deliver us from evil.
For thine is the kingdom,
the power and the glory,
for ever and ever.
Amen.

Heavenly Father,
we thank you for all those whom we love but see no longer.
As we remember N in this place,
hold before us our beginning and our ending,
the dust from which we come
and the death to which we move,
with a firm hope in your eternal love and purposes for us,
in Jesus Christ our Lord.

All **Amen.**

Other prayers may be used, ending with

God of hope,
grant that we, with all who have believed in you,
may be united in the full knowledge of your love
and the unclouded vision of your glory;
through Jesus Christ our Lord.

All **Amen.**

The Dismissal

May the infinite and glorious Trinity,
the Father, the Son, and the Holy Spirit,
direct our life in good works,
and after our journey through this world
grant us eternal rest with all the saints.

All **Amen.**

An Outline Order for a Memorial Service

For Notes, see page 334.

The Gathering

1   The minister welcomes the people and introduces the service.

2   Sentences of Scripture may be used.

3   Authorized Prayers of Penitence may be used.

4   The Collect may be said here or in the Prayers.

Readings and Sermon

5   One or more readings from the Bible is used.
Psalms or hymns may follow the readings.

6   Other songs and readings may be used and a tribute or tributes made.

7   A sermon is preached, testimony may be given and an authorized Creed or Affirmation of Faith may be used.

Prayers

8   The prayers usually follow this sequence:

¶   Thanksgiving for the life of the departed

¶   Prayer for those who mourn

¶   Prayers of Penitence (if not already used)

¶   Prayer for readiness to live in the light of eternity

Commendation and Dismissal

9   The dead person is commended to God with authorized words.

10   The service may end with a blessing.

An Outline Order
for a Memorial Service within a
Celebration of Holy Communion

For Notes, see page 334.

The Gathering

1   The minister welcomes the people and introduces the service.

2   Sentences of Scripture may be used.

3   Authorized Prayers of Penitence are used here or in the Prayers.

4   The Collect is said here or in the Prayers.

The Liturgy of the Word

5   One or more readings from the Bible, including a Gospel reading,
    is used.
    Psalms or hymns may follow the readings.

6   Other songs and readings may be used and a tribute or
    tributes made.

7   A sermon is preached, testimony may be given and an authorized
    Creed or Affirmation of Faith may be used.

Prayers

8   The prayers usually follow this sequence:

    ¶   Thanksgiving for the life of the departed

    ¶   Prayer for those who mourn

    ¶   Prayers of Penitence (if not already used)

    ¶   Prayer for readiness to live in the light of eternity

The Liturgy of the Sacrament

9   The Peace

10   Preparation of the Table
Taking of the Bread and Wine

11   The Eucharistic Prayer (any authorized Eucharistic Prayer may be used)

12   The Lord's Prayer (used here rather than in the Prayers)

13   Breaking of the Bread

14   Giving of Communion

15   Prayer after Communion

Commendation and Dismissal

16   The dead person is commended to God with authorized words.

17   The service may end with a blessing.

Notes

1 These Outline Orders are designed for use in church several weeks after the Funeral service has taken place. One way of amplifying the first Order is provided on pages 335–344.

2 If the memorial service takes place on the same day as, or very soon after, the Funeral, the Funeral service should be used, without the Committal.

3 For annual memorial services a provision such as that on pages 62–82 in *The Promise of His Glory* should be used.

4 Care should be taken to ensure that there is a clear president throughout, who introduces and concludes the service, and that the number of other speakers, musical items and non-biblical readings does not unbalance the service from its focus on the word of God, prayer and thanksgiving.

Memorial Service: A Sample Service

The Gathering

The minister welcomes the people and introduces the service.

Sentences of Scripture may be sung or said, and a hymn may be sung.

The minister says

We meet in the name of Jesus Christ,
who died and was raised to the glory of God the Father.
Grace and mercy be with you.

[*All*　**And also with you.]**

The minister introduces the service in these or other suitable words

We look not to the things that are seen
but to the things that are unseen;
for the things that are seen are transient
but the things that are unseen are eternal.
Today we come together
to remember before God our *brother/sister N*,
to give thanks for *his/her* life
and to comfort one another in our grief.

Opening Prayer

One of these prayers is said

Father in heaven,
we thank you because you made us in your own image
and gave us gifts in body, mind and spirit.
We thank you now for *N*
and what *he/she* meant to each of us.
As we honour *his/her* memory,
make us more aware that you are the one
from whom comes every perfect gift,
including the gift of eternal life through Jesus Christ.

All　**Amen.**

(or)

Father in heaven, we praise your name
for all who have finished this life loving and trusting you,
for the example of their lives,
the life and grace you gave them
and the peace in which they rest.
We praise you today for your servant *N*
and for all that you did through *him/her*.
Meet us in our sadness
and fill our hearts with praise and thanksgiving,
for the sake of our risen Lord, Jesus Christ.

All **Amen.**

Readings and Sermon

This canticle may be used

All **The ransomed of the Lord shall return,
and sorrow and sighing shall flee away.**

The wilderness and the dry land shall rejoice:
the desert shall burst into song.

They shall see the glory of the Lord:
the majesty of our God.

All **The ransomed of the Lord shall return,
and sorrow and sighing shall flee away.**

Strengthen the weary hands:
make firm the feeble knees.

Say to the anxious: Be strong, fear not,
your God is coming with judgement:
coming with judgement to save you.

All **The ransomed of the Lord shall return.
and sorrow and sighing shall flee away.**   *Isaiah 35.1,2b,3,4,10a*

A reading from the Old or New Testament may be used.
At the end the reader may say

This is the word of the Lord.
All **Thanks be to God.**

A reading from the New Testament (which may be a Gospel reading) is used. When the Gospel is announced the reader says

Hear the Gospel of our Lord Jesus Christ according to N.

All **Glory to you, O Lord.**

At the end

This is the Gospel of the Lord.

All **Praise to you, O Christ.**

Memories may be shared, a tribute or tributes may be made. Psalms, hymns and other songs and readings may be used.

A sermon is preached.

One of these prayers may be used to provide a link with the Affirmation of Faith or the Thanksgiving

Father in heaven,
we give you thanks for your servant N.
We praise you as we recollect *his/her* life and cherish
    his/her memory.
We bless you that in bearing your image
he/she has brought light to our lives;
for we have seen
    in *his/her* friendship reflections of your compassion,
    in *his/her* integrity demonstrations of your goodness,
    in *his/her* faithfulness glimpses of your eternal love.
Grant to each of us, beloved and bereft,
the grace to follow *his/her* good example
so that we with *him/her* may come to your everlasting kingdom;
through Jesus Christ our Lord,
who died and rose again and opened the gate of glory,
to whom be praise for all eternity.

All **Amen.**

(or)

Almighty Saviour,
those who have died in faith
have eternal joy in your presence.
For us who remain, be with us in our sadness
and turn our eyes to you.
By your death once for all upon the cross,
raise us to new life,
give us victory over death
and confidence to look forward to your coming.

All **Amen.**

Affirmation of Faith

This Affirmation of Faith may be used

Let us declare our faith
in the resurrection of our Lord Jesus Christ:

All **Christ died for our sins**
in accordance with the Scriptures;
he was buried;
he was raised to life on the third day
in accordance with the Scriptures;
afterwards he appeared to his followers,
and to all the apostles:
this we have received,
and this we believe.
Amen.   *cf 1 Corinthians 15.3-7*

Prayers

Prayers of Penitence

The minister may introduce the confession with these or other suitable words

God has shone in our hearts to give the light of the knowledge of his glory in the face of Christ. But we have this treasure in earthen vessels to show that the transcendent power belongs to God and not to us. As we acknowledge our human frailty, we call to mind our sins of word, deed and omission, and confess them before God our Father.

Silence is kept.

All **Father eternal, giver of light and grace,**
we have sinned against you and against our neighbour,
in what we have thought,
in what we have said and done,
through ignorance, through weakness,
through our own deliberate fault.
We have wounded your love,
and marred your image in us.
We are sorry and ashamed,
and repent of all our sins.
For the sake of your Son Jesus Christ,
who died for us,
forgive us all that is past;
and lead us out from darkness
to walk as children of light.
Amen.

The minister says an authorized absolution.

Prayers of Intercession

Suitable prayers are said (see pages 351–372).

This introduction and response may be used

In peace let us pray to the Lord, using the response:

Hear us, risen Lord,
All **our resurrection and our life.**

Prayers of Thanksgiving

Hymns may be sung and testimony given.

Either the whole of, or these verses from, the Te Deum may be used

You, Christ, are the King of glory,
the eternal Son of the Father.
When you took our flesh to set us free
you humbly chose the Virgin's womb.
You overcame the sting of death
and opened the kingdom of heaven to all believers.
You are seated at God's right hand in glory.
We believe that you will come and be our judge.
Come then, Lord, and help your people,
bought with the price of your own blood,
and bring us with your saints
to glory everlasting.

One or more of these thanksgivings may be used

You are worthy, our Lord and God,
to receive glory and honour and power.

All **For you have created all things,**
and by your will they have their being.

You are worthy, O Lamb, for you were slain,
and by your blood you ransomed for God
    saints from every tribe and language and nation.

All **You have made them to be a kingdom and priests**
    serving our God,
and they will reign with you on earth.

To the One who sits on the throne and to the Lamb
be blessing and honour, glory and might,
    for ever and ever.
Amen.

(or)

We give you thanks and praise, almighty Father,
that you sent your Son to die,
and raised him from the dead.
We praise you in the confidence that you save all your people,
living and dead.
Lord, hear us:

All **Lord, graciously hear us.**

We thank you for *N,*
who in baptism was given the pledge of eternal life
and is now admitted to the company of the saints.
Lord, hear us:

All **Lord, graciously hear us.**

We thank you for our *brother/sister* who shared the bread of life,
a foretaste of the eternal banquet of heaven.
Lord, hear us:

All **Lord, graciously hear us.**

We thank you for our relatives and friends
and for all who have helped us,
who enjoy the reward of their goodness.
Lord, hear us:

All **Lord, graciously hear us.**

We pray that the family and friends of our *brother/sister N*
may be consoled in their grief by the Lord,
who wept at the death of Lazarus his friend.
Lord, hear us:

All **Lord, graciously hear us.**

We pray for all of us assembled here to worship in faith,
that we may be gathered together again in God's kingdom.
Lord, hear us:

All **Lord, graciously hear us.**

(or)

Lord God, creator of all,
you have made us creatures of this earth,
but have also promised us a share in life eternal.
According to your promises,
may all who have died in the peace of Christ
share with your saints in the joy of heaven,
where there is neither sorrow nor pain
but life everlasting.

All **Alleluia. Amen.**

The Commendation

Almighty God,
in your great love
you crafted us by your hand
and breathed life into us by your Spirit.
Although we became a rebellious people,
you did not abandon us to our sin.
In your tender mercy
you sent your Son
to restore in us your image.
In obedience to your will
he gave up his life for us,
bearing in his body our sins on the cross.
By your mighty power
you raised him from the grave
and exalted him to the throne of glory.
Rejoicing in his victory
and trusting in your promise
to make alive all who turn to Christ,
we commend N to your mercy
and we join with all your faithful people
and the whole company of heaven
in the one unending song of praise:
glory and wisdom and honour
be to our God for ever and ever.

All **Amen.**

As our Saviour taught us, so we pray

All   **Our Father in heaven,**
hallowed be your name,
your kingdom come,
your will be done,
on earth as in heaven.
Give us today our daily bread.
Forgive us our sins
as we forgive those who sin against us.
Lead us not into temptation
but deliver us from evil.
For the kingdom, the power,
and the glory are yours
now and for ever.
Amen.

(or)

Let us pray with confidence as our Saviour has taught us

All   **Our Father, who art in heaven,**
hallowed be thy name;
thy kingdom come;
thy will be done;
on earth as it is in heaven.
Give us this day our daily bread.
And forgive us our trespasses,
as we forgive those who trespass against us.
And lead us not into temptation;
but deliver us from evil.
For thine is the kingdom,
the power and the glory,
for ever and ever.
Amen.

The Dismissal

Jesus said: Peace I leave with you. My peace I give to you.
Not as the world gives give I unto you. Do not let your
hearts be troubled, neither let them be afraid.

The peace of the risen Christ be always with you

All **and also with you.**

Conclusion

Neither death nor life
can separate us from the love of God
in Jesus Christ our Lord.

Grant to us, Lord God,
to trust you not for ourselves alone,
but also for those whom we love
and who are hidden from us by the shadow of death;
that, as we believe your power to have raised
  our Lord Jesus Christ from the dead,
so may we trust your love to give eternal life to all
  who believe in him;
through Jesus Christ our Lord,
who is alive and reigns with you and the Holy Spirit,
one God, now and for ever.

All **Amen.**

The God of peace,
who brought again from the dead our Lord Jesus,
that great shepherd of the sheep,
make *you* perfect in every good work to do his will;
and the blessing of God almighty,
the Father, the Son, and the Holy Spirit,
be among *you* and remain with *you* always.

All **Amen.**

Resources

Prayers for Use with the Dying and at Funeral and Memorial Services

These prayers follow the order of dying and mourning. They reflect the sequence found in the services, from the time of death until after the Funeral:

Other suitable prayers may be found in the sections Before the Funeral and After the Funeral (pages 236–254 and 318–322). Prayers suitable for a child may be found on pages 301–315.

Prayers with Dying People

1   Soul of Christ, sanctify me.
     Body of Christ, save me.
     Blood of Christ, refresh me.
     Water from the side of Christ, wash me.
     Passion of Christ, strengthen me.
     O good Jesus, hear me.
     Within your wounds hide me.
     Let me never be separated from you.
     From the power of darkness defend me.
     In the hour of my death, call me
     and bid me come to you,
     that with your saints I may praise you
     for ever and ever.
     Amen.

2   Christ be with me, Christ within me,
     Christ behind me, Christ before me,
     Christ beside me, Christ to win me,
     Christ to comfort and restore me,
     Christ beneath me, Christ above me,
     Christ in quiet, Christ in danger,
     Christ in hearts of all that love me,
     Christ in mouth of friend and stranger.

3   Lord Jesus Christ, we thank you
     for all the benefits you have won for us,
     for all the pains and insults you have borne for us.
     Most merciful redeemer,
     friend and brother,
     may we know you more clearly,
     love you more dearly,
     and follow you more nearly,
     day by day.
     Amen.

4   Lord,
     in weakness or in strength
     we bear your image.
     We pray for those we love
     who now live in a land of shadows,
     where the light of memory is dimmed,
     where the familiar lies unknown,
     where the beloved become as strangers.
     Hold them in your everlasting arms,
     and grant to those who care
          a strength to serve,
          a patience to persevere,
          a love to last
          and a peace that passes human understanding.
     Hold us in your everlasting arms,
     today and for all eternity;
     through Jesus Christ our Lord.
     Amen.

Gathering Prayers

5   God our refuge and strength,
     close at hand in our distress;
     meet us in our sorrow and lift our eyes
     to the peace and light of your constant care.
     Help us so to hear your word of grace
     that our fear will be dispelled by your love,
     our loneliness eased by your presence
     and our hope renewed by your promises
     in Jesus Christ our Lord.
All   **Amen.**

6   Gracious Father,
     in darkness and light,
     in trouble and in joy,
     help us to trust your love,
     to serve your purpose
     and to praise your name;
     through Jesus Christ our Lord.
All   **Amen.**

7 Heavenly Father,
   you have not made us for darkness and death,
   but for life with you for ever.
   Without you we have nothing to hope for;
   with you we have nothing to fear.
   Speak to us now your words of eternal life.
   Lift us from anxiety and guilt
   to the light and peace of your presence,
   and set the glory of your love before us;
   through Jesus Christ our Lord.
All **Amen.**

Prayers of Penitence

Kyries

8 Remember, Lord, your compassion and love,
   for they are everlasting.
   Lord, have mercy.
[*All* **Lord, have mercy.**]

   Remember not the sins of my youth or my transgressions,
   but think on me in your goodness, O Lord,
        according to your steadfast love.
   Christ, have mercy.
[*All* **Christ, have mercy.**]

   O keep my soul and deliver me;
   let me not be put to shame, for I have put my trust in you.
   Lord, have mercy.
[*All* **Lord, have mercy.**]

9   Lord Jesus, you have shown us the way to the Father:
Lord, have mercy.

[*All*   **Lord, have mercy.**]

Lord Jesus, your word is a light to our path:
Christ, have mercy.

[*All*   **Christ, have mercy.**]

Lord Jesus, you are the good shepherd,
leading us into everlasting life:
Lord, have mercy.

[*All*   **Lord, have mercy.**]

10   Praise the Lord, O my soul,
and forget not all his benefits:
Lord, have mercy.

[*All*   **Lord, have mercy.**]

Who forgives all your sin
and heals all your infirmities:
Christ, have mercy.

[*All*   **Christ, have mercy.**]

Who saves your life from destruction
and crowns you with mercy and loving-kindness:
Lord, have mercy.

[*All*   **Lord, have mercy.**]

11   Out of the depths I cry to you:
Lord, hear my voice.
Lord, have mercy.

[*All*   **Lord, have mercy.**]

If you should mark what is done amiss:
who may abide it?
Christ, have mercy.

[*All*   **Christ, have mercy.**]

Trust in the Lord, for with him there is mercy:
for with him is ample redemption.
Lord, have mercy.

[*All*   **Lord, have mercy.**]

12   May the God of love
      bring us back to himself,
      forgive us our sins
      and assure us of his eternal love
      in Jesus Christ our Lord.

All   **Amen.**

*The following absolution is particularly appropriate when the Funeral
service is set within Holy Communion*

13   May God our Father forgive us our sins
      and bring us to the fellowship of his table
      with his saints for ever.

All   **Amen.**

Collects for Funeral and Memorial Services

14   Merciful Father,
      hear our prayers and comfort us;
      renew our trust in your Son,
      whom you raised from the dead;
      strengthen our faith
      that [*N and*] all who have died in the love of Christ
      will share in his resurrection;
      who lives and reigns with you,
      now and for ever.

All   **Amen.**

15   Eternal God, our maker and redeemer,
      grant us [*with N*] and all the faithful departed
      the sure benefits of your Son's saving passion
          and glorious resurrection:
      that, in the last day,
      when you gather up all things in Christ,
      we may with them enjoy the fullness of your promises;
      through Jesus Christ your Son our Lord,
      who is alive and reigns with you,
      in the unity of the Holy Spirit,
      one God, now and for ever.

All   **Amen.**

Thanksgiving for the Life of the Departed

16   Blessed be the God and Father of our Lord Jesus Christ,
      who has blessed us all with the gift of this earthly life
      and has given to our *brother/sister N*
      his/her span of years and gifts of character.
      God our Father, we thank you now for all *his/her* life,
      for every memory of love and joy,
      for every good deed done by *him/her*
      and every sorrow shared with us.
      We thank you for *his/her* life and for *his/her* death,
      we thank you for the rest in Christ *he/she* now enjoys,
      we thank you for giving *him/her* to us,
      we thank you for the glory we shall share together.
      Hear our prayers through Jesus Christ our Lord.

All   **Amen.**

17   Merciful Father and Lord of all life,
      we praise you that we are made in your image
      and reflect your truth and light.
      We thank you for the life of your child *N*,
      for the love *he/she* received from you
      and showed among us.
      Above all, we rejoice at your gracious promise
      to all your servants, living and departed,
      that we shall rise again at the coming of Christ.
      And we ask that in due time
      we may share with our *brother/sister* that clearer vision,
      when we shall see your face in the same Christ our Lord.

All   **Amen.**

18   Lord of all, we praise you
      for all who have entered into their rest
      and reached the promised land where you are seen face to face.
      Give us grace to follow in their footsteps
      as they followed in the way of your Son.
      Thank you for the memory of those you have called to yourself:
      by each memory, turn our hearts from things seen
            to things unseen,
      and lead us till we come to the eternal rest
            you have prepared for your people,
      through Jesus Christ our Lord.

All   **Amen.**

19   Father in heaven, we praise your name
      for all who have finished this life loving and trusting you,
      for the example of their lives,
      the life and grace you gave them,
      and the peace in which they rest.
      We praise you today for your servant N
      and for all that you did through *him/her*.
      Meet us in our sadness
      and fill our hearts with praise and thanksgiving,
      for the sake of our risen Lord, Jesus Christ.
All   **Amen.**

20   Father in heaven,
      we thank you because you made us in your own image
      and gave us gifts in mind, body and spirit.
      We thank you now for N
      and what *he/she* meant to each of us.
      As we honour *his/her* memory,
      make us more aware that you are the one
      from whom comes every perfect gift,
      including the gift of eternal life through Jesus Christ.
All   **Amen.**

21   God our Father,
      we thank you that you have made each of us
          in your own image,
      and given us gifts and talents with which to serve you.
      We thank you for N,
      the years we shared with *him/her*,
      the good we saw in *him/her*,
      the love we received from *him/her*.
      Now give us strength and courage
      to leave *him/her* in your care,
      confident in your promise of eternal life
      through Jesus Christ our Lord.
All   **Amen.**

22 Eternal God and Father,
we praise you that you have made people
    to share life together
and to reflect your glory in the world.
We thank you now for *N*,
for all that we saw of your goodness and love in *his/her* life
and for all that *he/she* means to each one of us.
As we too journey towards death
may we do so in the company of Jesus,
who came to share our life
that we might share the life of eternity.
To him be glory with you and the Holy Spirit
for ever and ever.

All **Amen.**

23 Lord God, creator of all,
you have made us creatures of this earth
but have also promised us a share in life eternal:
receive our thanks and praise
that, through the passion and death of Christ,
your child *N*, our *brother/sister*,
whom we commend into your hands today,
shares with your saints in the joy of heaven,
where there is neither sorrow nor pain
but life everlasting. Alleluia.

All **Amen.**

24 Almighty God,
you love everything you have made
and judge us with infinite mercy and justice.
We rejoice in your promises of pardon, joy and peace
to all those who love you.
In your mercy turn the darkness of death into the dawn of new life,
and the sorrow of parting into the joy of heaven;
through our Saviour Jesus Christ,
who died, rose again, and lives for evermore.

All **Amen.**

25   Almighty God,
      we come before you, the supreme judge,
      and to Jesus, the mediator of the new covenant,
      and to the spirits of the righteous made perfect;
      we give you thanks for giving us an unshakeable kingdom
      and we worship you in reverence and awe,
      through Jesus Christ our Lord.

All   **Amen.**

Prayers for Those who Mourn

26   God of mercy,
      as we mourn the death of *N*
      and thank you for *his/her* life,
      we also remember times when it was hard for us to understand,
      to forgive, and to be forgiven.
      Heal our memories of hurt and failure,
      and bring us to forgiveness and life
      in Jesus Christ our Lord.

All   **Amen.**

27   Lord Jesus Christ,
      you comforted your disciples when you were going to die:
      now set our troubled hearts at rest
      and banish our fears.
      You are the way to the Father:
      help us to follow you.
      You are the truth:
      bring us to know you.
      You are the life:
      give us that life,
      to live with you now and for ever.

All   **Amen.**

28   O God, who brought us to birth,
     and in whose arms we die,
     in our grief and shock
     contain and comfort us;
     embrace us with your love,
     give us hope in our confusion
     and grace to let go into new life;
     through Jesus Christ.
All   **Amen.**

29   Father,
     you know our hearts and share our sorrows.
     We are hurt by our parting from *N* whom we loved:
     when we are angry at the loss we have sustained,
     when we long for words of comfort,
     yet find them hard to hear,
     turn our grief to truer living,
     our affliction to firmer hope
     in Jesus Christ our Lord.
All   **Amen.**

30   Gracious God,
     surround us and all who mourn this day
     with your continuing compassion.
     Do not let grief overwhelm your children,
     or turn them against you.
     When grief seems never-ending,
     take them one step at a time
     along your road of death and resurrection
     in Jesus Christ our Lord.
All   **Amen.**

31   Father, the death of *N* brings an emptiness into our lives.
     We are separated from *him/her*
     and feel broken and disturbed.
     Give us confidence that *he/she* is safe
     and *his/her* life complete with you,
     and bring us together at the last
     to the wholeness and fullness of your presence in heaven,
     where your saints and angels enjoy you for ever and ever.
All   **Amen.**

32   Lord, we pray for those who mourn,
      for parents and children,
      friends and neighbours.
      Be gentle with them in their grief.
      Show them the depths of your love,
      a glimpse of the kingdom of heaven.
      Spare them the torment of guilt and despair.
      Be with them as they weep beside the empty tomb
            of our risen Saviour,
      Jesus Christ our Lord.
All   **Amen.**

33   Most merciful God,
      whose wisdom is beyond our understanding,
      surround the family of N with your love,
      that they may not be overwhelmed by their loss,
      but have confidence in your goodness
      and strength to meet the days to come.
      We ask this through Christ our Lord.
All   **Amen.**

34   Father of all mercies and God of all consolation,
      you pursue us with untiring love
      and dispel the shadow of death
            with the bright dawn of life.
      [Give courage to this family in their loss and sorrow.
      Be their refuge and strength, O Lord,
      reassure them of your continuing love
      and lift them from the depths of grief
      into the peace and light of your presence.]
      Your Son, our Lord Jesus Christ,
      by dying has destroyed our death,
      and by rising, restored our life.
      Your Holy Spirit, our comforter,
      speaks for us in groans too deep for words.
      Come alongside your people,
      remind them of your eternal presence
      and give them your comfort and strength.
All   **Amen.**

35   Lord God,
      you are attentive to the voice of our pleading.
      Let us find in your Son
      comfort in our sadness,
      certainty in our doubt
      and courage to live.
      Make our faith strong
      through Christ our Lord.
All   **Amen.**

36   Risen Lord Jesus,
      draw near to us as we walk this lonely road.
      Pierce our weary sorrow
      and gladden our heavy hearts as you go with us,
      and bring us in the end to your heavenly table.
All   **Amen.**

37   O God, you do not willingly grieve or afflict
            your children.
      Look with pity on the suffering of this family
            in their loss.
      Sustain them in their anguish;
      and into the darkness of their grief
      bring the light of your love;
      through Jesus we pray.
All   **Amen.**

38   Almighty God,
      Father of all mercies and giver of all comfort:
      deal graciously, we pray, with those who mourn,
      that, casting all their care on you,
      they may know the consolation of your love;
      through Jesus Christ our Lord.
All   **Amen.**

39   Out of the darkness of our grief,
we cry to you, O Lord.
You gave *him/her* to us,
and you have taken *him/her* away.
Turn to us, Lord, and have pity on us,
and give us the comfort that you alone can give,
through Jesus Christ our Lord.

All   **Amen.**

After a short life

40   Lord our God,
you give and you take away.
You blessed us through the gift of N,
who is now taken from us
and whose loss we mourn.
Help us, through our tears and pain,
to glimpse your hand at work
to bring blessing out of grief.
To you be glory for ever.

All   **Amen.**

41   God of all mystery, whose ways are beyond understanding,
lead us, who grieve at this untimely death,
to a new and deeper faith in your love,
which brought your only Son Jesus
through death into resurrection life.
We make our prayer in Jesus' name.

All   **Amen.**

42   **After a sudden death**
God of hope,
we come to you in shock and grief and confusion of heart.
Help us to find peace in the knowledge
    of your loving mercy to all your children,
and give us light to guide us out of our darkness
into the assurance of your love,
in Jesus Christ our Lord.

All   **Amen.**

After a violent death

43   Merciful God,
hear the cries of our grief,
for you know the anguish of our hearts.
It is beyond our understanding
and more than we can bear.
Accept our prayer
that as *N* has been released from this world's cruelty
so may *he/she* be received
    into your safe hands and secure love.
We pray that justice may be done
and that we may treasure the memory of *his/her* life
more than the manner of *his/her* death.
For Christ's sake.

All **Amen.**

44   God of love,
we thank you that *N* is in your gentle and loving hands,
far from the cruelty, violence and pain of our world.
When the trouble was near,
we could not understand how you seemed
    to remain far away.
And yet it is to you we turn;
for in life and death
it is you alone whom we can trust,
and yours alone is the love that holds us fast.
We find it hard to forgive the deed
that has brought us so much grief.
But we know that, if life is soured by bitterness,
an unforgiving spirit brings no peace.
Lord, save us and help us.
Strengthen in us the faith and hope that *N*
is freed from the past with all its hurt,
and rests for ever in the calm security of your love,
in Jesus Christ our Lord.

All **Amen.**

After a suicide

45   Eternal God and Father,
look in mercy on those who remember *N* before you.
Let not the manner of *his/her* death
cloud the good memories of *his/her* life.
For *N* the trials of this world are over
and death is past.
Accept from us all that we feel
even when words fail;
deliver us from despair
and give us strength to meet the days to come
in the faith of Jesus Christ our Lord.

All   **Amen.**

46   God our strength and our redeemer:
you do not leave us in this life
nor abandon us in death.
Hear our prayer for those in despair,
when days are full of darkness
and the future empty of hope.
Renew in them your sustaining strength
for we believe that there is nothing in all creation
that can separate us from your love
in Christ Jesus our Lord.

All   **Amen.**

47   **After a long illness**
       Eternal God,
       our life is a fleeting shadow that does not endure.
       Our years pass quickly,
       our days are few and full of trouble.
       We thank you that *N* no longer has to suffer pain or fear,
       grappling with death, fighting for life;
       and that for *him/her*
       limitations are ended,
       weakness is overcome,
       and death itself is conquered.
       As *he/she* passes from our earthly sight,
       we thank you for the years of *his/her* presence among us.
       And while we feel the pain of the parting,
       we rejoice in the faith that *he/she* has gone to be with you,
       for in your presence is the fullness of joy,
       at your right hand are pleasures for evermore.
       Bless those who had the care of *him/her*,
       especially doctors, nurses and technicians.
       Guide and prosper all who are engaged in
            medical research:
       may they never lose heart
       in their search to discover the way of health and healing.
       Grant that by their vision and courage
       we may advance in our understanding of the world
       and be better able to help those in need.
All   **Amen.**

48   **In sorrow, guilt and regret**
       Forgiving God,
       in the face of death we discover
       how many things are still undone,
       how much might have been done otherwise.
       Redeem our failure.
       Bind up the wounds of past mistakes.
       Transform our guilt to active love
       and by your forgiveness make us whole.
       We pray in Jesus' name.
All   **Amen.**

Prayers for Readiness to Live in the Light of Eternity

49   Support us, O Lord,
all the day long of this troublous life,
until the shadows lengthen and the evening comes,
the busy world is hushed,
the fever of life is over
and our work is done.
Then, Lord, in your mercy grant us a safe lodging,
a holy rest, and peace at the last;
through Christ our Lord.

All **Amen.**

50   Grant us, Lord,
the wisdom and the grace
to use aright the time
that is left to us on earth.
Lead us to repent of our sins,
the evil we have done
and the good we have not done;
and strengthen us to follow the steps of your Son,
in the way that leads to the fullness of eternal life;
through Jesus Christ our Lord.

All **Amen.**

51   God, our Father,
we thank you that you sent your Son Jesus Christ
to die for us and rise again.
His cross declares your love to be without limit;
his resurrection, that death our last enemy is doomed.
By his victory we are assured of the promise
that you will never leave us or forsake us;
that neither death nor life,
nor things present nor things to come,
can separate us from your love
in Christ Jesus our Lord.

All **Amen.**

52   Almighty God, we pray that,
        encouraged by the example of your saints,
        we may run with patience the race that is set before us,
        looking to Jesus, the pioneer and perfecter of our faith;
        so that at the last we may join those whom we love
        in your presence where there is fullness of joy;
        through Jesus Christ our Lord.

All   **Amen.**

53   Almighty God,
        you have surrounded us by a great cloud of witnesses.
        As you strengthened them,
        inspire us to throw off all that weighs us down
        and the sin that clings so closely.
        As you sustained them,
        keep us running in the race that lies ahead,
        fixing our eyes on Jesus, the pioneer and perfecter of our faith.
        Hear us as we offer with them,
        in the power of the eternal Spirit,
        the unending song of praise,
        through Jesus Christ our Lord.

All   **Amen.**

54   Father, your Son has become the source of eternal salvation
        for all who follow him.
        When we are tempted to turn from your way:
        form in us the obedience of Christ, our brother.
        When our consciences are stained by sin:
        cleanse us with the sacrifice of Christ, our priest.
        When we fear our death and the death of those we love:
        strengthen us in the knowledge that Christ has gone before us
        and entered your holy presence, crowned with glory and honour,
        where he is alive and reigns with you and the Holy Spirit,
        one God, now and for ever.

All   **Amen.**

55   Eternal God,
      whose Son Jesus Christ said,
      'Do not let your hearts be troubled or afraid',
      take away our fear of death;
      bring us to the place he has gone to prepare for us;
      and give us his peace for ever.

All   **Amen.**

56   Living God,
      you have lit the day with the sun's light
      and the midnight with shining stars.
      Lighten our hearts with the bright beams
      of the Sun of Righteousness
      risen with healing in his wings,
      Jesus Christ our Lord.
      And so preserve us in the doing of your will,
      that at the last we may shine
      as the stars for ever;
      through the same Jesus Christ our Lord.

All   **Amen.**

57   Intimate God,
      you are able to accept in us
      what we cannot even acknowledge;
      you have named in us
      what we cannot bear to speak of;
      you hold in your memory
      what we have tried to forget;
      you will hold out to us
      a glory we cannot imagine.
      Reconcile us through your cross
      to all that we have rejected in ourselves,
      that we may find no part of your creation
      to be alien or strange to us,
      and that we ourselves may be made whole,
      through Jesus Christ, our lover and our friend.

All   **Amen.**

58   Eternal God,
you give light to those who sit in darkness
and in the shadow of death;
let your light shine on those who mourn
that they may rejoice in your holy comfort
and live in the light of the resurrection
    of Jesus Christ our Lord.

All   **Amen.**

59   Father of all,
by whose mercy and grace
your saints remain in everlasting light and peace:
we remember with thanksgiving
those whom we love but see no longer;
and we pray that in them
your perfect will may be fulfilled;
through Jesus Christ our Lord.

All   **Amen.**

60   Eternal Lord God, you hold all souls in life:
shed forth, we pray,
upon your whole Church in paradise and on earth
the bright beams of your light and heavenly comfort;
and grant that we,
following the good example of those who have loved
    and served you here and are now at rest,
may at the last enter with them
into the fullness of your eternal joy;
through Jesus Christ our Lord.

All   **Amen.**

Litanies and Responsive Prayers

61   In peace let us pray to the Lord.

Jesus, bread from heaven,
you satisfy the hungry with good things:
grant us a share with all the faithful departed
in the banquet of your kingdom.

Hear us, risen Lord,

All   **our resurrection and our life.**

Jesus, the light of the world,
you gave the man born blind the gift of sight
and opened the eyes of his faith:
bring those in darkness to your eternal light and glory.

Hear us, risen Lord,

All   **our resurrection and our life.**

Jesus, Son of the living God,
you summoned your friend Lazarus from death to life:
raise us at the last to full and eternal life with you.

Hear us, risen Lord,

All   **our resurrection and our life.**

Jesus, crucified Saviour,
in your dying you entrusted each to the other,
Mary your mother and John your beloved disciple:
sustain and comfort all who mourn.

Hear us, risen Lord,

All   **our resurrection and our life.**

Jesus, our way and truth and life,
you drew your disciple Thomas from doubt to faith:
reveal the resurrection faith to the doubting and the lost.

Hear us, risen Lord,

All   **our resurrection and our life.**

May God in his infinite love and mercy bring the whole Church,
living and departed in the Lord Jesus,
to a joyful resurrection
and the fulfilment of his eternal kingdom.

All   **Amen.**

62 Let us turn to Christ Jesus
with confidence and faith in the power of his cross and resurrection.

Risen Lord, pattern of our life for ever:
Lord, have mercy.

All **Lord, have mercy.**

Promise and image of what we shall be:
Lord, have mercy.

All **Lord, have mercy.**

Son of God who came to destroy sin and death:
Lord, have mercy.

All **Lord, have mercy.**

Word of God who delivered us from the fear of death:
Lord, have mercy.

All **Lord, have mercy.**

Crucified Lord, forsaken in death, raised in glory:
Lord, have mercy.

All **Lord, have mercy.**

Lord Jesus, gentle shepherd who brings rest to our souls,
give peace to *N* for ever:
Lord, have mercy.

All **Lord, have mercy.**

Lord Jesus, you bless those who mourn and are in pain.
Bless *N*'s family and friends who gather around *him/her* today:
Lord, have mercy.

All **Lord, have mercy.**

63   The Lord Jesus is the lover of his people and our only sure hope.
      Let us ask him to deepen our faith and sustain us in this dark hour.

      You became a little child for our sake, sharing our human life.

      To you we pray.
All   **Bless us and keep us, O Lord.**

      You grew in wisdom, age and grace
      and learned obedience through suffering.

      To you we pray.
All   **Bless us and keep us, O Lord.**

      You welcomed children, promising them your kingdom.

      To you we pray.
All   **Bless us and keep us, O Lord.**

      You comforted those who mourned the loss of children and friends.

      To you we pray.
All   **Bless us and keep us, O Lord.**

      You took upon yourself the suffering and death of us all.

      To you we pray.
All   **Bless us and keep us, O Lord.**

      You promised to raise up those who believe in you,
      just as you were raised up in glory by the Father.

      To you we pray.
All   **Bless us and keep us, O Lord.**

64   Dear friends, our Lord comes to raise the dead
       and comforts us with the solace of his love.
       Let us praise the Lord Jesus Christ.

       Word of God, creator of the earth to which *N* now returns:
       in baptism you called *him/her* to eternal life
       to praise your Father for ever:
       Lord, have mercy.
All **Lord, have mercy.**

       Son of God, you raise up the just
       and clothe them with the glory of your kingdom:
       Lord, have mercy.
All **Lord, have mercy.**

       Crucified Lord, you protect the soul of *N* by the power of
            your cross,
       and on the day of your coming
       you will show mercy to all the faithful departed:
       Lord, have mercy.
All **Lord, have mercy.**

       Judge of the living and the dead,
       at your voice the tombs will open
       and all the just who sleep in your peace
       will rise and sing the glory of God:
       Lord, have mercy.
All **Lord, have mercy.**

       All praise to you, Jesus our Saviour,
       death is in your hands
       and all the living depend on you alone:
       Lord, have mercy.
All **Lord, have mercy.**

65   We pray with confidence to God, the almighty Father,
      who raised Christ his Son from the dead for the salvation of all.

      For *N* who in baptism was given the pledge of eternal life,
      that through faith *he/she* may now rejoice with the saints in glory.

      Lord, in your mercy

All **hear our prayer.**

      For our *brother/sister* who shared the bread of life,
      that in Christ *he/she* may be raised up on the last day.

      Lord, in your mercy

All **hear our prayer.**

      For those who have fallen asleep in the hope of rising again,
      that they may see God face to face.

      Lord, in your mercy

All **hear our prayer.**

      For the family and friends of our *brother/sister N*,
      that they may be consoled in their grief by the Lord,
      who wept at the death of his friend Lazarus.

      Lord, in your mercy

All **hear our prayer.**

66　We give you thanks and praise, almighty Father,
that you sent your Son to die,
and raised him from the dead for the salvation of all.

Lord, hear us.
All　**Lord, graciously hear us.**

We thank you for *N* who in baptism was given the pledge of
　　eternal life,
and now through faith rejoices with the saints in glory.

Lord, hear us.
All　**Lord, graciously hear us.**

We thank you for our *brother/sister* who shared the bread of life,
a foretaste of the eternal banquet of heaven.

Lord, hear us.
All　**Lord, graciously hear us.**

We thank you for our deceased relatives and friends,
who have helped us in the faith
and now find rest from their labours.

Lord, hear us.
All　**Lord, graciously hear us.**

We thank you that the family and friends of our *brother/sister N*
may be consoled in their grief by the Lord,
who wept at the death of his friend Lazarus.

Lord, hear us.
All　**Lord, graciously hear us.**

We pray for all of us assembled here to worship in faith,
that we may be gathered together again in God's kingdom.

Lord, hear us.
All　**Lord, graciously hear us.**

67   Let us pray with confidence to God our Father,
      who raised Christ his Son from the dead for the salvation of all.

      Grant, Lord, that your servant may know the fullness of life
      which you have promised to those who love you.

      Lord, in your mercy
All   **hear our prayer.**

      Be close to those who mourn:
      increase their faith in your undying love.

      Lord, in your mercy
All   **hear our prayer.**

      May we be strengthened in our faith,
      live the rest of our lives in following your Son,
      and be ready when you shall call us to eternal life.

      Lord, in your mercy
All   **hear our prayer.**

      Show your mercy to the dying;
      strengthen them with hope,
      and fill them with the peace and joy of your presence.

      Lord, in your mercy
All   **hear our prayer.**

      Lord, we commend all those who have died to your unfailing love,
      that in them your will may be fulfilled;
      and we pray that we may share with them in your eternal kingdom;
      through Jesus Christ our Lord.
All   **Amen.**

Prayers of Entrusting and Commending

68   Lord Jesus, our redeemer,
       you willingly gave yourself up to death,
       so that all might be saved and pass from death to life.
       By dying you unlocked the gates of life
       for all those who believe in you.
       So we commend *N* into your arms of mercy,
       believing that, with sins forgiven,
       he/she will share a place of happiness, light and peace
       in the kingdom of your glory for ever.

All   **Amen.**

69   *N* has fallen asleep in the peace of Christ.
       We entrust *him/her*, with faith and hope in everlasting life,
       to the love and mercy of our Father
       and surround *him/her* with our love and prayer.
       [In baptism, *he/she* was made by adoption a child of God.
       At the eucharist *he/she* was sustained and fed.
       God now welcomes *him/her* to his table in heaven
       to share in eternal life with all the saints.]

All   **Amen.**

70   Heavenly Father,
       your Son Jesus Christ is the firstborn from the dead.
       We believe that he will raise up the bodies of his faithful people
          to be like his in glory.
       We commend *N* to your mercy
       and pray that as you gather *him/her* to yourself,
       you will give to us your blessing of peace;
       through Jesus Christ our Lord,
       who died and rose again to save us,
       and is now alive and reigns with you
       and the Holy Spirit in glory for ever.

All   **Amen.**

71   Heavenly Father,
     you have assured us
     that everyone who looks to your Son
     and believes in him
     shall have eternal life.
     Trusting in your faithfulness,
     we commend *N* to your mercy
     as we await that great day
     when you raise us with *him/her* to life in triumph
     and we shall stand before you,
     with all your whole creation made new in him,
     in the glory of your heavenly kingdom.
All **Amen.**

72   God our creator and redeemer,
     by your power Christ conquered death
     and returned to you in glory,
     bearing in his body the marks of his passion.
     Confident of your victory
     and claiming his promises,
     we entrust *N* into your keeping
     in the name of Jesus our Lord,
     who, though he died, is now alive
     and reigns with you and the Holy Spirit,
     one God, now and for ever.
All **Amen.**

73   Almighty God,
     as you bring us face to face with our mortality,
     we thank you for making each one of us in your own image
     and giving us gifts in body, mind and spirit.
     We thank you now as we honour the memory of *N*,
     whom you gave to us and have taken away.
     We entrust *him/her* to your mercy,
     and pray that you will show us the path of life,
     and the fullness of joy in your presence
     through all eternity.
All **Amen.**

74 Almighty God,
in your great love
you crafted us by your hand
and breathed life into us by your Spirit.
Although we became a rebellious people,
you did not abandon us to our sin.
In your tender mercy
you sent your Son
to restore in us your image.
In obedience to your will
he gave up his life for us,
bearing in his body our sins on the cross.
By your mighty power
you raised him from the grave
and exalted him to the throne of glory.
Rejoicing in his victory
and trusting in your promise
to make alive all who turn to Christ,
we commend *N* to your mercy
and we join with all your faithful people
and the whole company of heaven
in the one unending song of praise:
glory and wisdom and honour
be to our God for ever and ever.

All **Amen.**

At the time of death

75 Into your hands, Lord,
our faithful creator and most loving redeemer,
we commend your child *N*,
for *he/she* is yours in death as in life.
In your great mercy
fulfil in *him/her* the purpose of your love;
gather *him/her* to yourself in gentleness and peace,
that, rejoicing in the light and refreshment of your presence,
he/she may enjoy that rest which you have prepared
for your faithful servants;
through Jesus Christ our Lord.

All **Amen.**

76 Into your hands, O merciful Saviour,
we commend your servant N.
Acknowledge, we pray, a sheep of your own fold,
a lamb of your own flock,
a sinner of your own redeeming.
Enfold *him/her* in the arms of your mercy,
in the blessed rest of everlasting peace
and in the glorious company of the saints in light.

All **Amen.**

77 N, go forth from this world:
in the love of God the Father who created you,
in the mercy of Jesus Christ who redeemed you,
in the power of the Holy Spirit who strengthens you.
May the heavenly host sustain you
and the company of heaven enfold you.
In communion with all the faithful,
may you dwell this day in peace.

All **Amen.**

78 N, go forth upon your journey from this world,
in the name of God the Father almighty who created you;
in the name of Jesus Christ who suffered death for you;
in the name of the Holy Spirit who strengthens you;
in communion with the blessed saints,
and aided by angels and archangels,
and all the armies of the heavenly host.
May your portion this day be in peace,
and your dwelling the heavenly Jerusalem.

All **Amen.**

79

All **Give rest, O Christ, to your servant with the saints:**
where sorrow and pain are no more,
neither sighing, but life everlasting.
You only are immortal, the creator and maker of all:
and we are mortal, formed from the dust of the earth,
and unto earth shall we return.
For so you ordained when you created me, saying:
'Dust you are and to dust you shall return.'
All of us go down to the dust,
yet weeping at the grave, we make our song:
Alleluia, alleluia, alleluia.

All **Give rest, O Christ, to your servant with the saints:**
where sorrow and pain are no more,
neither sighing, but life everlasting.

Blessings and other Endings

80 And now to him who is able to keep us from falling,
and lift us from the dark valley of despair
to the bright mountain of hope,
from the midnight of desperation
to the daybreak of joy;
to him be power and authority, for ever and ever.

All **Amen.**

81 God be in my head,
and in my understanding;
God be in my eyes,
and in my looking;
God be in my mouth,
and in my speaking;
God be in my heart,
and in my thinking;
God be at my end,
and at my departing.

All **Amen.**

82 May Christ the good shepherd
enfold *you* with love,
fill *you* with peace,
and lead *you* in hope,
to the end of *your* days;
and the blessing of God almighty,
the Father, the Son, and the Holy Spirit,
be among *you* and remain with *you* always.

All **Amen.**

83 The Lord is here,
his Spirit is with us.
We need not fear,
his Spirit is with us.
We are surrounded by love,
his Spirit is with us.
We are immersed in peace,
his Spirit is with us.
We rejoice in hope,
his Spirit is with us.
We travel in faith,
his Spirit is with us.

84 May the eternal God
bless and keep us, guard our bodies,
save our souls
and bring us safe to the heavenly country,
our eternal home,
where Father, Son, and Holy Spirit reign,
one God for ever and ever.

All **Amen.**

For a Memorial Service

85   The love of the Lord Jesus draw *you* to himself,
the power of the Lord Jesus strengthen *you* in his service,
the joy of the Lord Jesus fill *your* hearts;
and the blessing of God almighty,
the Father, the Son, and the Holy Spirit,
be among *you* and remain with *you* always.

All   **Amen.**

86   May the infinite and glorious Trinity,
the Father, the Son, and the Holy Spirit,
direct our life in good works,
and after our journey through this world,
grant us eternal rest with the saints.

All   **Amen.**

87   The Lord God almighty,
Father, Son, and Holy Spirit,
the holy and undivided Trinity,
guard us, save us,
and bring us to that heavenly city,
where he lives and reigns for ever and ever.

All   **Amen.**

88   The Lord God almighty is our Father:
All   **he loves us and tenderly cares for us.**

The Lord Jesus Christ is our Saviour:
All   **he has redeemed us and will defend us to the end.**

The Lord, the Holy Spirit is among us:
All   **he will lead us in God's holy way.**

To God almighty, Father, Son, and Holy Spirit,
All   **be praise and glory today and for ever. Amen.**

Prayers for Use after Psalms

For use after Psalm 6

Our eyes, Lord, are wasted with grief;
you know we are weary with groaning.
As we remember our death
in the dark emptiness of the night,
have mercy on us and heal us;
forgive us and take away our fear
through the dying and rising of Jesus your Son.

All **Amen.**

For use after Psalm 32

Lord, our hiding place in times of trouble,
you bring our guilt to mind.
Your hand seems heavy;
our tongues dry up
and we openly confess our guilt.
Embrace us with your mercy.
Teach us to trust you,
and bring us at the last
to rejoice in your presence for ever and ever.

All **Amen.**

For use after Psalm 38

Lord, have mercy
on those who go about in mourning all the day long,
who feel numb and crushed
and are filled with the pain of grief,
whose strength has given up
and whose friends and neighbours are distant.
You know all our sighing and longings:
be near to us and teach us to fix our hope on you alone;
through Jesus Christ our Lord.

All **Amen.**

Lord Jesus Christ, Son of the living God,
grant that we may ever seek you
and feed on you all our days,
for you are in all and with all and through all,
now and for ever.

All **Amen.**

For use after Psalm 90

Teach us, Lord, to number our days;
to see the span of our life in the light of eternity.
Reveal your splendour to us.
Give us the wisdom and grace to know your love
and to rejoice in your forgiveness and life;
through Jesus Christ our Lord.

All **Amen.**

For use after Psalm 116

Lord of life,
we walk through eternity in your presence.
Lord of death,
we call to you in grief and sorrow:
you hear us and rescue us.
Watch over us as we mourn the death of your servant,
precious in your sight,
and keep us faithful to our vows to you.

All **Amen.**

For use after Psalm 120

God of mercy,
we are in trouble and we call to you.
Deliver us from lies and deceit
and the pain of the enemy's attack.
And give us peace, the peace Christ won upon the cross.

All **Amen.**

For use after Psalm 121

Faithful Lord, lift us up when we are down.
Watch over us and keep us safe.
Be with us in our going out and in our coming in,
now and for ever.

All **Amen.**

For use after Psalm 130

Lord of mercy and redemption,
rescue us, we pray, from the depths of sin and death;
forgive us what we do wrong,
and give us grace to stand in your presence,
to serve you in Jesus Christ our Lord.

All **Amen.**

For use after Psalm 138

Lord, do not abandon us in our desolation.
Keep us safe in the midst of trouble,
and complete your purpose for us
through your steadfast love and faithfulness,
in Jesus Christ our Saviour.

All **Amen.**

For use after Psalm 139

Lord,
you created and fashioned us,
you know us and search us out,
you abide with us through light and dark:
help us to know your presence in this life
and, in the life to come, still to be with you;
where you are alive and reign,
God, for ever and ever.

All **Amen.**

Bible Readings and Psalms for Use at Funeral and Memorial Services

Any suitable translation may be used.

¶ *New Testament Readings*

John 6.35-40

Jesus said to them, 'I am the bread of life. Whoever comes to me will never be hungry, and whoever believes in me will never be thirsty. But I said to you that you have seen me and yet do not believe. Everything that the Father gives me will come to me, and anyone who comes to me I will never drive away; for I have come down from heaven, not to do my own will, but the will of him who sent me. And this is the will of him who sent me, that I should lose nothing of all that he has given me, but raise it up on the last day. This is indeed the will of my Father, that all who see the Son and believe in him may have eternal life; and I will raise them up on the last day.'

John 11.17-27

When Jesus arrived, he found that Lazarus had already been in the tomb for four days. Now Bethany was near Jerusalem, some two miles away, and many of the Jews had come to Martha and Mary to console them about their brother. When Martha heard that Jesus was coming, she went and met him, while Mary stayed at home. Martha said to Jesus, 'Lord, if you had been here, my brother would not have died. But even now I know that God will give you whatever you ask of him.' Jesus said to her, 'Your brother will rise again.' Martha said to him, 'I know that he will rise again in the resurrection on the last day.' Jesus said to her, 'I am the resurrection and the life. Those who believe in me, even though they die, will live, and everyone who lives and believes in me will never die. Do you believe this?' She said to him, 'Yes, Lord, I believe that you are the Messiah, the Son of God, the one coming into the world.'

Jesus said to his disciples: 'Do not let your hearts be troubled. Believe in God, believe also in me. In my Father's house there are many dwelling places. If it were not so, would I have told you that I go to prepare a place for you? And if I go and prepare a place for you, I will come again and will take you to myself, so that where I am, there you may be also. And you know the way to the place where I am going.' Thomas said to him, 'Lord, we do not know where you are going. How can we know the way?' Jesus said to him, 'I am the way, and the truth, and the life. No one comes to the Father except through me.'

Romans 8.31-end

What then are we to say about these things? If God is for us, who is against us? He who did not withhold his own Son, but gave him up for all of us, will he not with him also give us everything else? Who will bring any charge against God's elect? It is God who justifies. Who is to condemn? It is Christ Jesus, who died, yes, who was raised, who is at the right hand of God, who indeed intercedes for us. Who will separate us from the love of Christ? Will hardship, or distress, or persecution, or famine, or nakedness, or peril, or sword? As it is written,

'For your sake we are being killed all day long;
we are accounted as sheep to be slaughtered.'

No, in all these things we are more than conquerors through him who loved us. For I am convinced that neither death, nor life, nor angels, nor rulers, nor things present, nor things to come, nor powers, nor height, nor depth, nor anything else in all creation, will be able to separate us from the love of God in Christ Jesus our Lord.

I should remind you, brothers and sisters, of the good news that I proclaimed to you, which you in turn received, in which also you stand, through which also you are being saved, if you hold firmly to the message that I proclaimed to you – unless you have come to believe in vain.

For I handed on to you as of first importance what I in turn had received: that Christ died for our sins in accordance with the scriptures, and that he was buried, and that he was raised on the third day in accordance with the scriptures, and that he appeared to Cephas, then to the twelve. Then he appeared to more than five hundred brothers and sisters at one time, most of whom are still alive, though some have died. Then he appeared to James, then to all the apostles. Last of all, as to one untimely born, he appeared also to me. For I am the least of the apostles, unfit to be called an apostle, because I persecuted the church of God. But by the grace of God I am what I am, and his grace towards me has not been in vain. On the contrary, I worked harder than any of them – though it was not I, but the grace of God that is with me. Whether then it was I or they, so we proclaim and so you have come to believe.

Now if Christ is proclaimed as raised from the dead, how can some of you say there is no resurrection of the dead? If there is no resurrection of the dead, then Christ has not been raised; and if Christ has not been raised, then our proclamation has been in vain and your faith has been in vain. We are even found to be misrepresenting God, because we testified of God that he raised Christ – whom he did not raise if it is true that the dead are not raised. For if the dead are not raised, then Christ has not been raised. If Christ has not been raised, your faith is futile and you are still in your sins. Then those also who have died in Christ have perished. If for this life only we have hoped in Christ, we are of all people most to be pitied.

But in fact Christ has been raised from the dead, the first fruits of those who have died. For since death came through a human being, the resurrection of the dead has also come through a human being; for as all die in Adam, so all will be made alive in Christ. But each in his own order: Christ the first fruits, then at his coming those who belong to Christ. Then comes the end, when he hands over the kingdom to God the Father, after he has destroyed every ruler and every authority and power. For he must reign until he has put all his enemies under his feet. The last enemy to be destroyed is death.

But someone will ask, 'How are the dead raised? With what kind of body do they come?' Fool! What you sow does not come to life unless it dies. And as for what you sow, you do not sow the body that is to be, but a bare seed, perhaps of wheat or of some other grain. But God gives it a body as he has chosen, and to each kind of seed its own body.

So it is with the resurrection of the dead. What is sown is perishable, what is raised is imperishable. It is sown in dishonour, it is raised in glory. It is sown in weakness, it is raised in power. It is sown a physical body, it is raised a spiritual body.

For this perishable body must put on imperishability, and this mortal body must put on immortality. When this perishable body puts on imperishability, and this mortal body puts on immortality, then the saying that is written will be fulfilled:

'Death has been swallowed up in victory.'
'Where, O death, is your victory?
Where, O death, is your sting?'

The sting of death is sin, and the power of sin is the law. But thanks be to God, who gives us the victory through our Lord Jesus Christ.

Therefore, my beloved, be steadfast, immovable, always excelling in the work of the Lord, because you know that in the Lord your labour is not in vain.

But in fact Christ has been raised from the dead, the first fruits of those who have died. For since death came through a human being, the resurrection of the dead has also come through a human being; for as all die in Adam, so all will be made alive in Christ. But each in his own order: Christ the first fruits, then at his coming those who belong to Christ. Then comes the end, when he hands over the kingdom to God the Father, after he has destroyed every ruler and every authority and power. For he must reign until he has put all his enemies under his feet. The last enemy to be destroyed is death. For 'God has put all things in subjection under his feet.' But when it says, 'All things are put in subjection,' it is plain that this does not include the one who put all things in subjection under him. When all things are subjected to him, then the Son himself will also be subjected to the one who put all things in subjection under him, so that God may be all in all.

Otherwise, what will those people do who receive baptism on behalf of the dead? If the dead are not raised at all, why are people baptized on their behalf?

And why are we putting ourselves in danger every hour? I die every day! That is as certain, brothers and sisters, as my boasting of you – a boast that I make in Christ Jesus our Lord. If with merely human hopes I fought with wild animals at Ephesus, what would I have gained by it? If the dead are not raised,

'Let us eat and drink,
for tomorrow we die.'

Do not be deceived:

'Bad company ruins good morals.'

Come to a sober and right mind, and sin no more; for some people have no knowledge of God. I say this to your shame.

But someone will ask, 'How are the dead raised? With what kind of body do they come?' Fool! What you sow does not come to life unless it dies. And as for what you sow, you do not sow the body that is to be, but a bare seed, perhaps of wheat or of some other grain. But God gives it a body as he has chosen, and to each kind of seed its own body. Not all flesh is alike, but there is one flesh for human beings, another for animals, another for birds, and another for fish. There are both heavenly bodies and earthly bodies, but the glory of the heavenly is one thing, and that of the earthly is another. There is one glory of the sun, and another glory of the moon, and another glory of the stars; indeed, star differs from star in glory.

So it is with the resurrection of the dead. What is sown is perishable, what is raised is imperishable. It is sown in dishonour, it is raised in glory. It is sown in weakness, it is raised in power. It is sown a physical body, it is raised a spiritual body. If there is a physical body, there is also a spiritual body. Thus it is written, 'The first man, Adam, became a living being'; the last Adam became a life-giving spirit. But it is not the spiritual that is first, but the physical, and then the spiritual. The first man was from the earth, a man of dust; the second man is from heaven. As was the man of dust, so are those who are of the dust; and as is the man of heaven, so are those who are of heaven. Just as we have borne the image of the man of dust, we will also bear the image of the man of heaven.

What I am saying, brothers and sisters, is this: flesh and blood cannot inherit the kingdom of God, nor does the perishable inherit the imperishable. Listen, I will tell you a mystery! We will not all die, but we will all be changed, in a moment, in the twinkling of an eye, at the last trumpet. For the trumpet will sound, and the dead will be raised imperishable, and we will be changed. For this perishable body must put on imperishability, and this mortal body must put on immortality. When this perishable body puts on imperishability, and this mortal body puts on immortality, then the saying that is written will be fulfilled:

'Death has been swallowed up in victory.'
'Where, O death, is your victory?
Where, O death, is your sting?'

The sting of death is sin, and the power of sin is the law. But thanks be to God, who gives us the victory through our Lord Jesus Christ.

Therefore, my beloved, be steadfast, immovable, always excelling in the work of the Lord, because you know that in the Lord your labour is not in vain.

I Thessalonians 4.13-end

We do not want you to be uninformed, brothers and sisters, about those who have died, so that you may not grieve as others do who have no hope. For since we believe that Jesus died and rose again, even so, through Jesus, God will bring with him those who have died. For this we declare to you by the word of the Lord, that we who are alive, who are left until the coming of the Lord, will by no means precede those who have died. For the Lord himself, with a cry of command, with the archangel's call and with the sound of God's trumpet, will descend from heaven, and the dead in Christ will rise first. Then we who are alive, who are left, will be caught up in the clouds together with them to meet the Lord in the air; and so we will be with the Lord for ever. Therefore encourage one another with these words.

Revelation 21.1-7

I, John, saw a new heaven and a new earth; for the first heaven and the first earth had passed away, and the sea was no more. And I saw the holy city, the new Jerusalem, coming down out of heaven from God, prepared as a bride adorned for her husband. And I heard a loud voice from the throne saying,

'See, the home of God is among mortals.
He will dwell with them;
they will be his peoples,
and God himself will be with them;
he will wipe every tear from their eyes.
Death will be no more;
mourning and crying and pain will be no more,
for the first things have passed away.'

And the one who was seated on the throne said, 'See, I am making all things new.' Also he said, 'Write this, for these words are trustworthy and true.' Then he said to me, 'It is done! I am the Alpha and the Omega, the beginning and the end. To the thirsty I will give water as a gift from the spring of the water of life. Those who conquer will inherit these things, and I will be their God and they will be my children.'

¶ Further Readings

Old Testament and Apocrypha

Genesis 42.29-end *The sorrow you would cause me would kill me*
2 Samuel 1.17,23-end *David's lament for Saul and Jonathan*
2 Samuel 12.16-23 *David's son dies*
Job 19.23-27 *I know that my Redeemer lives*
Isaiah 53.1-10 *The suffering servant*
Isaiah 61.1-3 *To comfort all who mourn*
Lamentations 3.22-26,31-33 *The love of the Lord never ceases*
Daniel 12.1-3[5-9] *Everyone whose name shall be found written in the book*
Wisdom 2.22 – 3.5,9 *The souls of the righteous are in the hand of God*
Wisdom 3.1-5,9 *The souls of the righteous are in the hand of God*
Wisdom 4.8-11,13-15 *Age is not length of time*
Ecclesiasticus 38.16-23 *Do not forget, there is no coming back*

Psalms

Psalm 6	Psalm 32	Psalm 116
Psalm 23	Psalm 38.9-end	Psalm 118.4-end
Psalm 25	Psalm 42	Psalm 121
Psalm 27	Psalm 90	Psalm 139

New Testament

The passages printed on pages 383–389 are included in this list.

Matthew 25.31-end *The final judgement*
Mark 10.13-16 *Let the little children come to me*
Mark 15.33-39; 16.1-6 *He has risen, he is not here*
Luke 12.35-40 *The coming of the Son of Man*
Luke 24.1-9[10-11] *The Resurrection*
John 5.[19-20]21-29 *Whoever hears my word and believes him who sent me, has eternal life*

John 6.35-40[53-58] *All that the Father gives me will come to me*
John 11.17-27 *I am the resurrection and the life*
John 14.1-6 *In my Father's house are many rooms*
John 19.38-end *The burial of Christ*
John 20.1-11 *The Resurrection of Christ*
Romans 6.3-8[9-11] *All of us who have been baptized into*
                               Christ Jesus were baptized into his death
Romans 8.18-25[26-30] *The future glory*
Romans 8.31-end *Nothing can separate us from the love of Christ*
Romans 14.7-12 *Christ the Lord of the living and the dead*
1 Corinthians 15.1-26,35-38,42-44a,53-end *The resurrection of the dead*
1 Corinthians 15.20-end *The resurrection of the dead*
2 Corinthians 4.7-15 *We carry in our mortal bodies the death of Jesus*
2 Corinthians 4.16 – 5.10 *The heavenly body*
Ephesians 3.14-19[20-21] *The power to understand Christ's love*
Philippians 3.10-end *God's purposes for us*
1 Thessalonians 4.13-18 *So we shall always be with the Lord*
2 Timothy 2.8-13 *If we have died with him, we shall also live with him*
1 Peter 1.3-9 *We have been born anew to a living hope*
1 John 3.1-3 *We shall be like him*
Revelation 7.9-end *The crowd worshipping in heaven*
Revelation 21.1-7 *Behold I make all things new*
Revelation 21.22-end; 22.3b-5 *The Lord God will be their light*

Other readings may be more suitable for a particular occasion, for instance, at the Funeral of a child:

Psalm 84.1-4
Song of Solomon 2.10-13
Isaiah 49.15-16
Jeremiah 1.4-8
Jeremiah 31.15-17
Matthew 18.1-5,10
John 10.27,28
1 Corinthians 13.1-end

Canticles for Use at Funeral and Memorial Services

A Song of the Redeemer

Refrain:

All **Proclaim the time of the Lord's favour,**
and comfort all who grieve.

1   The Spirit of the Lord is upon me, ♦
    because he has anointed me.

2   He has sent me to bind up the brokenhearted, ♦
    to announce release from darkness for the prisoners,

3   To proclaim the time of the Lord's favour, ♦
    and to comfort all who grieve,

4   To give them oil of gladness instead of mourners' tears, ♦
    a garment of splendour for the heavy heart.

5   They will be called trees of righteousness, ♦
    planted by the Lord for his praise.

6   For God shall make his righteousness and praise ♦
    blossom before all the nations.

7   Buildings long in ruins will be rebuilt ♦
    and the desolate cities restored.

8   And you shall be called the Redeemed of the Lord, ♦
    a city no longer forsaken.   *Isaiah 61.1-3,11b,4; 62.12*

    Glory to the Father, and to the Son
    and to the Holy Spirit;
    as it was in the beginning is now
    and shall be for ever. Amen.

The Song of Manasseh

Refrain:

All   **Full of compassion and mercy and love
is God, the Most High, the Almighty.**

1   O Lord almighty and God of our forebears, ✦
you who made heaven and earth in all their glory:

2   All things tremble with awe at your presence, ✦
before your great and mighty power.

3   Immeasurable and unsearchable is your promise of mercy, ✦
for you are God, Most High.

4   You are full of compassion and very merciful, ✦
and you relent at human suffering.

5   O God, according to your great goodness, ✦
you have promised repentance and forgiveness
      to those who have sinned against you.

6   The sins I have committed against you ✦
are more in number than the sands of the sea.

7   I am not worthy to look up and see the heavens, ✦
because of my many sins and iniquities.

8   And now my heart bows before you, ✦
imploring your kindness upon me.

9   I have sinned, O God, I have sinned, ✦
and I acknowledge my transgressions.

10   Unworthy as I am, I know that you will save me, ✦
according to your great mercy.

11   For all the host of heaven sings your praise, ✦
and your glory is for ever and ever.

Manasseh 1a,2,4,6,7,9a,9c,11,12,14b,15b

Glory to the Father, and to the Son
and to the Holy Spirit;
as it was in the beginning is now
and shall be for ever. Amen.

A Song of the Righteous

Refrain:

All **God has found the righteous worthy
and their hope is of immortality.**

1 The souls of the righteous are in the hand of God ♦
and no torment will ever touch them.

2 In the eyes of the foolish, they seem to have died; ♦
but they are at peace.

3 For though, in the sight of others, they were punished, ♦
their hope is of immortality.

4 Having been disciplined a little,
they will receive great good, ♦
because God tested them and found them worthy.

5 Like gold in the furnace, God tried them ♦
and, like a sacrificial burnt offering, accepted them.

6 In the time of their visitation, they will shine forth ♦
and will run like sparks through the stubble.

7 They will govern nations and rule over peoples ♦
and God will reign over them for ever.   *Wisdom 3.1,2a,3b-8*

Glory to the Father, and to the Son
and to the Holy Spirit;
as it was in the beginning is now
and shall be for ever. Amen.

Nunc dimittis (The Song of Simeon)

Refrain:

All   **Awake may we watch with Christ:**
      asleep may we rest in peace.

1   Now, Lord, you let your servant go in peace: ♦
     your word has been fulfilled.

2   My own eyes have seen the salvation ♦
     which you have prepared in the sight of every people;

3   A light to reveal you to the nations ♦
     and the glory of your people Israel.   *Luke 2.29-32*

Glory to the Father, and to the Son
and to the Holy Spirit;
as it was in the beginning is now
and shall be for ever. Amen.

1   Lord, now lettest thou thy servant depart in peace :
     according to thy word.

2   For mine eyes have seen :
     thy salvation;

3   Which thou hast prepared :
     before the face of all people;

4   To be a light to lighten the Gentiles :
     and to be the glory of thy people Israel.   *Luke 2.29-32*

Glory be to the Father, and to the Son :
and to the Holy Ghost;
as it was in the beginning, is now, and ever shall be :
world without end. Amen.

A Song of the Justified

All **We are justified by faith,**
we have peace with God through our Lord Jesus Christ.

1 God reckons as righteous those who believe, ♦
who believe in him who raised Jesus from the dead;

2 For Christ was handed over to death for our sins, ♦
and raised to life for our justification.

3 Since we are justified by faith, ♦
we have peace with God through our Lord Jesus Christ.

4 Through Christ we have gained access
to the grace in which we stand, ♦
and rejoice in our hope of the glory of God.

5 We even exult in our sufferings, ♦
for suffering produces endurance,

6 And endurance brings hope, ♦
and our hope is not in vain,

7 Because God's love has been poured into our hearts, ♦
through the Holy Spirit, given to us.

8 God proves his love for us: ♦
while we were yet sinners Christ died for us.

9 Since we have been justified by his death, ♦
how much more shall we be saved from God's wrath.

10 Therefore, we exult in God through our Lord Jesus Christ, ♦
in whom we have now received our reconciliation.

Romans 4.24,25; 5.1-5,8,9,11

Glory to the Father, and to the Son
and to the Holy Spirit;
as it was in the beginning is now
and shall be for ever. Amen.

A Song of God's Children

Refrain:

All **The Spirit of the Father,
who raises Christ Jesus from the dead,
gives life to the people of God.**

1   The law of the Spirit of life in Christ Jesus ◆
     has set us free from the law of sin and death.

2   All who are led by the Spirit of God are children of God; ◆
     for we have received the Spirit that enables us to cry, 'Abba, Father'.

3   The Spirit himself bears witness that we are children of God ◆
     and if God's children, then heirs of God;

4   If heirs of God, then fellow-heirs with Christ; ◆
     since we suffer with him now, that we may be glorified with him.

5   These sufferings that we now endure ◆
     are not worth comparing to the glory that shall be revealed.

6   For the creation waits with eager longing ◆
     for the revealing of the children of God.   *Romans 8.2,14,15b-19*

     Glory to the Father, and to the Son
     and to the Holy Spirit;
     as it was in the beginning is now
     and shall be for ever. Amen.

A Song of Faith

Refrain:

All **God raised Christ from the dead,
the Lamb without spot or stain.**

1   Blessed be the God and Father ✦
    of our Lord Jesus Christ!

2   By his great mercy we have been born anew to a living hope ✦
    through the resurrection of Jesus Christ from the dead,

3   Into an inheritance that is imperishable, undefiled and unfading, ✦
    kept in heaven for you,

4   Who are being protected by the power of God
        through faith for a salvation ✦
    ready to be revealed in the last time.

5   You were ransomed from the futile ways of your ancestors ✦
    not with perishable things like silver or gold

6   But with the precious blood of Christ ✦
    like that of a lamb without spot or stain.

7   Through him we have confidence in God,
        who raised him from the dead and gave him glory, ✦
    so that your faith and hope are set on God.   *1 Peter 1.3-5,18,19,21*

    Glory to the Father and to the Son
    and to the Holy Spirit;
    as it was in the beginning is now
    and shall be for ever. Amen.

A Song of the Redeemed

Refrain:

All **Salvation belongs to our God,**
   who will guide us to springs of living water.

1   Behold, a great multitude ♦
    which no one could number,

2   From every nation,
        from all tribes and peoples and tongues, ♦
    standing before the throne and the Lamb.

3   They were clothed in white robes
        and had palms in their hands, ♦
    and they cried with a loud voice, saying,

4   'Salvation belongs to our God
        who sits on the throne, ♦
    and to the Lamb.'

5   These are they
        who have come out of the great tribulation, ♦
    they have washed their robes
        and made them white in the blood of the Lamb;

6   Therefore they stand before the throne of God, ♦
    whom they serve day and night within the temple.

7   And the One who sits upon the throne ♦
    will shelter them with his presence.

8   They shall never again feel hunger or thirst, ♦
    the sun shall not strike them,
        nor any scorching heat.

9   For the Lamb at the heart of the throne ♦
    will be their Shepherd,

10 He will guide them to springs of living water, ♦
    and God will wipe away every tear from their eyes.

Revelation 7.9,10,14b-17

   To the One who sits on the throne and to the Lamb
   be blessing and honour and glory and might,
       for ever and ever. Amen.

A Song of the Lamb

Refrain:

All　**Let us rejoice and exult
and give glory and homage to our God.**

1　Salvation and glory and power belong to our God, ♦
　whose judgements are true and just.

2　Praise our God, all you his servants, ♦
　all who fear him, both small and great.

3　The Lord our God, the Almighty, reigns: ♦
　let us rejoice and exult and give him the glory.

4　For the marriage of the Lamb has come ♦
　and his bride has made herself ready.

5　Blessed are those who are invited ♦
　to the wedding banquet of the Lamb.

Revelation 19.1b,2b,5b,6b,7,9b

To the One who sits on the throne and to the Lamb
be blessing and honour and glory and might,
　　for ever and ever.　Amen.

A Song of St Anselm

Refrain:

All   **Gather your little ones to you, O God,
as a hen gathers her brood to protect them.**

1   Jesus, like a mother you gather your people to you; ◆
you are gentle with us as a mother with her children.

2   Often you weep over our sins and our pride, ◆
tenderly you draw us from hatred and judgement.

3   You comfort us in sorrow and bind up our wounds, ◆
in sickness you nurse us, and with pure milk you feed us.

4   Jesus, by your dying we are born to new life; ◆
by your anguish and labour we come forth in joy.

5   Despair turns to hope through your sweet goodness; ◆
through your gentleness we find comfort in fear.

6   Your warmth gives life to the dead, ◆
your touch makes sinners righteous.

7   Lord Jesus, in your mercy heal us; ◆
in your love and tenderness remake us.

8   In your compassion bring grace and forgiveness, ◆
for the beauty of heaven may your love prepare us.

from Anselm of Canterbury

Glory to the Father, and to the Son
and to the Holy Spirit;
as it was in the beginning is now
and shall be for ever. Amen.

General Rules for Regulating Authorized Forms of Service

1   Any reference in authorized provision to the use of hymns shall be construed as including the use of texts described as songs, chants, canticles.

2   If occasion requires, hymns may be sung at points other than those indicated in particular forms of service. Silence may be kept at points other than those indicated in particular forms of service.

3   Where rubrics indicate that a text is to be 'said' this must be understood to include 'or sung' and vice versa.

4   Where parts of a service make use of well-known and traditional texts, other translations or versions, particularly when used in musical compositions, may be used.

5   Local custom may be established and followed in respect of posture but regard should be had to indications in Notes attached to authorized forms of service that a particular posture is appropriate for some parts of that form of service.

6   On any occasion when the text of an alternative service authorized under the provisions of Canon B 2 provides for the Lord's Prayer to be said or sung, it may be used in the form included in *The Book of Common Prayer* or in either of the two other forms included in services in *Common Worship*. The further text included in Prayers for Various Occasions (page 106 in *Common Worship: Services and Prayers for the Church of England*) may be used on suitable occasions.

7   Normally on any occasion only one Collect is used.

8   At Baptisms, Confirmations, Ordinations and Marriages which take place on Principal Feasts, other Principal Holy Days and on Sundays of Advent, Lent and Easter, within the Celebration of the Holy Communion, the Readings of the day are used and the Collect of the Day is said, unless the bishop directs otherwise.

Authorization Details

¶ The following services and other material in *Common Worship: Pastoral Services* are authorized pursuant to Canon B 2 of the Canons of the Church of England for use until further resolution of the General Synod:

¶ Wholeness and Healing
¶ The Marriage Service
¶ The Marriage Service within a Celebration of Holy Communion
¶ Supplementary Texts (Marriage)
¶ Emergency Baptism
¶ Thanksgiving for the Gift of a Child
¶ The Outline Order for Funerals
¶ The Funeral Service
¶ The Funeral Service within a Celebration of Holy Communion
¶ The Blessing of a Grave
¶ The Burial of Ashes
¶ Collects for Funeral and Memorial Services
¶ Prayers of Entrusting and Commending
¶ Bible Readings and Psalms for Use at Funeral and Memorial Services
¶ Nunc dimittis
¶ General Rules for Regulating Authorized Forms of Service

¶ The following material has been commended by the House of Bishops of the General Synod pursuant to Canon B 2 of the Canons of the Church of England and is published with the agreement of the House (authorized texts are, however, incorporated in some of these forms):

¶ Canticles (Marriage)
¶ An Order for Prayer and Dedication after a Civil Marriage
¶ Thanksgiving for Marriage
¶ Ministry at the Time of Death
¶ Receiving the Coffin at Church before the Funeral
¶ The Outline Order for the Funeral of a Child
¶ The Outline Order for the Funeral of a Child
   within a Celebration of Holy Communion
¶ Resources for the Funeral of a Child
¶ At Home after the Funeral
¶ An Outline Order for a Memorial Service
¶ An Outline Order for a Memorial Service
   within a Celebration of Holy Communion
¶ Memorial Service: A Sample Service
¶ Prayers for Use with the Dying
   and at Funeral and Memorial Services
¶ Canticles for Use at Funeral and
   Memorial Services

Under Canon B 4 it is open to each bishop to authorize, if he sees fit, the form of service to be used within his diocese. He may specify that the services shall be those commended by the House, or that a diocesan form of them shall be used. If the bishop gives no directions in this matter the priest remains free, subject to the terms of Canon B 5, to make use of the services as commended by the House.

Copyright Information

The Archbishops' Council of the Church of England and the other copyright owners and administrators of texts included in *Common Worship: Pastoral Services* have given permission for the use of their material in local reproductions on a non-commercial basis which comply with the conditions for reproductions for local use set out in the Archbishops' Council's booklet, *A Brief Guide to Liturgical Copyright.* This is available from:

Church House Bookshop
Great Smith Street
London SW1P 3BN
Telephone: 020 7898 1300/1/2/4/6
Fax: 020 7898 1305
Email: bookshop@c-of-e.org.uk

or from www.cofe.anglican.org/commonworship. A reproduction which meets the conditions stated in that booklet may be made without an application for copyright permission or payment of a fee, but the following copyright acknowledgement must be included:

> *Common Worship: Pastoral Services*, material from which is included in this service, is copyright © The Archbishops' Council 2000.

Permission must be obtained in advance for any reproduction which does not comply with the conditions set out in *A Brief Guide to Liturgical Copyright.* Applications for permission should be addressed to:

The Copyright and Contracts Administrator
The Archbishops' Council
Church House
Great Smith Street
London SW1P 3NZ
Telephone: 020 7898 1557
Fax: 020 7898 1449
Email: copyright@c-of-e.org.uk

Acknowledgements and Sources

The publisher gratefully acknowledges permission to reproduce copyright material in this book. Every effort has been made to trace and contact copyright holders. If there are any inadvertent omissions we apologize to those concerned and undertake to include suitable acknowledgements in all future editions.

Published sources include the following:

The Archbishops' Council of the Church of England: *The Prayer Book as Proposed in 1928; The Alternative Service Book 1980;* both of which are copyright © The Archbishops' Council of the Church of England.

Cambridge University Press: Extracts (and adapted extracts) from *The Book of Common Prayer,* the rights in which are vested in the Crown, are reproduced by permission of the Crown's Patentee, Cambridge University Press.

The Division of Christian Education of the National Council of Churches in the USA: Unless otherwise stated, Scripture quotations are from *The New Revised Standard Version of the Bible,* copyright © 1989 by the Division of Christian Education of the National Council of Churches in the USA. Used by permission. All rights reserved.

International Bible Society: Scripture quotations taken from the *Holy Bible, New International Version.* Copyright © 1973, 1978, 1984 by International Bible Society. Used by permission of Hodder and Stoughton, a member of the Hodder Headline Group. All rights reserved. 'New International Version' is a trademark of International Bible Society. UK trademark number 1448790.

Thanks are also due to the following for permission to reproduce copyright material:

The Anglican Church in Aotearoa, New Zealand and Polynesia: Pastoral Introduction (Marriage, p. 102), Blessing 2 (lines 1-9; Marriage, p. 153), Thanksgiving 6 (Marriage, p. 161), prayer for the support of friends (Marriage, p. 168), the alternative opening prayer (Funeral, p. 260), prayer at the time of death ('N, go forth from this world: in the love of God the Father …'; Funeral, pp. 229 and 376), prayers 21 (Funeral, p. 352), 24 (p. 353), 26 (p. 354), 30 (p. 355), 31 (p. 355) and 42 (p. 358). Taken/adapted from *A New Zealand Prayer Book – He Karikia Mihinare O Aotearoa*, copyright © The Church of the Province of New Zealand 1989.

The Anglican Church of Australia: Longer prayers and litanies 2 (Marriage, p. 157), prayers for grace to live well (Marriage, p. 162), for discipleship (Marriage, p. 162), the joy of loving (Marriage, p. 164), the healing of memory (Marriage, p. 164), the joy of companionship (Marriage, p. 164), faithfulness (prayer 18) (Marriage, p. 165), children and family (Marriage, p. 167), an existing family (Marriage, p. 167) and the families of the couple (Marriage, p. 168); and prayer when a coffin has come to its place (Funeral, p. 243). Taken/adapted from *A Prayer Book for Australia*, copyright ©1995 The Anglican Church of Australia Trust Corporation. All rights reserved.

The General Synod of the Anglican Church of Canada: Prayer after communion (Marriage, p. 131). Adapted from (or excerpted from) *The Book of Alternative Services of the Anglican Church of Canada*, copyright © 1985 by the General Synod of the Anglican Church of Canada. Used with permission.

The English Language Liturgical Consultation: The Lord's Prayer, Nunc dimittis and a prayer of thanksgiving ('You, Christ, are the King of glory …'; p. 340) prepared by the English Language Liturgical Consultation, based on (or excerpted from) *Praying Together*, copyright © ELLC 1988.

The International Commission on English in the Liturgy: 'You raise the dead to life in the Spirit ...' (Wholeness and Healing, p. 19), the Collect (Marriage, pp. 107 and 121), prayer for the preparation of the table and gifts (Marriage, p. 130), the Collect (Funeral, pp. 262, 278 and 350), Eucharistic preface (b) (Funeral, p. 283), 'Christ yesterday and today ...' (Funeral, p. 247). English translations based on (or excerpted from) *The Roman Missal*, copyright © 1973 International Committee on English in the Liturgy (ICEL). Prayers of entrusting and commending ('Lord Jesus, our Redeemer ...', Funeral, p. 373 and 'N has fallen asleep in the peace of Christ ...', Funeral, p. 373), and prayers for those who mourn 33 (Funeral, p. 356), 34 (p. 356) and 35 (p. 357). Based on (or excerpted from) the *Order of Christian Funerals*, copyright © 1985 ICEL. All rights reserved.

The Joint Liturgical Group of Great Britain: Blessing 4 (Marriage, p. 154), prayer for a glimpse of eternal love (Marriage, p. 163), prayer for grace and delight (Marriage, p. 165), prayer for faithfulness ('Gracious God ...', Marriage, p. 165) from *An Order of Marriage for Christians from Different Churches*, copyright © The Joint Liturgical Group of Great Britain, 1999. Used by permission.

The Episcopal Church in the USA: Prayer after communion (Funeral, p. 286) and 'Into your hands, O merciful Saviour ...' (Funeral, p. 376) from *The Book of Common Prayer* according to the use of the Episcopal Church of the USA, 1979. The ECUSA Prayer Book is not subject to copyright.

The Continuum International Publishing Group Ltd: Prayers after a stillbirth (Funeral, p. 313), miscarriage (p. 313), a violent death 43 (p. 359) and a suicide (p. 360) from *Pastoral Prayers* edited by Stephen Oliver, copyright © Mowbray 1996, an imprint of The Continuum International Publishing Group Ltd. Used by permission.

Darton, Longman and Todd: 'Lord, we pray for those who mourn ...' (Prayer 32, Funeral, p. 356) from *Good Friday People* by Sheila Cassidy, published and copyright ©1991 by Darton, Longman and Todd Ltd, and used by permission of the publishers.

The European Province of the Society of St Francis: 'God of all consolation …' (Funeral, pp. 260 and 276), Psalm 139 prayer (Funeral, pp. 248 and 382) and Psalm 27 prayer (Funeral, p. 250) from *Celebrating Common Prayer*, copyright © The Society of St Francis European Province 1992 and 1996.

Grove Books: Thanksgiving for the life of the departed 18 (Funeral, p. 351), 19 (p. 352) and 20 (p. 352), prayers for those who mourn 27 (Funeral, p. 354) and Ending 72 (Funeral, p. 374) from *Liturgy and Death* (Grove Books, 1974) © Trevor Lloyd.

Intellectual Properties Management, Atlanta, Georgia (executive licensor of the Martin Luther King estate): Conclusion (Funeral, p. 239) (also shown as Blessing 80, p. 377) from *I Have a Dream*, HarperCollins New York. Copyright © 1963 by Martin Luther King, Jr., copyright renewed 1991 by Coretta Scott King.

Jubilate Hymns: Confession and Absolution (a) (Marriage, p. 117) from *Church Family Worship*. Words: Michael Perry © Mrs B Perry/ Jubilate Hymns 1986. Used by permission.

The Methodist Publishing House: Blessing 2 (lines 10-15; Marriage, p. 153) and Litanies and responsive prayers 66 (Funeral, p. 371) from *The Methodist Worship Book*, copyright ©1999 Trustees for Methodist Church Purposes. Used by permission of Methodist Publishing House.

Oxford University Press: Prayer for readiness to live in the light of eternity 51 (Funeral, p. 362) and 52 (p. 363). Taken from *The Service Book of the United Reformed Church in the United Kingdom*, copyright © The United Reformed Church 1989. Reproduced by permission of Oxford University Press.

The Saint Andrew Press, Edinburgh: Prayer for the gift of love (Marriage, p. 163), 'We have come together to worship God …' (Funeral, p. 301), gathering prayer 7 (Funeral, p. 348), prayer after a violent death 44 (Funeral, p. 359), prayer after a long illness 47 (Funeral, p. 361) and prayer for readiness to live in the light of eternity 56 (Funeral, p. 364) from *The Book of Common Order*, copyright © The Church of Scotland Panel on Worship 1994.

SPCK: Prayer for those who mourn 28 (Funeral, p. 355) and prayer for readiness to live in the light of eternity 57 (Funeral, p. 364) from *All Desires Known,* SPCK. Copyright © Janet Morley 1992. Litanies and responsive prayers 67 (Funeral, p. 372) taken from *Tides and Seasons* by David Adam, Triangle/SPCK, 1989. Used by permission of the publishers.

The Rt Revd Dr David Stancliffe: Greeting (Wholeness and Healing, p. 14), Introduction (Wholeness and Healing, p. 14), prayers of intercession (Wholeness and Healing, p. 17), prayers of penitence (Wholeness and Healing, p. 18), 'Blessed are you sovereign God ...' (Wholeness and Healing, p. 20) and Sending Out (Wholeness and Healing, p. 23). Used by permission.

Index